D1293507

GENTLE TIGER

GENERAL CHATHAM ROBERDEAU WHEAT

GENTLE TIGER

THE GALLANT LIFE OF
ROBERDEAU
WHEAT

by Charles L. Dufour

Louisiana State University Press   BATON ROUGE

for

MARIE JEANNE DUFOUR
in proof that
I do love her
more than I love Roberdeau Wheat

PREFACE

This is the story of a man born six or seven hundred years too late. Chatham Roberdeau Wheat would have been more at home in the age when knighthood was in flower than in the mid-nineteenth century. He was a dreamer whose dreams never came true until the last fateful one. He was an idealist whose idealism did not exclude an unquenchable thirst for gold and glory.

Wheat's story is that of a man who learned to play soldier late in youth and thereafter was never able to shake off the fascination that battle held for him. He hitched his life to a Latin motto

> " Non per sylvas, sed per castra
> Nobis iter est ad astra "

which he freely translated

> " Through rural quiet doth thy pathway lead,
> Undying conflicts bear me to the sky."

Virginia-born and Tennessee-bred, Wheat led an adventurous life which admirably demonstrated that a born leader of men, even though he be a gentleman among rogues, can command the wildest of soldiers. This he did on foreign

shores for almost half his life, but when the Civil War broke
over the land he hurried back from the camp of Garibaldi
to offer his sword to the Confederacy. In 1861, he went
forth eagerly at the head of the Louisiana Tigers to win a
hero's grave at thirty-six on the bloody field of Gaines's Mill.

". . . Ere his end," wrote Douglas Southall Freeman of
Wheat, "he shares in three of the most dramatic scenes of
the drama."

Dr. Freeman, in his monumental *Lee's Lieutenants* gives
the best sketch of Roberdeau Wheat's life, but no full-length
biography of this fantastic young soldier of fortune has been
published.

Without the sympathetic assistance of Mrs. Burton
Craige and Mrs. Chatham Roberdeau Wheat, Jr., both of
Winston-Salem, North Carolina, this book could not have
been written. Mrs. Craige, Wheat's grandniece, made available, and Mrs. Wheat, wife of Wheat's nephew, organized
a collection of Wheat's letters, family papers and pictures
which the author had in his possession for months. Gratitude
is hereby expressed to them and to other Wheat relatives,
especially Chatham Roberdeau Wheat III of Devon, Pennsylvania; Mrs. Harold Ello and James Keith, both of New
Orleans; J. C. Wheat, Jr., of Richmond, and Mrs. William
Elam of Greenville, Mississippi.

It is impossible to name everyone from whom the author
has received help, but he would be grossly unappreciative if
he did not specify Joseph Abraham of New Orleans; Mrs.
Eleanor Ashby Bancroft of the Bancroft Library, University
of California; William M. Boothe of Episcopal High School,
Alexandria, Virginia; Vergil Bedsole, Director of Archives
at Louisiana State University, and his research assistant, Mrs.
Marcelle F. Schertz; Josiah Collins, Seattle, Washington;
Mrs. R. B. Critz, Manteo, Virginia; Miss Betty Cocke, Char-
lottesville, Virginia; Arthur Ben Chitty, Sewanee, Tennessee;
Arthur L. Crabb of Peabody College in Nashville, Tennessee;
Ralph W. Donnelly, Washington, D. C.; Harbart Davenport,

Brownsville, Texas; Miss Llerena Friend, Barker Texas History Center, University of Texas; Stanley F. Horn, Nashville, Tennessee; Mrs. Telfair Hodgson, Sewanee, Tennessee; Congressman F. Edward Hebert of Louisiana; Holman Hamilton, University of Kentucky; Major J. H. Mills of Manassas, Virginia; Rex B. Magee, Washington, D. C.; Fred Russell, Nashville, Tennessee; Miss Margaret Ruckert, archivist, New Orleans Public Library; Dr. Garland F. Taylor, Director of Libraries at Tulane University, and his excellent staff; Mrs. Carolyn A. Wallace of the Southern Historical Collection, University of North Carolina; Mrs. George A. Washington of New Orleans; Francis Wilshin, National Park Superintendent at the Manassas battlefield; Lee Wallace, National Park Historian, formerly stationed at Petersburg, Virginia, who, with Jim Holland, National Park Regional Historian, helped the author to understand the Gaines's Mill battlefield; Richard G. Woods, formerly of War Records Branch, National Archives, and his staff, especially E. O. Parker and Miss Mabel Deutrich; and Mrs. Gertrude Morton Parsley of the Tennessee State Library and Archives, Nashville, Tennessee. Special thanks are due Douglass V. Freret and Jack Freret for the excellent maps throughout the text; to Thomas Harrison and Kenneth Urquhart for making their knowledge of Louisiana Confederate units available; and to Mrs. Dorothy Lawton of Tulane University's Howard-Tilton Library for assistance in preparing the bibliography.

To John Hall Jacobs and his wife Frances the author is deeply indebted for making the index and similar obligation is acknowledged to Miss Polly LeBeuf for meticulously typing the manuscript in all stages of its development. Thanks are due Crozet Duplantier for reading the manuscript for typographical and other errors and for his excellent suggestions.

Two distinguished students and writers on the Civil War—Clifford Dowdey and Bell I. Wiley—read the manuscript in its first draft and made valuable suggestions for its revision. A third Civil War scholar and biographer, John P. Dyer, read the final draft and made several vital suggestions for revision. To all three the author is grateful for their friendly criticism and he hereby absolves them of any responsibilities for whatever inadequacies remain.

C. L. D.

CONTENTS

ILLUSTRATIONS

LIST OF MAPS

GENTLE TIGER

CHAPTER I

THE TIGERS AND THEIR TAMER

The Yankees seemed to have forgotten that there was a war going on, and the Confederates on the Virginia side of the Potomac were not very interested in reminding them of it. Nothing of any importance had occurred since that hot, dusty July Sunday a few months earlier when the Northern boys had hotfooted it from the plains of Manassas and scurried back over Bull Run to the safety of Washington. One Southern soldier admirably summed up the military situation during the do-nothing days of the winter of 1861-1862: "The only reason we did not fight was that the enemy was afraid of us and we of them and that was all that kept us apart." [1]

As the weeks of inactivity succeeded each other, winter added a convincing argument to the mutual reluctance of the Confederate and Union forces to resume the fighting: it was simply too cold to fight. The men in the Confederate camps around Centreville, Virginia, had a bad time of it. They improvised shacks which afforded some protection against the bitter weather, but as they moved about the camps many wrapped themselves in blankets and tied handkerchiefs or even shirttails around their heads. Measles and dysentery and other diseases struck severe blows at the shrinking morale. And where cold and illness left off, monotony and boredom commenced. Many men took off without leave to visit the

3

home folks; those who lived too far away found other means
to kick over the traces.

On a particularly disagreeable day, Captain Jim Nisbet
of the Twenty-first Georgia Regiment sat reading before a
comfortable fire in his quarters. Suddenly there broke out
in the company street a frightful din. Captain Nisbet hurried
to the window to discover a furious and unequal brawl underway between the men of his company and ten or twelve
gaily clad intruders. From their scarlet skull caps, their red
shirts and open brown jackets, their baggy Turkish trousers
of blue and white striped bed ticking, he recognized the
belligerent visitors as Louisiana Tigers, already universally
considered the most extraordinary outfit in the Confederate
army.[2]

Captain Nisbet ran out into the snow-filled street and
ordered the fighting to stop, but it was with considerable
difficulty that the company sergeants were able to restore
order. In the snow lay several Tigers who been knocked
down by Nisbet's men. The captain demanded an explanation. One of the Tigers spoke up: The Georgia boys had
stolen their whiskey. They had asked for a drink and when
the Tigers had passed them the bottles the Georgians had
run off with them. The Tigers had come to get satisfaction.

"You seem to have gotten it from the looks of your
bloody heads," declared Nisbet. He took the Tigers to his
quarters and after they had washed their wounds, he gave
each of them a drink.

"I'm sorry you were robbed," said Captain Nisbet, "but
to come in that company for a row was a dangerous business.
These men would have killed some of you if I had not
stopped 'em."

Grudgingly, the Tigers departed. They were reluctant
to leave behind unfinished business with the Georgians. One
of them called over his shoulder to Nisbet as they moved off:
"We are much obliged, sor, but Wheat's Battalion kin clean
up the whole dam 21st Georgia anytime."[3]

Such conduct as this explains why no brigade commander in General Joseph E. Johnston's army wanted the Louisiana Tigers around except when a battle was brewing. If there weren't any Yankee soldiers handy the "gentle Tigers," as General Richard (Dick) Taylor called them, were not above promoting a scrap with another unit—or even with each other. To be true, these brawls were pale substitutes for killing Yankees. This was a mission to which the Tigers always dedicated themselves with enthusiasm, not only for the immediate satisfaction it provided, but for the opportunities it offered to practice two of the arts of war in which they were second to none—looting and robbing the dead.

The evil fame of the Louisiana Tigers spread rapidly throughout the Southern army. One company of Zouaves, the Tiger Rifles, had given their name and character to the entire battalion. "They neither fear God, man or the Devil," confided a Virginia soldier to his diary. "They are the lowest scrapings of the Mississippi and New Orleans." Another soldier unashamedly confessed: "Tigers they were, too, in human form. I was actually afraid of them, afraid I would meet them somewhere and that they would . . . knock me down and stamp me half to death." A lad from South Carolina called the Tigers "the worst men I ever saw," and added, "I understand that they are mostly wharf rats from New Orleans, and Major Wheat was the only man that could do anything with them. They were continually fighting with each other. They were always ready to fight, and it made little difference to them who they fought." [4]

The Tigers didn't fight exactly according to the textbook. They rushed gaily into battle under their ridiculous standard, a picture of a lamb with the legend " as gentle as "; and once engaged, anything went. Frequently they'd drop their rifles and take after the enemy with knives. At the Battle of Manassas when some South Carolina troops fired into them by mistake, the Tigers didn't hesitate to fire back. An English observer noted the Tigers in action and the effect they had on Union soldiers opposing them: "Now the battalion would keep up a lively fire from the woods, creep through brush, make a sudden charge, upset a cannon or two and retire. Again, they would maintain a death-like silence until the foe was not more than 50 paces off; then delivering a withering volley, they would dash forward with unearthly yells and [when] they drew their knives and rushed to close quarters, the Yankees screamed with horror." [5]

Commanding this band of hooligans was a handsome giant of a man, a gentleman by birth, a lawyer by profession and a soldier of fortune by preference. Major Chatham Roberdeau Wheat made "a magnificent battle figure." He was active as an athlete and his six-foot-four frame carried his 275 pounds with ease and grace. In the saddle, one of his comrades noted, Wheat resembled "a mounted Falstaff." He had black hair and moustaches and flashing black eyes that seemed to light up in battle. His voice was loud but musical.

When the Civil War broke out Wheat was perhaps the most experienced campaigner in either the Confederate or Union armies. Almost half his thirty-five years had been dedicated to soldiering in Mexico, Cuba, Nicaragua and Italy, whenever, as General Taylor put it, "the pleasant business of killing was going on." [6] Everyone agreed that this picturesque giant was the only man in the Confederate army who could handle so unruly a command as the Louisiana Tigers. These wild, looting, brawling worthies idolized Wheat, who was a leader after their hearts, rushing into battle as recklessly and enthusiastically as they themselves did.

"Rob" Wheat was universally liked in the army and by those who knew him well he was genuinely beloved. All his life he had the gift of making friends. A Cuban associate called him "a noble fellow, young and ardent in dangerous enterprise." To one who filibustered with him in Nicaragua, he was a "warmhearted and chivalrous gentleman . . . brave as the bravest." He was "dear, affectionate, tender Major Wheat," to an impressionable girl in New Orleans. He was "gallant, big hearted," to one of Stonewall Jackson's staff, and General Jackson himself said Wheat was "too brave ever to think of himself." To Dick Taylor, his immediate commander, he was a "gallant spirit." [7]

It remained, however, for a lady of wartime Richmond to depict Wheat and his men with graphic accuracy: "The battalion of 'Tigers' from New Orleans, commanded by the intrepid Wheat, were, as their name denotes, men of desperate courage but questionable morals. They were well suited to the shock of battle, but wholly unfitted for the more important details of the campaign. Among them were many of lawless character, whose fierce passions were kept in abeyance by the superior discipline of their accomplished commander. . . . Educated under influences the most pious and refining, he was gentle, easy, graceful and dignified in society; toward the men under his command he was kind, but grave and reserved, and exacting in the performance of duty; in battle he was fiery, impetuous and resolute." [8]

Of Major Wheat and his Louisiana Tigers, a fellow officer wrote after the war: "It required the iron hand of discipline tempered with fatherly kindness, to make soldiers of them. Wheat had these two good qualities of a commander in a remarkable degree. His men loved him—and they feared him—the power or spell he had over his men was truly wonderful." [9]

From his camp near Centreville, Wheat could almost discern the smoke curling from the chimneys of Alexandria where thirty-five years earlier, he had been born. For almost half his life, he had breathlessly pursued adventure in many lands and lent a willing blade to many causes not his own. And now, in the supreme adventure of all, Rob had made the long circuit back to the land of his birth to draw his sword in its defense.

When Wheat was born on April 9, 1826, the family had already been established in America for more than a hundred years. The founder of the line, Francis Wheate, came from

England in 1724, settled in Prince Georges County, Maryland, and married. Although no record of his wife's name nor of the number of children exists, there were at least two sons, John, born about 1730, and Francis, born about 1745. John Wheate married Mary Mullikan, about 1753, and from the union came nine children, one of whom, Thomas, married Mary Chatham. The latter couple had six children, one of whom, John Thomas, became the father of Rob.

John Thomas Wheat—he dropped the final " e " from his name—was an Episcopal minister who, while completing his studies at the Theological Seminary in Alexandria, fell in love with Selina Blair Patten and married her on March 10, 1825. Eleven months later a son was born. The happy parents named the boy for his two grandmothers, Chatham for Mr. Wheat's mother, and Roberdeau for Mrs. Wheat's mother.

The Wheats had seven other children. Selina Patten, named for her mother, was born on June 12, 1827. The next child died at birth, but on December 3, 1830, John Thomas, named for his father, arrived. Josephine May, born on February 22, 1833, was followed by another child who died at birth, and Reginald Heber, who died in 1839 at the age of two. The last child, Leonidas Polk, named for the distinguished Episcopal bishop who became a Confederate major general, was born on May 5, 1841. He was, accordingly, Rob's junior by fifteen years.[10]

During Rob's early boyhood, the Reverend Mr. Wheat made frequent changes of parishes. When the boy was a year old his father was rector of St. John's Church in Anne Arundel County, Maryland. He moved to Wheeling, then in Virginia, in 1829, to become rector of St. Matthew's Church. In January, 1833, Mr. Wheat transferred his little family, which now numbered three children, to Marietta, Ohio, where he was rector of St. Luke's for three years.

Despite the family's frequent moves, Roberdeau's childhood was a normal one. They were a closely knit and happy group, although the minister's stipends barely met the family's needs. When Roberdeau was ten years old, his father went to New Orleans to recuperate from a severe illness. While there, he was engaged for three months by the vestry of Christ Church, temporarily without a rector. Shortly after he returned to his parish in Marietta, the Domestic Committee of the Episcopal Church sent the minister back to New Orleans to establish a mission in the upper part of the city. He had made many friends in New Orleans and these supported his mission to such an extent that it soon grew into St. Paul's, a self-supporting parish.[11]

By now, the Wheat family had grown to seven by the addition of Mrs. Wheat's orphaned niece, Mary de Nealle Wolfe. "Sister Mary," as the children called her, was a marriageable young lady, whose beauty and charm caught the eye of young Judge J. N. Morgan of New Orleans. The Reverend Wheat's journal of his New Orleans sojourn provides an intimate picture of the family life. The health of Ma and Pa and the children; the arrival of the new baby, Reginald Heber; the courtship and winning of Sister Mary by the Judge; the daily attendance at family prayers; the lessons learned or neglected; the behavior of the children; impatience over parish affairs; crises, real or imaginary, major or minor, all found their way into the daily records.

Frequently the entries were accompanied by comments which give an insight into the mind and heart of the rector of St. Paul's, expressing, with Christian piety, his hopes and fears for his growing brood. On one occasion young Roberdeau went out with an uncle who was visiting the Wheats, and when they did not return at the expected hour, the family was concerned. Finally, at dusk, "Uncle Thomas" and Roberdeau arrived home safely. With anxiety dispelled, the rector was "deeply grieved and mortified" that Roberdeau had been to a theater and he promised himself to take appropriate measures "to counteract the evil already done."

Reverend Wheat was happy at St. Paul's, but two

events combined to induce him to leave New Orleans. A subscription of $40,000 to build a church was wiped out by the panic of 1837. And during this financial crisis, he was called to Christ Church, Nashville, to which he removed his family in 1837.[12]

Roberdeau grew into adolescence and young manhood in Nashville, being away from the family only during the school term of 1841-1842, when he attended Episcopal High School on the outskirts of Alexandria, Virginia. An intensive reader, Roberdeau lost himself in books that appealed to him. When he was about twelve, an accident confined him to the house. His mother gave him *Thaddeus of Warsaw*, a best-seller of the early nineteenth century. Soon the boy was engrossed in the story. Moved by a particular passage in which the hero was subjected to injustices, he wept bitterly.

His mother attempted to soothe him: "This is not a true story; it is just made up by the author."

"Not true!" exclaimed Roberdeau, drying his tears. "And you, a Christian mother, give your child lies to read!"

Throwing the book into a corner, he could never be induced to read it again. Roberdeau was more intent on reading than studying, judging from Mrs. Wheat's comments to her absent husband: "Roberdeau has commenced Caesar and has brought home only a tolerable report. I shall be very strict in compelling a better one."[13]

Rob was fifteen when his parents sent him to Episcopal High School, founded in 1839 by Bishop Meade of Virginia and conducted at Alexandria by the Reverend William Nelson Pendleton, a high-ranking West Point graduate of the class of 1833. He had served three years in the artillery and then had resigned from the army to become a teacher. In 1837 Pendleton had entered the ministry. Years later he was to leave the pulpit to serve as Lee's Chief of Artillery and the story would pass through the Confederate army that when directing a gun, he would say reverently before each discharge: "The Lord have mercy on their souls . . . fire!"

When young Wheat arrived at Episcopal High School, it had grown from its original 35 students to an enrollment of 111 in three years, despite the difficult and almost unreasonable terms on which the school was placed in Mr. Pendleton's hands. There was no endowment, or hope of one in the future. Tuition fees, which were $200 per annum for full-pay students and $100 for sons of clergymen, had to cover everything—food, fuel, furniture, scientific apparatus, salaries of teachers and repairs.

According to Pendleton's daughter, " harmony and kindliness prevailed among scholars and teachers." Pendleton governed with " gentleness and firmness." When his authority was defied on infrequent occasions, the ex-West Pointer knew how to enforce discipline. He insisted on good scholarship and wholesome religious influence. He was kept very busy with school administration, teaching advanced classes in mathematics, chemistry, astronomy and engineering and conducting religious services during the week and often on Sunday as well. And yet the soldier-turned-clergyman, who was still young and active, found time to join the boys in their sports.[14]

Such was the headmaster to whom fifteen-year-old Rob Wheat was introduced in October, 1841. From the youngster's background and training, he should have been admirably suited to the Reverend Pendleton's school. But such was not the case. Barely a month of the school term had passed before Roberdeau began to send home complaining letters. He chafed at the restraints which prevented him from going to town when he pleased or into Washington when Congress was in session. He bitterly resented being limited to four hours of play daily. He found fault with Pendleton and the faculty and with some of his schoolmates. He begged to come home, coupling his plea with the threat that if he didn't come home he might become " a blackguard and a low-lifed boy."

The truth was that Rob was desperately homesick. This doesn't seem to have occurred to his father and mother, who

sorrowfully expressed their "shame and mortification . . .
mingled with serious apprehension" over their son's "mis-
conduct."

"I am grieved at the disingenuousness—the want of hearty
sincerity and manly honesty," his father wrote Roberdeau.
"I gather, from under all the disguises of your letter, these
facts: (1) you are under strict restraint; not allowed to go
to town, the mill, etc., as often as you wish; (2) you are
unwilling to submit to this; (3) you rake up and spread out
every little matter (which I do not doubt occurred just as you
say) with the idea that I shall be alarmed, and bring you
home."

Mr. Wheat was obviously much upset over Rob's "mis-
conduct" and he made no attempt to conceal it. At the same
time, he could not obscure his affection for his oldest child.

"Roberdeau! You are my first born," he continued. "I
love you most tenderly. I *always shall love you* most tenderly,
even if (and God forbid it!) you should disappoint my
fondest hopes. I own you possess many good traits, character
for one, affectionate, and in the main, a dutiful child; but
you have one capital fault—it is conspicuous in this letter—
You are not, at all times, under all circumstances, thoroughly
sincere, fearlessly honest."

Wheat's mother wrote, too, upbraiding her son for
blaming others for his behavior, reminding him of his fret-
fulness and constant inclination to find fault at home. She
blamed herself for having indulged him too much. She
warned Rob that he "shall not come home except with
honor"; she appealed to his pride in the lofty goals his parents
had set for him.

The Wheats had unnecessarily concerned themselves
over Roberdeau, who, as a normal adolescent away from home
for the first time, was now homesick, now rebellious and
now a little of both at the same time. It was not until some
months later, after they had compared notes with friends
who also had sons off at school that they discovered that

Rob's conduct wasn't so reprehensible after all. They began to take a more relaxed attitude toward the lad, especially when Reverend Wheat's uncle, Benoni Wheat of Alexandria, looked into Rob's affairs at his mother's request and reported that the boy's hardships were merely the contrast from parental indulgence at home.

Roberdeau weathered the crisis and settled down to do good work. To his mother's regret, he was not among the first ten students in his class, but he graduated with sufficient credit to his parents. They welcomed him back to Nashville in the summer of 1842.[15]

CHAPTER II

VOLUNTEER FROM TENNESSEE

Rob Wheat entered the University of Nashville in the fall of 1842. He had already made up his mind to become a lawyer. He had so informed his parents from Episcopal High and now that he was working for his degree he was impatient to begin the reading of law. Wheat found the university small, poorly equipped and financially pinched, but it had a distinguished faculty which struggled valiantly against frustration. Girard Troost, eminent Dutch geologist, held the chair of science. Nathaniel Cross taught languages and James Hamilton mathematics. The students, most of whom graduated to become leading citizens of Nashville, were generally brilliant, high-spirited youngsters.

This is not to suggest that all went smoothly at the University of Nashville. Life among the students was frequently turbulent. One boy, having entered the university, quickly withdrew, because he found his classmates "very wild." Expulsions were frequent and midnight escapades, which often grew riotous, sometimes wound up with equipment destroyed and heads bashed. One student was expelled because "Professor Cross saw him in an intoxicated condition on the street at 2 a. m."[1]

Because he lived at home, Rob probably avoided the more serious scrapes of his fellows, but there is no reason

to suspect that he didn't join in the milder forms of sky-
larking. Wheat's parents were just beginning to understand
their boy and he, on his part, was making an honest effort
to be understood. On one occasion, when Mr. Wheat was
away on church business, Mrs. Wheat wrote him that Rob
was "trying to be good." He replied: "I will incur any
expense for his good, and to make his home pleasant to him
if he will keep on trying." [2]

One of Rob's classmates was James Walker, whose
brother William Walker, a dozen years later, would capture
Roberdeau's imagination in a compelling way. Wheat's main
extra-curricular interest at the university was the literary
society. This group afforded him opportunities to practice
oratory, for which he had a definite flair. His natural wit,
mental agility and easy delivery soon gave him a reputation
for eloquence which followed him the rest of his life. In
his junior year, he was selected to represent the literary
society in an oratorical competition and, discarding tradition,
he delivered an extemporaneous speech which won him great
acclaim.

At one time, Wheat hoped to get an appointment to West
Point, but when this was not forthcoming, he concentrated
on a career in law. He began to read Blackstone at home in
his spare time. Rob's sisters, Selina and Joe May, were reading
at this time in weekly installments Eugene Sue's *The
Wandering Jew*. Frequently, the girls would interrupt his
studies to read him passages that pleased them. "Put down
that foolish book and listen to this," Rob demanded. And
he would read several utterly incomprehensible paragraphs
to the girls. Efforts to get him interested in the novels of
the day were futile. History and biographies were his fare.
When, several years later, his mother put the latest Dickens
novel in his bag, he brought it back from Mexico with the
pages still uncut.[3]

Wheat received his Bachelor of Arts degree at the fall
commencement in 1845, and on the platform with him,

receiving an honorary degree of Doctor of Divinity, was his
father. The day was a gala one for the family which turned
out in force for the ceremonies. It was, perhaps, a happy
occasion, too, for fifteen-year-old Marina Cheatham, a school-
mate of Selina's and the sister of Rob's friend, Will Cheatham.
Marina was already a lovely young woman and had attracted
Rob's attention for some time. He began to look on Marina
as someone other than just Selina's companion and Will's
sister. He became captivated by her sweet disposition, her
character and her charming grace as well as by her exceptional
beauty.[4]

Wheat was convinced that some day Marina would be
his wife, but before he could propose marriage seriously he
had to make his way in the world. He decided that New
Orleans was the place to launch his career, inasmuch as he
had relatives there. Rob's cousin, Sister Mary, Judge Morgan's
wife, lived in New Orleans and so, too, did her brother,
Cousin Tom Wolfe. In mid-October, 1845, Roberdeau kissed
Ma, Pa and the children goodbye, boarded a steamboat at
Nashville for the long voyage to New Orleans. He was
nineteen, tall, lean and handsome.

Rob had a miserable trip, which in itself required ten
days. To add to the tedious journey, the steamboat was very
crowded, not only with passengers but also with cargo, hogs,
turkeys and horses. Part of the way, the gentlemen aboard
had to sleep on the floor, for the ladies occupied the state-
rooms. Will Cheatham was on board to Memphis, and he
and Rob held many long conversations to while away the
time. "Whenever he would turn his eyes on me, Marina
stared me in the face," Rob wrote his mother. "How much
in every movement they are alike. I love them both." At
Vicksburg the cook fell overboard and drowned. "Poor fellow,
he was soon forgotten, sooner than the dinner he had just
cooked," wrote Wheat. That day he became ill with a violent
bilious attack, but by the time the boat reached New Orleans
he was well again.

Rev. Dr. J. T. Wheat   Mrs. Wheat   Selina Wheat Seay

John Thomas Wheat   Josephine   Leo Wheat
May Wheat Shober

ROBERDEAU WHEAT'S FAMILY

(*Courtesy Mrs. Burton Craige*)

MARINA CHEATHAM
(*Courtesy Mrs. George A. Washington*)
She was Rob Wheat's first and greatest love

He located a furnished room at No. 80 Camp Street and boarded at the nearby Globe Restaurant for $3.50 a week. Roberdeau loved to eat and he was delighted with the bill of fare placed before him at his private table. One day, being quite hungry, he commenced at the head of the bill of fare and went right down about one third of the way. A bit ashamed of his appetite, Roberdeau, when the servant went to change his plate, got up and left. Oysters were a favorite article with Roberdeau. " I eat them until I can't eat anything else," he wrote.

Roberdeau set about finding a situation which would support him while he was studying law. Doubtless, and with reason, he expected work in his cousin's law office. Thomas Wolfe had settled in New Orleans in 1843 and within five years had become one of the city's more successful lawyers. What would be more natural than for his young cousin to work for him and read law under his supervision? At least Rob thought so and he called immediately on his cousin.[5]

Apparently, Cousin Thomas had no place for him, for Roberdeau, two months later, hearing of a possible opening at the Custom House, hastened to enlist his mother's help in getting the post. He wrote:

"I have just had an interview with Mr. Reader who is in the Custom House here who tells me that I can be admitted, too, by these means . . . if you who are so well acquainted with Mrs. James K. Polk will write to her asking her influence with the President to get me this situation, that a mere mention of my name to the Custom House officer here by the President will be a law and I shall have an independent support of $90 a month and study Law in the bargain until the close of this administration and then be admitted. Write then, dear Mother, let your words be winged. . . . I shall not take a free breath until the mail returns from Washington with my commission."[6]

In a postscript, Roberdeau pointed out the advantages of the position, which in addition to good pay, threw him into

daily contact with the men among whom, as a commercial
lawyer, he would make his living. Moreover, he assured his
mother, there would be the satisfaction of supporting himself
and contributing to the family's support as well.

While waiting impatiently for his appointment to the
Custom House, Rob worked every day at his law books. He
conserved his slender funds by cutting his daily expenses
" including everything," to less than eighty cents a day.

If Mrs. Wheat wrote Mrs. Polk to intercede with the
President on Roberdeau's behalf, she was not successful. For
Roberdeau did not get the Custom House appointment and
within three months he was in Memphis, " happy and studying hard" and working in the law office of a " Mr. D."

Perhaps " Mr. D." was a friend of the family, with whom
Dr. Wheat had arranged for Roberdeau to study law. Or
perhaps the youngster, frustrated and disappointed in New
Orleans, had gone up the river on his own initiative and
landed a job in Memphis.

On his twentieth birthday, April 9, 1846, Roberdeau
revealed how busy he was: "Mr. D. is engaged in a suit
involving five millions of dollars. . . . He is writing his opinion
which is to cover 100 sheets of foolscap. . . . I am copying as
fast as he writes. . . . I have been writing all day without
intermission until my hand aches. . . . O how I long to put
my armor on and try my lance." [7]

As he worked and studied in Mr. D.'s office, Roberdeau
couldn't have been unmindful of the news from Texas. The
year before, the annexation of Texas had been approved by
both houses of Congress and relations with Mexico immediately became strained. John Slidell, who had been sent by
President Polk as minister to Mexico, had not been received.
Indignantly, he had informed the President " that nothing
is to be done with these people until they shall have been
chastised."

The President had ordered Zachary Taylor and his force
of nearly four thousand men to the Rio Grande to defend

Texas and the inevitable had happened. On the night of April 25 a Mexican force had crossed the Rio Grande and killed or wounded sixteen Americans in a scouting party. Word of this reached Washington on the evening of May 8, the very day Slidell had returned from Mexico with the news of the violent war fever in Mexico City. And on that very day, General Taylor, in retaliation for the ambush, had met and defeated Mexican troops in hard-fought border battles at Palo Alto and Resaca de la Palma, and had driven them across the Rio Grande.

President Polk sent to Congress on May 11 a "ferocious war message . . . with its howling catalogue of grievances." To his inflammatory words, "Mexico has passed the boundary of the United States, has invaded our territory, and shed American blood upon American soil," there could be only one Congressional answer. Quickly, Congress declared that war existed by virtue of Mexico's act, authorized calling for 50,000 volunteers and appropriated $10,000,000 for the prosecution of the war.[8]

The President requisitioned the states for volunteers and on May 24 the Governor of Tennessee issued a call to fill three regiments, two of infantry and one of cavalry. Roberdeau Wheat dropped his law books and Mr. D.'s briefs and hastened to put his name on the rolls.

Dr. Wheat wrote to Roberdeau immediately, urging him to wait a while before volunteering and promising that he might go if there was another call for volunteers. But before Roberdeau got this letter he had already dispatched one to his father to this effect: "Dear Pa: 'A chip of the old block,' I knew you would be ashamed of me if I did not volunteer as soon as the call came. My name, I am proud to say, is the very first on the list. I have been unanimously elected second lieutenant in a company of cavalry. Please send Jim by some careful hand." Jim was his blooded horse, a spirited, highly trained animal, just the mount for a young lieutenant of dragoons.

Wheat volunteered in the Eagle Guards, one of the ten mounted companies that were mustered into service on June 15, 1846, and organized into the First Tennessee Mounted Regiment. In those days, as later in the Civil War, the officers were elected by the men. Roberdeau was elected assistant second lieutenant of Company G, commanded by Captain William N. Porter. The other company officers were First Lieutenant James L. Penn and Second Lieutenant Robert M. Anderson. When the regimental officers were elected, the men picked Private Jonas E. Thomas from Captain Cooper's company and elevated him to colonel of the regiment. Robert Allison was named lieutenant colonel and Richard Waterhouse major.[9]

The First Tennessee Mounted Regiment gathered at Memphis and then encamped at Big Spring, two miles east of town. The men, all expert horsemen, went into serious training to become soldiers. The Regiment, wholly composed of 12-months volunteers, remained at Camp Carroll until July 17, when it crossed the Mississippi and camped opposite Memphis to complete preparations for the long march to the Rio Grande. On July 27 the orders came and the regiment, a fine body of men about 940 strong, mounted on the best of horses, moved out for Little Rock, 160 miles away.[10] It was an exciting moment for twenty-year-old Roberdeau Wheat.

As they rode along, choking in the dust, under a blistering sun, his thoughts doubtless lingered behind on the law career he had just set aside for a future day. Perhaps they journeyed back to Nashville to Ma and Pa and the children—and to Marina Cheatham, who had given him her picture taken especially for him to take along to Mexico.

CHAPTER III

THE SCHOOL OF THE SOLDIER

Twelve days after breaking camp on the Mississippi, the First Tennessee Mounted Regiment, begrimed and saddle-weary, rode into Little Rock.

Rob Wheat and his comrades were expert horsemen, but a dozen days of riding dusty roads under the midsummer sun were enough to take a toll in both men and mounts.

Many of the Volunteers were ill and some of the horses were badly fatigued. The order for a three-day halt was welcomed by all. During this break in the march Wheat was exposed for the first time to the exercise of military law. One of the Volunteers was courtmartialed and drummed out of camp for horse-stealing.

Complying with the courtmartial order called for ingenuity, for the First Mounted Tennessee Volunteers had no drums. The disgraced soldier was forced to run the gauntlet between two lines of his comrades, each of whom beat furiously with knives, forks and spoons on frying pans, canteens and whatever else made a noise.

When the order to saddle up came, more than fifty of the Volunteers were too ill to march and they were left behind in Little Rock. A week later, at Washington, Arkansas, more sick soldiers dropped out and those who weren't ailing were "sour and angry" because they expected to collect their pay and didn't. The regiment reached the Red River at Fulton on August 23, where the ferrying operation took two days, with two small flatboats requiring eighty trips each to get men and horses across. Two days later, at 9 A. M., the Texas border was crossed.

Soon after this young Wheat got a lesson in the responsibilities of a leader to his men which he never forgot. He had joined Captain Porter and the two other lieutenants, Penn and Anderson, on an all-night excursion from camp. Next morning when they returned, preparations for resuming the march were already underway. But when they reached Company G's area, they found the company in a disgruntled mood.

The men were disgusted with their officers, for when all the other companies were saddling up, Company G had no officer on the ground of higher rank than second sergeant, so the company did nothing until Porter, Penn, Anderson and Wheat arrived hurriedly on the grounds together.

"Saddle up! saddle up!" shouted the officers in one voice, but the men made no effort to speed up. "They fretted, fumed and threatened, but not a whit faster did the men move," recorded a private in the company. "If they had been in their place, the men would have been in season, but their neglect of duty was too plain."

Early in September the Tennessee Mounted was caught in the backlash of a tropical hurricane and the men suffered bitterly from cold, rain, wind and mud. Everybody got drunk and Colonel Thomas remarked later that "out of a thousand men, teamsters and all, in the regiment, there were 1100 intoxicated."

Rob weathered the "Rainy Day"—September 8, when the storm was at its worst—and was in fine health when Colonel Thomas dispatched him to Houston, sixty miles to the south, to replenish the regiment's dwindling medical supplies.[1]

Wheat left the regiment on September 14, fully expecting to rejoin it in a reasonable time. But Rob was seized by

a bilious attack in Houston and for several weeks he was
desperately sick. From Galveston, where he went to recuperate, he wrote his parents on October 9: "I thank God that
I am in the land of the living. . . . I never was so sick in all
my life." He had been imprudent, Rob admitted, for in the
worst stages of his illness he had gotten up from bed to take
passage on a schooner for La Boca. "I was so anxious to
join my regiment," he declared. However, when the schooner's captain found Rob in his cabin with high fever, he
signalled a ship heading to Galveston and Wheat was transferred to this vessel and returned to port.

By this time the battle of Monterrey had been fought
and Rob was much chagrined that his regiment was not within
six hundred miles of battle. He hoped that the Tennessee
Mounted would get an opportunity for action in the near
future. "Grandpa and Pa have been in the wars and I must,
too." he wrote. "I want to give my bride a soldier's breast
to lay her head upon. My children, too, shall play around
Jim and say that's the horse my Pa rode to wars."

Roberdeau next addressed a letter to his "dear friend"
Marina Cheatham's mother. He apologized for not having
written during "our very long and tedious journey through
an almost uninhabited region upon which there was nothing
to be seen but marshes and prairies much less a postoffice
to which one could entrust an epistle." Wheat opened his
heart to the mother of the girl he loved: "I have often
thought of your words of prophecy still ringing in my ears—
'Some dark-eyed girl of the South will win your heart' but
without being fulfilled. I am now as I have been as I ever
expect to be and you know how that is. . . ."

Roberdeau found Galveston society "inferior in no respect to Nashville" and he met many of the town's most
beautiful girls, including the "acknowledged Queen" who
reminded him of Marina Cheatham. "She is beautiful indeed," he confided to Mrs. Cheatham, "but how could she
compare with your peerless Marina." [2]

Wheat regained his strength rapidly, but his face and
chin were covered with annoying fever blisters. He planned
an early departure for Matamoros as soon as his doctor released
him. However, Rob changed his mind, and instead of sailing
for Port Isabel, he took passage for New Orleans where he
arrived on October 20.

On November 18, from Camp Ringgold, near Matamoros,
Rob wrote his parents of his trip: "I was in New Orleans
about two or three weeks ago. I saw Cousin Thomas and
Cousin Maria and her children. Cousin was delighted to
see me. I enjoyed myself very much—put up at the St. Charles
and lived on oysters. . . ."

Wheat's regiment had reached Matamoros on November
7, about a week before he rejoined. He learned that Captain
Porter, commander of Company G, had resigned because of
severe illness, which several weeks later proved fatal in New
Orleans. The company had elected as Porter's successor the
popular regimental Sergeant-Major, John L. T. Sneed.

"He is a noble fellow," wrote Wheat of his new commanding officer. "He is not yet placed in command, so the
company is immediately under my supervision and sole command and the way I drill them and play the officer is no
man's business. I am splendidly equipped—I bought the best
sabre, the finest belt, and fine uniform, cavalry gloves, spurs
and the finest horse in the regiment and the way I ride
through the streets of Matamoros is death to the Signorittas
[sic]."

But his thoughts, Rob assured his parents, were on "one
little beauty" and he asked them to tell him all about her
in their next letter. "I have selected a place for us to live,"
he continued. "It is upon one of the most beautiful lakes
in Mexico, it is where our camp is now situated." Apparently,
Rob had forgotten that a few weeks earlier in a letter home
he announced he had picked out "a little home in Texas not
far from Houston" for himself and Marina.

Although Roberdeau assured his parents that he was

well again "save for a little weakness of the bowels," he was soon back in the hospital. It was there that he met Dick Taylor, son of General Zachary Taylor, who was destined to be his commanding officer in the Civil War fifteen years later. Taylor's interest was captured by the "bright-eyed youth . . . wan with disease, but cheery withal," and he arranged for Rob's removal to army headquarters, where he soon recovered health and became a pet. Muster rolls of Wheat's company show that on December 12 he was detailed to the artillery for an indefinite period, and he doesn't appear back for duty with his company until February.[3] No records have been found to indicate with what artillery unit he served, so the assignment may have been merely a convenient way of bringing the youngster to army headquarters until he regained his health. When General Zachary Taylor occupied Victoria on December 29 Lieutenant Wheat was still attached to headquarters, but he rejoined his company in time to march to Tampico to join General Winfield Scott's army assembled there for an attack on Vera Cruz.

On March 9, 1847, the Tennesseans crowded with other troops aboard the *Essex* and after more than a week's buffeting by storms, which drove them off their course, they landed on the beach beyond Vera Cruz and joined Scott's forces investing the city.

On March 25 some of the Tennessee Mounted engaged in a spirited action at Puente de Moreno. A large company of Mexican lancers had been attacked in the rear about nine miles southward by an American detachment. After being repulsed, the Americans called for reinforcements. Wheat's company was among the force sent to their assistance and a lively engagement took place, culminating in a charge on a stone bridge which the Mexicans had defended stoutly. The Americans rushed the bridge "with a wild yell, that resounded far and near," and the Mexicans broke and ran for it. The Americans continued the chase for about four miles until General Robert Patterson called it off. The usually taciturn

Patterson, carried away by the moment, took off his hat and
waved it enthusiastically as the pursuers rode by. "Hurrah
for Tennessee!" he cried, to the surprise of the troops.[4]

Four days later Vera Cruz fell and General Scott lingered
little before beginning his march on Mexico City. On April
8 the American force took up the route and on April 18 it
fought and won the bloody battle of Cerro Gordo. On that
day the rear elements of Scott's army, under General John
Quitman, left Vera Cruz for the scene of action. In it were
four companies of the Tennessee Mounted, two hundred
strong, including Wheat's company.

General Quitman must have been very much impressed
with Lieutenant Wheat on the march, for a few years later,
in New Orleans, when both were interested in the Cuban
enterprise, he told Roberdeau that he was "the best natural
soldier he ever knew." As for Wheat, he seemed to have
found in Quitman the qualities of a soldier on which he could
model himself, for a dozen years later he was to refer to the
General as "my military father."

Wheat's outfit arrived at Plan del Rio, near Cerro Gordo,
two days after the battle, much to the chagrin of Wheat and
some of the more venturesome Tennnessee Volunteers. "I
have had several skirmishes with the enemy in small parties,"
Wheat wrote home, "and fortunately every time been in command." For some days the First Tennessee Mounted engaged
itself in burning ammunition, burying the dead and removing
cannon.

To the many harassments of General Scott, who had
been wrestling with shortages and deficiencies in his army,
there was now added the problem of the twelve-months volunteers whose time of service would expire at various dates
between May and July, 1847. They were asked to volunteer
for further service but they declined. As their time drew
near they were passed through Vera Cruz and discharged.[5]

Among the departing troops was the First Tennessee
Mounted Regiment, which returned home with a clean slate,

having had no one killed in action, no one wounded in action, no one killed accidentally and no one wounded accidentally. But Lieutenant Chatham Roberdeau Wheat did not leave with them. He, " by great exertions, induced a sufficient number to remain to form a company, which . . . elected Wheat captain, and served to the end of the war." A fragment of a letter to his mother on May 3, 1847, reveals Wheat's pride in his new command: "Here I am at Jalappa [sic] the prettiest place in Mexico—I am enjoying the finest health and spirits—I am busily employed in selecting such men as I wish my troops to be composed of—I have about 100 as strong, hearty and healthy a lot of men as you would wish to see. . . . I am already in quiet possession of my title (Captain Wheat) Oh, grand the appellation when it is known that I command 100 mounted men—They will all be mustered in about the 1st of June." Wheat went to Vera Cruz to recruit for his company but despite his optimism about having a hundred men, the records show he was able to secure but four officers and fifty-five men.

While recruiting, Roberdeau was seized with yellow fever. When his company was ordered out, he was carried on a litter, between two mules, to Jalapa, where the company arrived on May 21. The fever was at its height while he was on the road, and to make matters worse, the company was under attack several times by Mexican guerillas.[6]

Wheat came very near dying in Vera Cruz and he credited his recovery to being brought into the mountains. His company went on to Puebla under the command of Rob's first lieutenant, while he remained in Jalapa to recuperate.

Roberdeau was eager for action and a chance to distinguish himself. " I have a fine active troop," he wrote home, " and my men are of the very best kind, so thus if we have a fight I stand a chance."

Wheat's service during the next six months is vague. His brother, Leo, in a biographical sketch which appears in at

least three versions, makes a number of statements, utterly
without foundation, which, accordingly, cast doubt on the
reliability of other information he offers on Roberdeau's Mexican War exploits. There is the story of how Lieutenant Wheat
at the battle of Resaca de la Palma captured the distinguished
General La Vega and treated him with such courtly kindness
and consideration that his prisoner presented him with a
handsome sword. General Scott, present on the occasion,
commended the young officer for his gallant behavior, says
Leo Wheat.

Inasmuch as the battle of Resaca de la Palma was fought
several weeks before Wheat volunteered and six months
before he actually reached Mexico, he couldn't have captured General La Vega. And General Scott, in any event,
couldn't have commended Rob's nobility on the occasion for
Scott was still in Washington on May 9, 1846.

Leo Wheat confused this with a subsequent incident at
Churubusco, where Roberdeau, arriving after the battle had
been fought, did have for his prisoner General Villareal.
Perhaps General Villareal gave young Wheat a sword as a
token of his thanks for the young man's consideration to a
prisoner. "He embraced me," Roberdeau wrote years later
upon meeting General Villareal again, "for I had treated
him very kindly when a prisoner." Perhaps General Scott
did, on this occasion, say to Lieutenant Wheat: "Sir, this
is a rare compliment for one so young and a soldier to receive!"
Perhaps Roberdeau did say: "It is the gray hairs of the
general's head I honored, for I knew not the high rank of my
prisoner. I was ever taught to honor old age." [7]

Wheat missed the battle of Puebla which was fought
on May 15, for at that time he was in Vera Cruz outfitting
his new recruits. On May 22 Rob's company, together with
all other cavalry units in Scott's army, was placed under the
command of Colonel W. S. Harney. For the rest of the campaign until the fall of Mexico City the only source of specific

information on Roberdeau is the dubious testimony of Leo Wheat. There is, however, no reason to question such statements as these: "His men being well mounted, handsomely uniformed, splendidly equipped and perfect in drill, 'did the ornamental,' as he laughingly said 'on great occasion for general officers and triumphal entries into conquered cities'," and "His command . . . suffered severely in killed and wounded. . . ." But Leo's claim that Roberdeau was the first to gaze upon Mexico City may be discounted as fraternal exuberance. Leo wrote: "Accompanying a party making a reconnaissance, as they drew near to the City of Mexico, he pushed ahead and was the first to catch a distant view of the city as it lay, to use his words, 'glorified by the morning sun in the midst of the loveliest landscape the eye ever beheld.'" [8]

Wheat's company probably rode with Colonel Harney in the van of the army on the march from Puebla which began early on August 7. Old General Twiggs waved his hat around his white head and exclaimed: "Now, my lads, give them a Cerro Gordo shout!" And while a lusty cheer went up and the band, mounted on white horses, played national airs, the cavalry rode out to lead the way to Mexico City.

Precisely what fighting Roberdeau engaged in cannot be determined. It is possible that Captain Wheat's company served as General Scott's bodyguard as the *National Cyclopedia*, without citing any authority, asserts. Sometime after the fall of Mexico City, Wheat's company was ordered to Jalapa and attached to the Maryland–District of Columbia Regiment. On December 2 Wheat received orders to return to the United States on recruiting service, an assignment which Roberdeau relished, for it meant seeing Marina Cheatham and his family and parading his military splendor before them and his Nashville friends. Roberdeau recruited fifty-four men in Nashville, which with the four officers and fifty-five men he had in Jalapa, brought his company up to strength. [9]

Before returning to Mexico, Wheat was presented with a handsome flag by the young ladies of Professor Ingraham's school. He listened with delight to Miss Emma Baxter's flowery effusion: " Captain: You are too well tried a soldier to need the inspiration of our words to nerve your arms. Already you have won unfading laurels on the battlefields of Mexico! . . . The brilliance of the past proclaim the splendor of your future career! "

Roberdeau " out-effused " Miss Baxter with garlands of extravagant eloquence: " Away, across the sea, thousands of miles, the tear-moistened eye of the rough soldier at Jalapa will be lifted up to Heaven with heartfelt benediction upon the lovely school girls of Nashville. . . . This beautiful banner shall be as you wished it—our 'guiding star' through the thickest gloom of strife. . . . Wherever and whenever, upon the toilsome march or in the tented field, amid the shock of armies, or in the triumphal procession, this bright banner shall be unfurled at the head of my column, like a magic mirror it shall fling back to our admiring gaze with true fidelity your forms of innocence and beauty." Roberdeau had been to war, and he liked it. Now he was beginning to like making speeches and he piled bombast upon bombast. " The sight of it [the flag] shall nerve the tired arm of the combatant to renewed exertion, shall mitigate the sufferings of the wounded, and with kindred, holier thoughts assuage the agony of the dying." [10]

Meanwhile, in Mexico, things had happened while Roberdeau was gathering troops in Nashville. On February 2 the treaty of peace was signed and on March 10 the Senate approved it. So when Captain Wheat and his men set out for Mexico, all that sufficed to end the war was acceptance of the treaty by the Mexican Congress.

Wheat took command of his company at Jalapa on May 10, 1848, and was immediately engaged in scouting expeditions, escorting supply trains and rounding up deserters, " of

whom there are quite a host in this immediate neighborhood."
Not knowing that on the day prior, the Mexican Congress
had ratified the treaty of peace, thus ending the war, Roberdeau wrote on May 25, " My presentiments are against peace,
I hope they are not true."

Two months later, to the day, Captain Wheat and his
company were mustered out of service in Memphis.[11]

CHAPTER IV

MANIFEST DESTINY GAINS A SWORD

Wheat returned to Nashville in the summer of 1848 with two things on his mind—to marry Marina Cheatham and to return to the study of law.

It is evident from his letters home from Mexico that he considered the matter all settled with Marina. As late as May 25, shortly before sailing for the United States, he had sent, through his father, his love to "the Mrs. Wheat that is to be if you can guess who the distinguished personage is." [1]

But the lovely and accomplished Marina, with Roberdeau off to war, had not sat pining for her soldier. It is possible that Marina considered him only one of several eligible young gentlemen who were contending for her hand.

Late in 1846 Marina had written relatives in North Carolina describing her beaux, and from the reply of her uncle, David Outlaw, we can get some idea of Marina's estimates of the eager suitors. His advice undoubtedly was prompted by her description of young Wheat: "You say you would like to marry some man of genius, who would confer distinction upon you. . . . You say you are not ambitious of wealth. Let me assure you my dear a competency and independence, and even wealth are very convenient things to be looked to, as the means but not the end of happiness. Love and a cottage is all nonsense, found no where except in silly novels. . . . No woman ought to marry a man until he is able to support her in the same style of life to which she has been accustomed. And where she is a belle and courted by rich and poor, I do not see why she had not as well love a man who has something as one who has nothing. . . . Of your beaux now I confess Mr. Woods is my favorite even though he has 'a sledge hammer nose' if he possesses the qualities of head and heart which you ascribe to him." [2]

Perhaps Marina was influenced by this letter, perhaps Mr. Woods's presence in Nashville and Roberdeau's absence in Mexico during the next year and a half helped her to make up her mind. Perhaps it was a combination of these factors. At any rate, on October 12, 1848, less than three months after Wheat's return, Marina Cheatham was married to Robert Woods, a young banker and iron merchant with plantation holdings on Bayou Lafourche in Louisiana. Dr. Wheat performed the ceremony. [3]

Marina's marriage was a great shock to Roberdeau, but he never fell out of love with her. Four years later he wrote his mother: "I would rather have her now were she a widow than any maid in the world. I love her still. Perhaps I may yet make her regret the refusal of my hand." [4]

In the fall of 1848 Wheat went to New Orleans to complete his legal studies and he was admitted to the Louisiana bar early in 1849. His mother, in a letter to her husband's family in Wheeling, proudly declared: "Mary [Mrs. Judge Morgan] writes that few young men make as good an impression as R. has done among the old men at the Bar."

Roberdeau, struggling to establish himself, was lonely in New Orleans, although his cousins, Thomas Wolfe and Mary Wolfe Morgan, lived there. His spirit was still wounded by Marina Cheatham's marriage. He pleaded with his mother to visit him. "I need your society," he wrote. "I feel like an isolated being I have no ties, no restraint, if you do not come I shall be miserable. . . . I am in fine health and look forward to the coming season for a support by my profession." Roberdeau had expected that his Cousin Thomas would take him into his prosperous firm, but he never did and Wheat never forgave him. "I shall always remember," he wrote several years later, "that Cousin T. promised me that he would take me into partnership when I got my license."

Young Wheat, disappointed in love and in his professional progress, too, turned to politics, which he entered as a Whig. But soon more compelling things attracted his attention.

A new political philosophy was abroad in the land. After the Mexican War, many Americans held that it was the manifest destiny of the United States to be the instrument of Divine Providence in bringing enlightenment and civilization to the benighted people of the Western hemisphere. Manifest Destiny—the phrase is credited to Editor John L. O'Sullivan of the *Democratic Review* who coined it in 1845—appealed to people North and South and for various reasons. It was essentially a land-grabbing idea, but one which was rooted "in a national or sectional superiority complex."

Editors, local and national politicians, influential business and professional men and even ministers from the pulpit, all joined the movement, and Americans generally, from one end of the country to the other, believed devoutly in Manifest Destiny. To Southern leaders it meant the extension of slavery and the strengthening of the South, economically and politically. To the free North, expansion southward meant bringing to backward Catholic states the blessings of Protestant civilization and the spreading of American political doctrines.

"The North Americans *will* spread out far beyond their present bounds," wrote the influential J. D. B. DeBow, in 1848. "They *will* encroach again and again on their neighbors. New territories *will* be planted, declare their independence and be annexed! We have new Mexico and California! We will have Old Mexico and Cuba! The isthmus cannot arrest—nor even the St. Lawrence!! Time has all this in her womb." [5]

When Wheat arrived in New Orleans in the fall of 1848, he found the papers full of Manifest Destiny, with Cuba as the immediate goal of the expansionists. When Spain refused American offers to buy the island in 1848 and again in 1849, the expansionists launched a propaganda campaign against Spanish despotism and brutality. It was pointed out, too, that Cuba in the hands of some other nation than Spain was a threat to the security of the United States. Moreover, a free Cuba meant commercial expansion and American control of the world sugar market.

In New Orleans, the closest of the great American cities to Cuba, the desire to possess the island was almost universal, although the motives for possession were different. Some sought Cuba for expanding commerce, others sought land, while still others desired it for political advantages to the South. This reached its peak in the late summer of 1849, when an expedition at Round Island, near New Orleans, prepared to descend on Cuba, in concert with a similar expedition from New York. General Narciso Lopez, a proscribed Cuban official, was to lead both forces after they had landed on Cuba.

Lopez, a native of Venezuela, entered the Spanish army as a boy and rose rapidly to colonel before he was twenty-four. Stationed in Cuba, he married well. He went to Spain where he became a field marshal. Returning to Cuba, Lopez held high office for a while. After engaging unsuccessfully in several business ventures he began to dream of Cuban independence, to which he dedicated the rest of his days and ultimately his life itself.

An abortive Cuban uprising in 1848 collapsed and Lopez escaped to the United States, where his plans and those of the expansionists met on common ground. The fifty-year-old general was just what the expansionists in the United States needed. And they were exactly what Lopez needed to push his plan for Cuban independence. Twin expeditions to Cuba were mounted at Round Island and New York. But before either sailed in September, 1849, they were broken up by United States authorities, who seized the filibusters' vessels.

Young Wheat was infected early with the Manifest Destiny virus. His Mexican experiences made him highly susceptible for he had come home from the war certain that it was a mistake for the United States to give up any part of the conquered Mexican territory.

Shortly after the suppression of the Round Island expedition, New Orleans became the center of Lopez's operations. Disgusted with the lukewarm support for the Cuban enterprise in the North, Lopez, in the spring of 1850, traveled to New Orleans by way of the Ohio and Mississippi rivers.

In Cincinnati and Louisville he held interviews which resulted in the raising of a force of Kentuckians for the liberation of Cuba although ostensibly they were being organized to go to California. Lopez made munificent offers to them. They were offered a bounty, $4,000 in cash, with Cuban lands also promised to those who served a year. Until the venture was successful, they would draw the pay of privates in the American army. For officers the bounty was $10,000, with promised high rank in the Republic of Cuba. Many young men became soldiers of fortune under Lopez's banner, some in answer to the presumed cries of the oppressed, and others for the less altruistic motives of gain and glory.[6]

General Lopez, accompanied by his young chief of staff, Colonel Ambrosio José Gonzales, reached New Orleans about March 15, and began at once to organize the expedition to Cuba. Upon arrival Lopez met John Henderson, former United States Senator from Mississippi and brigadier general of militia in that state. An ardent expansionist, Henderson introduced the general to men of similar ideas, including L. J. Sigur, editor of the *Delta*, General John A. Quitman, governor of Mississippi, and several other influential men in New Orleans and in Mississippi.

By April 1 filibustering activities in New Orleans were well underway. To raise funds for the campaign, bonds redeemable in the name of the Republic of Cuba and signed by Lopez were printed and sold at ten cents on the dollar. Henderson, buying himself ten or fifteen thousand dollars worth of bonds, disposed of about 400,000 of them. "With the money collected, about $40,000," wrote Gonzales years later, "the little steamer *Creole*, that had been plying between New Orleans and Mobile, was purchased, repaired, coaled, officered, manned and provisioned, arms and uniforms were procured, and the bark *Georgiana* was chartered as a transport." Plans for a Mississippi regiment to join the already organized Kentucky unit were launched.

It was at this stage of the expedition that Roberdeau Wheat joined his fortunes with those of Lopez.

Colonel Gonzales, to whom Wheat applied, later wrote: "Col. Robert [sic] Wheat, who had served in the Mexican war, presented himself to me, begging to be allowed to go. I told him we had no transportation for him, but he removed the objection by offering to procure it if I only gave him the authority to form also a skeleton regiment of Louisianians. This having been done, he obtained money from young gentlemen friends of his, to charter the brig *Susan Loud*, provisioned her, etc., all for the mere privilege of going."

However much Roberdeau believed, as Leo Wheat asserts, "that the acquisition of Cuba as a new slave state would enable the South to withstand the further aggressions of Northern fanaticism"; however much General Lopez "won him to the cause of Cuban independence"; however much he might justify the Cuban enterprise by comparing it to risking one's life to rescue "a weak woman, gagged, manacled, dungeoned, and completely in the power of a brutal ravisher," [7] there is every reason to suspect that fame and fortune were the greatest inducements to Wheat's engaging in the venture.

He was young and ambitious and frustrated; he had served two years in Mexico, thirsting in vain for an oppor-

tunity to win glory before returning to civil life; he was poor,
and perhaps in debt; and to top off everything he was restless,
without a mooring since Marina Cheatham turned him down.
The Lopez expedition offered Roberdeau opportunities for
the things he wanted—leadership, action, fame and wealth.

The first miscalculation in the expedition occurred when
the Kentucky regiment arrived above New Orleans in the
early hours of April 11, only to learn that transportation was
not yet ready for them. "Owing to some woeful misunder-
standing," wrote one of the officers, "we had arrived ten or
fifteen days too soon." The Kentuckians moved the next
day to Lafayette, which was on the outskirts of New Orleans,
stating that they were "a California company" and would
be detained a few days. They probably fooled no one, for the
officer wrote: "Our object and destination was then as well
known in New Orleans as it could be. We had been the
subject of several newspaper notices, and the Cuban expedition was the barroom conversation all over the city."

Wheat, meanwhile, was busy recruiting men for his
skeleton regiment and raising funds with which to charter
the *Susan Loud*. His rendezvous soon attracted "many of
the worthless characters and blackguard rowdies composing
no small part of the population of New Orleans." Soon the
plan of the Lopez expedition was revealed. It would embark
in three sections. The Kentuckians would sail first on the
brig *Georgiana* and make for the island of Mujeres, off Yu-
catan. About a week later Colonel Wheat and his Louisiana
contingent would sail on the *Susan Loud* for a rendezvous
in the Gulf with the *Creole* which, after taking on Wheat's
men would then steam to Mujeres and pick up the Kentuckians.

In order to give an air of legality to the whole affair and
to forestall government interference before the expedition
sailed, each man was supplied with a ticket to Chagres as
if in reality the expedition were bound for California via the
Isthmus. Everything was ready by April 25, and the Ken-

tuckians, each with his personal belongings in a bundle, boarded the *Georgiana* that afternoon. At nine o'clock a tug came alongside and shortly thereafter, while a large crowd cheered from the docks, the *Georgiana* was towed towards the Gulf. Standing on the wharf and waving until the ship was gathered up in the darkness were Lopez, Gonzales and Henderson.[8]

In a few days it would be Roberdeau's turn to lead his men on the desperate adventure. In the interval of feverish activity, the filibusters in the Louisiana regiment had an opportunity to estimate the worth of their twenty-four-year-old commander. One of them, a fellow New Orleanian, provided this picture: "Col. Wheat is a noble fellow, young and ardent, in dangerous emprize. He was a pet with the generals of the Mexican war. The ladies of the Crescent City frequently speak of his flashing, dark eyes, his frank ingenuous countenance, and his Herculean, but graceful, frame. A favored mortal, who at his age, can win the confidence of rough soldiers and arouse to palpitation and fluttering the swelling bosom of fair maiden."[9]

CHAPTER V

FIASCO IN CUBA

On the night of May 2, 1850, the brig *Susan Loud*, " bound " for Chagres, cast off her moorings and slipped down the Mississippi with Colonel Wheat and his Louisiana regiment.

For three days squalls and rain accompanied their south-eastward sailing, but by daylight on May 6 the wind died down, the clouds scudded off and at noon the sun was shining brightly.

Captain Pendleton took a reading, and issued instructions to the steward for an early dinner. The men knew something was up, for Colonel Wheat and his staff, Lieutenant Colonel William H. Bell and Major George B. Hayden, were seriously conversing apart. They hurriedly ate their meal in a state of expectancy and quickly assembled aft the mainmast when summoned on deck. Colonel Wheat mounted the quarter-deck and raised his hand for silence.

" Fellow citizens," he began, " we have now arrived at our point of destination and organization in the gulf. You are aware that we cleared New Orleans for Chagres. Captain Pendleton informs me that it is a matter of perfect indifference with him whether we proceed to Chagres or not."

Colonel Wheat waved a piece of paper in his hand and said dramatically that it had been given to him by one of General Lopez's aides with instructions to break the seal when the *Susan Loud* was in Latitude 26° N. and Longitude

87°. "I find on opening this paper that I am directed to remain near this spot until the 7th day of May, on which day . . . we are to sail on a direct line for the Balize, and by Thursday evening [May 9] may expect to see the *Creole* and the Old General."

Wheat then launched into the main points of his speech: "I have addressed you as Fellow Citizens, because it is perhaps the last time I shall ever address you as Citizens of the United States. Long ere the sun has sunk beneath the world of waters which now surround us, we shall perhaps have consummated an act that will throw us beyond the protection of the Stars and the Stripes under whose auspices we have sailed thus far. This act is simply organizing our little band into a skeleton regiment for the purpose of landing on, and wrenching Cuba from the grasp of bigoted and besotted Spain. The moment we organize, that moment we pass beyond the protection of our own government we have no longer any right to sail under her flag. . . . I shall therefore henceforth address you as Soldiers of the Liberating Army of Cuba."

There was no longer need to keep up any pretense. Colonel Wheat reminded his men that they all knew where they were bound and for what purpose. Wheat justified the assault on Cuba by recalling how Lafayette had come to the aid of the American colonies to help them repel oppression; what was once a patriot's devotion was now his duty; true patriotism consisted not in merely helping those who could throw off oppression after they are in rebellion, but rather in striking the first blow for them, as this expedition would do for the Cubans.

This, apparently, was a prearranged signal, for at that moment the Cuban flag was run up the masthead and as it whipped free in the breeze, Wheat pointed to it and exclaimed: "Liberators! Behold your flag! Three cheers for the Cuban flag!" Three tremendous cheers went up, "reverberating over the billows, and arousing the listless sharks."

For thirty minutes Roberdeau talked on. ". . . You are aware fellow soldiers that we have come from the United States, without arms, without organization, without previous concert to commit any overt act which may, by any possibility, compromise the dignity, or disturb the harmony of our own government. Nor do we expect or intend to violate any law of nations, unless revolution be so considered, and this cannot be, because successful rebellion is always pronounced patriotism, while a failure is branded as piracy. We then shall soon be patriots, purer than Cato, or conspirators more dark than Catiline. Then Soldiers of the Liberating Army of Cuba, while you gaze on that flag with its lone star, resolve to make it your winding sheet on the field of battle, or your beacon in the camp of victory."

Colonel Wheat directed the men to divide into ten equal companies, forming a skeleton regiment, and to elect officers who would then draw by lot for rank. Before breaking up, the men gave three cheers for Wheat, three for Cuba and three cheers more for General Lopez.[1]

After organizing their companies the men killed time by playing poker with bonds of the future Cuban republic as the stakes.

On May 7 the *Creole*, with General Lopez, Colonel Gonzales and 130 Mississippians aboard sailed from New Orleans to keep its rendezvous in the Gulf with the *Susan Loud*. To create the flimsy fiction that when it left the United States, the expedition was not armed, boxes of arms were taken on during the night at a point in the Mississippi near its mouth.

The *Creole* and *Susan Loud*, each flying the Cuban flag, met on schedule. The brig came alongside the steamer, and Wheat's regiment boarded the *Creole*, which then headed for the island of Mujeres to pick up Colonel Theodore O'Hara and his Kentuckians.

Meanwhile, the *Georgiana* had been blown off her course and had put into the island of Contoy, ten miles from

Mujeres. Here the Kentuckians disembarked, but unfortunately the little island had no water fit to drink and unfavorable winds prevented the *Georgiana* from making Mujeres for a fresh supply. Discontent, growing almost to mutiny, quickly developed among the men. Colonel O'Hara and other officers were able to revive their spirits somewhat. Fortunately, at precisely this time the *Creole*, which was running close to shore to avoid a suspicious vessel, spotted the *Georgiana* at anchor and made for the harbor. It was May 14, and the filibuster force was now together at last.[2]

It was decided to send the *Creole* to Mujeres for water while the men drilled on the beach at Contoy. Lopez issued a proclamation to the men urging them to show all the virtues as well as all the valor of the American citizen-soldier and by "discipline, good order, moderation in victory, and sacred respects for all private rights, you will put to shame every insolent calumny of your enemies." After the *Creole* sailed, the Louisiana filibusters began whispering discontentedly among themselves. They feared that the already crowded *Creole* could not take on the Kentuckians without risk. Someone recalled that two years earlier the *Creole* had been condemned in the lake trade. Another one heard how just a year earlier it had been chartered for a Havana trip, but got only forty miles into the Gulf when it had to turn back because of leaks. Such comment served to bring their discontent into the open.

Colonel Wheat, recognizing the sagging morale of his men, decided he had to act quickly. The Louisiana regiment was assembled on the beach and Wheat stepped out in front of the line of dejected filibusters. As he silenced the hum of voices with a gesture, he realized that the men had reason on their side. The *Creole* was, indeed, an old tub, its seaworthiness suspect. And there was no denying what was evident to all, that the Liberating Army, about to embark on a hazardous adventure, barely numbered six hundred men. Wheat knew he could not answer such arguments with logic.

He could not prove to their satisfaction that the *Creole* was safe or that General Lopez had all the men he needed to seize and hold Cuba. The young commander was "impressed with the necessity of remedying by rhetoric that which he could not answer by reason."

The twenty-four-year-old lawyer had never pleaded before so stubborn a jury nor had he ever argued a case with the facts so much against him. But Roberdeau, his countenance aglow, staked all on his eloquence and in doing so, revealed the unmistakable mark of leadership, an ability to gain the confidence of the most desperate and unruly men.

"Fellow soldiers," he began, "this day a perfect organization of the Army of Liberators has been effected. Your wishes, previously expressed, have been carried out by our noble head—I now bear the commission of Colonel of this detachment."

Cheers broke out among the men and Roberdeau paused for them to subside. He would give his views on the expedition, he said, with the line of conduct he would follow with the assistance of Divine Providence. Then he pulled out all the rhetorical stops. "While yet within the borders of our beloved country [he forgot, apparently, that he had told the men aboard the *Susan Loud* that they had passed from the protection of the United States government] the distant wail of the oppressed Cubans, to whose rescue we are now rushing, saluted our pained ears, every breeze from the southward that should have been laden with the sweet perfume of tropical flowers, was freighted with cries of anguish and despair."

More cheers interrupted Wheat when he said that Cuba "is made the theatre of a brutal oppression, unprecedented in the most diresome periods of a Nero or a Caligula, and this too, within a short distance of a land that boasts of a Washington, an Adams, a Hancock and a Patrick Henry!"

Continuing to hammer heavily on Spanish brutality in Cuba, where "the bloody eye of the monster never sleeps,"

Colonel Wheat said the Cubans were begging: " 'Will not
. . . the hardy offsprings of revolutionary sires facilitate them
in making an effort for manhood and nationality?' You my
worthy comrades heard those rending cries and warm appeals.
When did a deserving American listen to the cry of distress,
and not fly to succor and relieve."

"Nary a time," answered a lieutenant.

"Never," added another.

"Never," thundered from the ranks.

When order was restored, Wheat continued: "I glory
in being connected with so noble an enterprise, I thank God
that I have contributed my mite, in furtherance of the great
cause of human rights, I thank you from my inmost heart
that you have placed me in your van!"

The men cheered again and Wheat took advantage of
the pause to mop the perspiration off his face.

"The kindly interposition of a superintending Providence is clearly apparent in every step we have taken," he
continued. "Land us in Cuba, let the standard of liberty be
raised, let us make a successful stand, and that mighty engine,
public opinion, will sustain us at home while our arms will
sustain us in Cuba, and soon, 'we shall feed in green pastures
by the side of still waters,' in this gem Republic of the Ocean."

More cheers went up from Louisianians, this time with
evidences of returning enthusiasm for the venture. Colonel
Wheat returned to his eloquence. Their little vessel, he
thanked God, had carried them safely thus far, free from
perils and dangers. "I tell you, my noble soldiers, success
must perch upon our banner. . . . Cuba shall yet be free! I
need not, soldiers, utter one word to stimulate you to deeds
of daring and hardy valor. The daring of American troops
is part of their nature and being. . . . We may die perhaps
. . . but there is no such word as fail. . . . And now, my brave
boys, let us, under the command of our noble chieftain, rush
to the field of glory. . . ."

When Wheat finished, flushed and almost breathless,

deafening cheers broke out from the men, their morale once again restored.

When the troops re-embarked on the *Creole* it was discovered that a number of desertions had cut the strength of the force to 521. It was with this "army" that Lopez hoped to establish himself on Cuba. Each man was given sixty rounds of ammunition. The Louisianians were supplied with muskets, the Kentuckians with rifles and the Mississippians with Jaegers. The men wore red flannel shirts, black cloth caps with a Lone Star cockade. The captains generally wore white trousers while the lieutenants wore black and the men wore pants of various shades and stripes.[3]

The *Creole* steamed toward Cuba with mounting tension on board. Heavy seas made progress difficult for the overloaded little steamer. The men were crowded below deck and in the hold as well as on deck, and it took the strictest discipline to keep groups from passing from one part of the ship to the other.

As the filibusters neared the island, General Lopez grew increasingly restless. When he wasn't below, studying maps and conferring with his aides, all the while smoking *cigarritos*, he paced the deck rapidly, examining with his spyglass the many ships which came into sight. Whenever the *Creole* ran close to a suspicious vessel the order came: "Off with your red shirts!" and the men didn't put them on again until all was clear.

By now the plan of attack had been revealed to the officers. Matanzas was the objective, but since it was heavily fortified by sea and Lopez had no artillery, the filibusters would land at Cárdenas, take the town by surprise and then advance by railroad to Matanzas before the word of the invasion could spread.

Lopez counted heavily upon the Cubans rushing immediately to his standard. He expected them quickly to swell his army to 5,000, with which he would advance on Havana. By the time he reached the capital, the chief of the "Liberating Army " expected a force of thirty thousand men, which would make him master of the island.

A full moon, so bright one could almost read by its light, was out on the night of May 18 as the *Creole* neared its destination. The steamer, idling along until the moon set, passed the lighthouse, fifteen miles from Cárdenas, at ten o'clock and began to grope its way slowly up the bay. As the

stealthily moving ship passed in and out of fleets of vessels and a number of tiny islands, hushed excitement gripped the men. They stood motionless and silent for hours, with only the low call of the leadsman, or the whispered orders of officers and now and then the clank of a sabre breaking the dead silence.

At one o'clock, the Liberators caught their first glimpse of Cárdenas; an hour later the *Creole* nosed noiselessly towards the wharf. But here Lopez's luck, good up to now, began to turn. A few yards from the dock, the *Creole* ran aground.

The mate, a plucky little fellow named Callender Fayssoux—
he later became famous as commander of William Walker's
one-vessel navy in Nicaragua—jumped overboard with a rope
and a plank and, climbing the wharf, soon made the *Creole*
secure. Fayssoux placed the plank on a gunnel and sat on
the other end to steady it. Over this precarious bridge came
the Liberators.

Insisting that he precede Lopez in order to test the
strength of the plank, Colonel Gonzales, adjutant general
of the expedition, was the first ashore. After pausing midway
to make sure the plank was firm, he beckoned from the wharf
to Lopez to cross. Then one by one, Lopez's staff landed,
followed by the Kentucky, Mississippi and Louisiana regiments in that order.

The delay in putting ashore more than five hundred
men who walked single file over a narrow plank eliminated
all element of surprise in Lopez's landing. The alarm was
given and the Spanish garrison prepared itself for the defense
of the town. Thwarted in his plan to seize Cárdenas before
the Spaniards realized what was taking place, Lopez was
now compelled to take the town by force.[4]

A detachment of Kentuckians rushed to seize the railroad
to Matanzas. Although they did so without opposition, the
station was a mile and a half from the wharf and this added
to the delay. Finally, about 5 A. M., three hours after he
landed, Lopez began his march on the plaza, which was
flanked on one side by the barracks, with the governor's
house directly opposite across the square. The Liberators
advanced in three columns, Colonel O'Hara's Kentuckians
moving up the main street and the Louisiana and Mississippi
regiments taking parallel streets.

At the first volley from the fortress-like barracks, Colonel
O'Hara was wounded and was forced to retire to the *Creole*.
When Wheat heard the firing, he assumed that it was a
salute to Lopez. He cried out "Lopez and Liberty" and
rushed into the plaza at the head of his Louisianians.[5] They

THE GREAT ADVENTURERS

Narciso Lopez (top, *courtesy Bettmann Archives*),
William Walker (left), and Garibaldi (right, *courtesy Frederick H. Meserve*)

MAJOR CHATHAM ROBERDEAU WHEAT, C. S. A.
(*Courtesy Mrs. William Elam*)

arrived in time to receive a volley from the Spanish troops, who, having engaged the Kentuckians in front of the governor's house, were now retreating into the building. Struck in the shoulder, Wheat cried out as he fell: "Louisianians! Your colonel is killed! Go on and avenge his death!" Wheat quickly realized, however, that this wound, far from mortal, was relatively slight. But it was painful and he was forced to withdraw from the fight. He returned to the *Creole* for treatment and took no further part in the action. Wheat's Louisianians, now commanded by Lieutenant Colonel Bell, made several fruitless charges on the governor's house before the filibusters were able to set fire to the structure. Then they surrounded the burning building and waited for the Spaniards either to try to escape or to surrender. At 8 A. M., a white flag was displayed from a window and Cárdenas was in Lopez's possession.

But now that he had the town, what was he going to do with it? There was no stampede of revolutionists to Lopez. The Cubans, in fact, showed a marked apathy to being liberated. The "distant wail of the oppressed Cubans," which Wheat had "heard" on the beach at Contoy, was wholly inaudible in Cárdenas. Some Cubans expressed surprise that Lopez's force was so small and protested that before the next day five thousand Spanish troops would be upon them. Accordingly, they feared to join Lopez, or show him any support, claiming that to do so would bring their ruin and destruction. The filibusters, with reason, asked each other: "Where is that 'host of friends' who were to have welcomed us?"

The Liberators soon became disorganized and the men scattered about the town seeking food and rest. Soon rumors were spread that three thousand Spaniards were on the road from Matanzas and would reach Cárdenas near midnight. "Never were 600 men"—actually, at least a hundred less— "in a more hopeless, lost and desperate situation. . . . The men drank a great deal of liquor, of every description."[6]

Lopez called a council of war. To fight three thousand
men with five hundred, many of whom were in no condition
for a fight, was out of the question. At any moment, too,
Spanish warships might block the harbor of Cárdenas, cutting
off retreat by sea, and leaving no alternative to annihilation
by vastly superior forces on their front.

Lopez decided to re-embark his men on the *Creole*, and
sail speedily to the western part of the island to make a new
landing at Mantua. Then, while all the Spanish energies
were directed to meeting an attack from Cárdenas, the liberators would approach Havana on its "blind side." Lopez
still indulged himself in the belief that the Cubans would
rise up against their Spanish masters once his little band
landed in their midst.

The re-embarkation was effected at dusk, under cover of
a rear guard of Kentuckians. The filibusters, after holding
Cárdenas for ten hours, sailed away with the Spanish governor,
his staff and a number of soldiers as prisoners, and with a
large quantity of ammunition seized in the town. But the
Creole did not sail very far. Soon, once again, the shoals of
the tricky harbor at Cárdenas held her fast. The vessel ran
aground at 8 P. M. Every effort to get the *Creole* off the bar
failed and as a last resort, Lopez ordered that everything that
could lighten the steamer, ammunition and provisions included, be thrown overboard. A hundred filibusters left the
vessel for a nearby island, to further relieve the *Creole's*
burden. Finally, the rising tide and the reduced load
combined to free the ship and at daybreak on May 20, the
Creole reached the Cárdenas light, where Lopez landed the
governor and other prisoners.

Although another landing was now impossible, Lopez
persisted in wanting to land at Mantua. But opposition to
this hopeless plan quickly arose. At a conference of the
officers, Colonel Wheat, Major Hardy, Adjutant Titus and
Captain Allen of Kentucky supported Lopez. Colonel O'Hara
denounced the idea as madness and the rest of the officers

agreed with him. Finally someone suggested leaving the
decision to the men. Wheat pledged that his Louisianians
would be willing to land again, but when a vote was taken
only seven of his men voted to land.

Lopez, crushed by the turn of events, begged to be put
ashore with whatever men would follow him, but his irra-
tional request was refused. With the expedition now a failure
the *Creole* made for Key West. At this moment the filibusters
saw the fast Spanish warship *Pizarro* on the horizon, entering
the harbor of Cárdenas. The Spanish admiral, once apprised
of what had happened, would surely take up the pursuit.

LOPEZ'S CARDENAS
EXPEDITION
MAY 19, 1850

By evening the *Creole* was in the shallows, forty miles
east of Key West. A pilot came aboard, but it was daylight
before the *Creole* proceeded again. As dawn broke on May
21, the filibusters saw the *Pizzaro*, barely four miles off,
making for the *Creole* at full speed. Between the two vessels
lay the reef which the *Creole*, drawing only five feet of
water, had safely navigated. The *Pizzaro*, drawing sixteen
feet, would have to circle the reef. With this slight advantage,
the *Creole* began the race to Key West in grim earnestness.
The filibusters depended on the *Creole* reaching Key West
before the Spanish warship caught up.

The *Creole* had taken on some coal at Cárdenas but it
was, recorded Colonel Gonzales, "a miserable black dust"
which hardly produced more than a speed of five knots.

The *Pizarro* could make thirteen knots. The *Creole* had thirty barrels of rosin which Gonzales had ordered aboard for an emergency. Now was the time to use them. " The ax was put to every available piece of wood in the boat, bunks, furniture, etc . . ." wrote Gonzales, " and with this and the rosin and the bacon we had saved and the coal dust, we made ten knots, and our next danger anticipated was the explosion of our boiler." [7]

Providentially, the *Pizarro* lost time taking on a pilot and then it went aground for fifteen to twenty minutes trying to get across the reef. The furious Spanish admiral threatened to have the Key West pilot hanged.

The Spanish man-of-war gained steadily as the ships raced on and on. But finally, with the *Pizarro* now only a cannon's shot astern, the *Creole* steamed into the harbor of Key West.

Ten minutes after the *Creole* docked she was deserted; the filibusters dispersed hurriedly to avoid arrest by United States authorities. Wheat's first attempt at filibustering had ended in a fiasco. But it nevertheless proved beyond any doubt that Rob was one of those " young men whose tastes for civil pursuits had been destroyed by the Mexican War." [8] Henceforth his law office would be mainly a place to hang his sword between far-off campaigns.

CHAPTER VI

THE END OF THE AFFAIR

On June 21 the United States Marshal at New Orleans received a *capias* for the arrest of Chatham Roberdeau Wheat, but he was unable immediately to execute the warrant because the young filibuster was not in the city.[1] Rob had not lingered in Key West after the *Creole* won its race to safety, but had taken off for Chapel Hill, North Carolina, where his father was now a member of the faculty of the University of North Carolina.

Wheat doubtless read in the newspapers of the aftermath of the ill-fated Cárdenas expedition. Narciso Lopez had been arrested in Savannah, to which he had gone from Key West. The Government, however, could not produce evidence that Lopez had violated the Neutrality Act of 1818 and he had been released. Emboldened by this turn of events, Lopez returned to New Orleans where he was promptly arrested again by United States authorities, who had received instructions from the White House to bear down heavily on all connected with the Cuban enterprise.

"It is the earnest desire of the President that all leaders engaged in organizing and setting on foot the late expedition against Cuba shall be brought to trial and punishment," wrote the Secretary of the Interior to the Federal District Attorney at New Orleans. "It is a matter in which the good faith of the nation is implicated and it shall not do to confine the retribution of justice to an obscure and worthless foreigner and suffer our own citizens who know the law which they have violated to escape unpunished." [2]

Practically all of the New Orleans newspapers agreed that the cards were stacked in favor of Lopez and the filibusters. " If the evidence against Lopez were a thousand fold stronger," declared the *Orleanian* in a typical comment, " no jury could be impaneled to convict him because public opinion makes a law, and public opinion is in favor of Lopez's striving for Republican institutions." [3]

At Lopez's preliminary hearing before the United States Commissioner, practically all witnesses refused to answer questions. Some did so on the grounds that they might incriminate themselves—a procedure to gain considerable vogue a century later—and others maintained that to do so would be to violate confidences. Despite difficulties in the Government's path, a grand jury eventually brought in true bills against sixteen of the leaders in the Cuban enterprise.

Active participants indicted were Wheat, Lopez, Theodore O'Hara, John Pickett, R. Hayden, Thomas T. Hawkins, W. H. Bell, N. J. Bunch, Peter Smith and A. J. Gonzales, all of whom held the rank of major or higher in the Cárdenas expedition. Indicted also, as leaders of the expedition, were L. J. Sigur, editor of the *Delta*, Donatien Augustin of the Louisiana Legion, Governor John A. Quitman and Supreme Court Justice Cotesworth Pinckney Smith of Mississippi, J. L. Sullivan, former editor of the *Democratic Review*, and John Henderson, former United States Senator. [4]

Throughout the summer and into the fall, Rob remained with his parents. Long before he decided to return to New Orleans to face the music, he met and fell in love with Sallie Jones, lovely seventeen-year-old daughter of Colonel Cadwallader Jones of West Hill, North Carolina. The young colonel of the filibusters was captivated by Sallie's beauty and charm. And, at least temporarily, she made him forget Marina

Cheatham. Regularly, Rob covered the fifteen miles between Chapel Hill and West Hill to·pay his respects to Sallie.

There can be little doubt that she was responsible for his postponing his return to New Orleans. His letters during the next four or five years indicate how much the young lady impressed him: " I wish I could win Sallie Jones "; " I wish I could get Sallie Jones "; " Please court Sallie Jones for me "; " One of the Senoritas here reminds me very much of Miss Sallie Jones."

But eventually Wheat bade farewell to Sallie and in October he reached New Orleans, where he was quickly brought into court by the United States Marshal. On October 25 Rob posted a surety bond of a thousand dollars and was released to await trial. He immediately resumed the practice of law.

Because John Henderson had been a prime mover in organizing the Cárdenas expedition, he was brought to trial first. Inasmuch as the charge against Wheat and the other filibusters was identical with that against Henderson, the latter's trial thus became a test case. The issue involved was not participation in the Lopez expedition, but the construction, meaning and application of the Neutrality Law of 1818 to the Cárdenas incident. The big question was whether, in a legal sense, the Cárdenas affair was a military expedition. If it was, Henderson, Wheat and the other filibusters were guilty of violating the Neutrality Law. If not, conviction of the filibusters was impossible.

Judah P. Benjamin, noted New Orleans lawyer and later to be called the " Brains of the Confederacy," was retained to assist in the prosecution of the filibusters. The government tried persistently to get a conviction, but three times a hung jury resulted in mistrials for Henderson. Finally, after almost three months of wasted effort, the government in March, 1851, dropped the suit against Henderson. At the same time the charges against Wheat and the other filibusters were also dismissed.[5]

At the time the first Henderson trial opened, Roberdeau reported to his parents that he was "hard at work upon my great Rail Road cases." He was in "fine health despite the cholera . . . in the city." His weight, unbelievably, was 126 pounds. He suggested that his brother, John Thomas, come to New Orleans, where "he can live at any rate he choses, from 1000 $ to 100,000 $ per annum."[6]

But despite Roberdeau's apparent new-found zeal for his profession he was soon lured away again from the bar by a revival of the Cuban business.

As early as April 25, 1851, President Millard Fillmore issued a proclamation stating there were reasons to believe that an expedition was in preparation and that the leaders were foreigners abusing the hospitality of the United States. The President warned that those who violated the neutrality laws would not only subject themselves to penalties, but would "forfeit their claim to the protection of this government, or any interference on their behalf, no matter to what extremities they may be reduced in consequence of their illegal conduct."

Narciso Lopez, undaunted by the failure at Cárdenas, was, indeed, actively engaged in mounting another invasion of Cuba. Lopez had the moral, if not the financial support, of his original backers. "I need not tell you," wrote John Henderson to a friend, "how much I desire to see him move again, and it is more useless to tell you also how wholly unable I am to assist him to make this move. With my limited means, I am under the extremest burdens from my endeavors on the former occasion. . . . Yet I still believe in the importance, the morality, and the probability of the enterprise; and I believe it is one the South should steadfastly cherish and promote."

Such, also, along with the hope of gain and glory were the views of young Colonel Wheat, who soon plunged wholeheartedly again into the Cuban adventure. News of a revolution in Cuba reached New Orleans on July 22, and the

city, already excited over Lopez's preparations, was swept
to a pitch of enthusiasm similar to that during the Mexican
War when news of military successes reached the city. Mass
meetings were held; speakers, urging that aid be dispatched
at once to Cuba, were enthusiastically cheered. Hundreds
of volunteers, many prominent residents of New Orleans,
enlisted. Cuban bonds to finance the venture were printed
and quickly sold and with the proceeds a ship and equipment
were purchased. Cuban flags, Cuban posters were seen all
over town.

Excitement was high when Lopez and about 450 filibusters sailed from New Orleans on the *Pampero* early on
the morning of August 3, 1851. Everybody in New Orleans
except government officials seemed to know about the expedition's departure and despite the predawn hour a large and
excited crowd was at the wharf to give Lopez a sendoff.

Rob Wheat did not sail on the *Pampero*. He was to
follow Lopez with the second wave of Liberators. This was
to include a Kentucky regiment which was on the way to
New Orleans, and two regiments which Wheat and Colonel
Bell were empowered to raise. Lopez expected that these
three regiments, totaling not less than three thousand men
would follow shortly after his departure.

While Lopez's reinforcements prepared to join him, all
New Orleans speculated on the venture, eagerly devouring
all rumors concerning the Cuban revolution that sifted into
the city. On August 21 rumors gave way to shocking facts.
The news reached the city that Colonel W. L. Crittenden
and fifty men, having been separated from Lopez, had been
captured by the Spaniards while trying to make their escape
in small boats. They were quickly tried, condemned to death
and shot.

Immediately New Orleans seethed with rage over this
new evidence of "Spanish brutality." Riots, fanned by inflammatory pieces in the press, broke out, the victims being
Spanish shopkeepers and the Spanish paper, *La Union*. A

mob descended upon the Spanish consulate, from which the consul had fled to the safety of a friend's house. Before the authorities could divert its fury, the mob wrecked the consulate. The rioting continued all day and into the night. Finally city authorities called upon law-abiding citizens to aid police in restoring order.[7]

At a Cuban mass meeting held in Lafayette Square the night of the riots, "excitement was irresistible, overwhelming." Young Colonel Wheat was among the speakers, all of whom called for suppression of the riots and direction of the city's anger against the Spanish authority in Cuba. Several days later, the *Daily Delta* published a letter describing an incident during Roberdeau's address:

"When Col. Wheat was speaking of the murdered fifty-one, he said: 'Were I to die this moment, I would have the proud satisfaction of knowing that I leave others behind to prosecute the good cause, and I would join the spirits of the gallant Crittenden and his companions in the land of Dreams.' At this moment a large sea-gull, white as the driven snow, floated slowly over the speaker's head, and then disappeared behind the trees. . . . What was this bird of the ocean doing so far from its accustomed haunts? A feeling of awe crept over me at that moment—it seemed as if the spirits of the gallant dead were hovering over us, and invoking us to revenge their 'most foul and unnatural murder.' To see that snow-white bird floating, with scarce a perceptible motion of its pinions, over the speaker when he spoke of the dead—did it not seem as if the spirit answered the call?"

Mass meetings were held almost nightly, the purpose being to raise funds to send the several thousand filibusters in New Orleans to Lopez's support. Wheat spoke at practically all of them. On August 26, before an overflow crowd at Banks's Arcade, he "made a truly brilliant and spirit-stirring address in which anecdote and argument were so happily mixed up, that the effect on the audience was indeed electrifying." Frequently interrupted by loud outbursts of applause, Wheat "spoke of the hope of the patriots of Cuba, of those who had periled their lives to assist in achieving independence, of those men who had been martyred and murdered in the cause, and of the necessity of wiping out, with the arm of the avenger, the indignity which had been offered to the American character and name." He told a story of a poor Irish woman, whose husband was bedridden, who had contributed $2.50 for her husband and $2.50 for her son, and a dime each for herself and daughters to the Cuban committee. "Let her example be followed by the wealthy," concluded Wheat, "and soon will the thousands now panting to take a part in the affairs of Cuba, have that opportunity."

The *Orleanian*, which was opposed to the Cuban expedition, commented on this speech: "He has a good, honest face, this Col. Bob Wheat; and no doubt, is right earnest and sincere in his devotion to the Cuban enterprise."

Two nights later at King's Pavilion, Wheat addressed a crowd so immense as to cover "the entire street for fifty yards around." The *Courier* said Colonel Wheat delivered "a splendid speech, worthy of the man and the occasion," and characterized Roberdeau as "a progressive: one of the young republicans who had an unfailing confidence in the people." When Wheat was introduced, "there was stretching of necks, glistening eyes and tremendous cheering." He spoke "in his usual powerful manner for about twenty minutes. He eulogized the dead, he said their bodies were buried in rude graves, but their spirits were indestructible, and invoked our vengeance. In the same pathetic manner as spoke Anthony over the body of Caesar, Col. Wheat alluded to our butchered countrymen. He pointed to their mutilated bodies; and painted the blackness of the officials who could advise it. . . . He desired to see Cuba annexed, and as it was blessed by nature, it should be exalted by the civilizing genius of our institutions." [8]

Despite the popular enthusiasm, money came in slowly

to the Cuban committee. Less than $8,000 was raised and practically all of it was expended as fast as it was collected to support the filibusters in the city. And then, on September 4, the ship *Cherokee* brought to New Orleans "melancholy and startling" information from Cuba. Lopez was defeated, his band dispersed and captured and Lopez himself executed.

With this shocking news the Cuban enterprise collapsed. A reaction set in almost immediately; the New Orleans press began to point out the impracticality of the Cuban scheme. Before New Orleans closed out the Lopez affair, however, there was one important task yet to be performed—getting the filibusters, variously estimated at from 1,500 to 3,000, out of town. The filibusters asked for passage money to their homes, and when the Cuban committee was unable to meet their demands they raised a disturbance. But the police, acting quickly and effectively, dispersed the filibusters, cleared their camp, and brought to an end the fantastic Lopez adventure.[9]

CHAPTER VII

THE FRUSTRATED FILIBUSTER

Had Roberdeau Wheat settled down after the collapse of the Cuban venture and applied himself to the serious practice of his profession, there is little doubt that he would have become one of the leading lights of the Louisiana bar in a few years.

He possessed, it appeared, every ingredient for success. His bright, active mind had been trained by a sound liberal education. He was young, handsome, personable, well-mannered, friendly and cheerful, attractive qualities which opened for him the doors to the best homes in New Orleans. In conversation he was witty and fluent. Wheat's participation in the Lopez expedition had made him well known and he had gained the friendship and confidence of some of the most influential men in town.

If ever a young lawyer appeared likely to become "one of the brightest ornaments" of the bar, as Cousin Thomas Wolfe had written his parents,[1] it was twenty-five-year-old Roberdeau Wheat in September, 1851.

But one thing was missing, one all-important ingredient from Roberdeau's otherwise admirable collection of natural talents, social graces and professional skills: his mind was on soldiering, and not the law.

All summer Wheat had prepared himself for the Cuban

junket. Now, with the Lopez debacle a reality, Roberdeau was restless for action, eager for adventure. He did not have long to wait. From the Rio Grande rumors had come in mid-August of an impending revolution in northern Mexico under the leadership of Colonel José Maria J. Carvajal. Soon Wheat was off to the border to offer his sword to the Mexican insurgent.

Carvajal (his name was variously spelled, Carbajal, Caravajal and Carabajal) was born in San Antonio about 1810 and as a youth was educated in the United States. Returning to Texas, he voted for its independence. However, when the Mexican War broke out, Carvajal joined the Mexican army, and fought against the Americans in northern Mexico.

The idea of establishing an independent republic in northern Mexico, detached from the Mexican federal government, had long appealed to Carvajal. Indeed, his Mexican War activities were said to have been directed toward establishing "The Republic of Sierra Madre" south of the Rio Grande.

After the Mexican War, restrictions on imports from the United States encouraged smuggling along the border and "the best people" engaged in this highly profitable business. "Practically every Anglo-American along the line," states one authority, "chose the pursuit of a merchant rather than that of stock-raising or agriculture, and smuggling, ceasing to be blame-worthy, soon became meritorious."

Mexican authorities, when they could, seized the smuggled goods and frequently the merchants would try to recapture them with organized armed bands. To enforce the law, Mexican army units were put on guard at the frontier.

In the early fall of 1851 Carvajal launched his revolution, known as the Plan de la Loba. It had, ostensibly, a four-point program: constitutional reforms, withdrawal of the army from northern Mexico, reduction of duties, and the free admission into Mexico for five years of certain articles.

Merchants on both sides of the Rio Grande lent support

to Carvajal, hoping to flood northern Mexico with large quantities of goods virtually free of duties. Their contributions enabled Carvajal to offer attractive pay as an inducement for several Americans to enlist; others, among them Rob

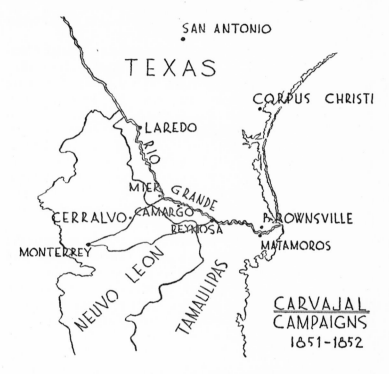

Wheat, moved by the filibustering spirit of the times, joined Carvajal for adventure; still others recognized the opportunity to profit by the recapture of runaway slaves.[2]

Carvajal framed his revolution in altruism. He raised the standard of liberation, he declared, because his " aggrieved countrymen " were " oppressed and borne down by the organized military despotism of the Central Government." Because they could not cope with the Federal troops unassisted he had invited Americans to join his cause. These would bring no shame either to their country or themselves for they were fighting in a cause as righteous as that which brought Lafayette, Kosciusko and Pulaski to the side of Washington.

Some, however, did not take such a generous view of Carvajal's motives. The New Orleans *Picayune* recalled that this "guardian of the liberties of Northern Mexico" had emerged from the Mexican War with a reputation as "the most miserable freebooter and rapacious robber" in the Rio Grande Valley. This journal marvelled at the magical transformation of Carvajal into a revolutionary patriot who was actually leading American citizens into battle.

Along the border people generally regarded Carvajal's revolution as nothing more than a smuggling undertaking. The dimmest view of all was taken by the American Consul at Matamoros, J. F. Waddell, who denounced to Washington the barbarity of the revolutionists, and also the "misguided men" who had taken service with the rebel leader for no other purpose but plunder.[3]

Such was the cause to which young Rob Wheat lent his burgeoning military skill in the fall of 1851. Rob had already developed the art of rationalizing his motives in taking up the sword and he easily convinced himself that Carvajal was a great patriot dedicated to a great purpose. No doubt Carvajal himself helped Wheat to reach this conclusion. Of medium height and weight, Carvajal was well formed and made a distinguished military figure. His features were regular; his eyes reflected latent energy and enterprise. And of his bravery, there could be no doubt. Wheat always referred to Carvajal as "our youthful general."

On September 16 Carvajal proclaimed the revolution, and his force quickly captured the towns of Camargo, Mier and Reynosa. On October 9 his "army," now about four hundred strong, moved on Matamoros. Reaching the outskirts of the town on October 19, Carvajal attacked and captured Fort Parades, an earthwork thrown up during the

Mexican War. Seizure of this position caused great jubilation in the ranks of the insurgents and Carvajal ordered the band to strike up some music.

But the celebration was premature. The resistance of the defenders stiffened as Carvajal advanced into the town and reached the Custom House. For ten days the fighting was inconclusive. "The species of warfare carried on in . . . the siege was of the most cowardly nature," Consul Waddell reported to Washington. He charged that Carvajal's men first set fire to a large building and, when the people turned out to fight the flames which threatened the heart of town, then fired upon the crowd, killing and wounding several persons. Waddell was among the wounded.

During the siege of Matamoros Wheat directed Carvajal's " artillery "—a single six-pounder. When he ran out of ammunition Wheat ordered a blacksmith to cut bars of iron into the right lengths and these were fired instead of grape and cannister. During the operations Wheat always got in as close to his target with his gun as he could. He told General Carvajal jokingly that he was converting his six-pounder into a twelve-pounder by taking half the distance.

As the inconclusive fighting dragged on, Carvajal's " army," losing strength daily by illness and desertion, was reduced to about three hundred men, all close to exhaustion. Carvajal decided to raise the siege, after eleven days of attacking, sacking, burning and pillage.[4] He ordered his men to fall back to Las Rucias, a ranch three or four miles from Matamoros. Carvajal's retirement was not at first a hasty one. It was planned, his friends later explained, to lure the government troops out of town for a battle in the open. However, a rumor spread that Mexican cavalry was descending upon the insurgents' rear. Panic then broke out when Carvajal ordered his " army " to retreat.

Wheat and his six-pounder were in the van of the troops as they retreated to Rancho Perdenal, eighteen miles from Matamoros. Here the weary Americans, most of whom were

on foot, refused to march any further. Many crossed the
river into the United States.

At this very time, Carvajal got word that his rear guard
was surrounded. In vain did Wheat and the other officers
appeal to the men to return. Only eight or ten responded.
Wheat sent word to Carvajal that only two men remained
with his piece. The harness by which Wheat's gun was
drawn had broken, and for ten miles his horsemen had drawn
it by rope attached to their saddles. Carvajal sent orders back
to Rob to spike the six-pounder and push it over the bank.
At first Wheat couldn't execute this order because too few
remained to move the gun. However, the rear guard, having
extricated itself from encirclement, rode up and Rob pressed
them into service to dispose of his " artillery." [5]

While the siege of Matamoros was underway President
Millard Fillmore issued on October 22, 1851, a proclamation
warning Americans not to participate in the military expedition against Mexico. " All persons who shall connect themselves with any enterprise in violation of the laws and national
obligations of the United States . . . will thereby subject
themselves to the heavy penalties denounced against such
offenses; that if they be captured within the jurisdiction of
the Mexican authorities they must expect to be tried and
punished according to the laws of Mexico, and will have no
right to claim the interposition of the Government on their
behalf," declared the President.

And, on October 29 United States Minister Robert
Perkins Letcher wrote from Mexico City to Secretary of State
Webster about the suspension of negotiations on the Tehuan-
tepec Canal Treaty: " The recent revolt on the Rio Grande,
which is attributed solely to our countrymen, has furnished
an additional cause of hostility to the treaty, and I must say
has embarrassed all my negotiations exceedingly." [6]

In New Orleans the *Picayune*, commenting on the
revolution unfavorably, probably had Rob Wheat in mind
when it wrote: " Of those Americans engaged in the move-

ment with whom we are acquainted, we entertain favorable opinions. In private life they are gentlemen of urbanity and honorable bearing. . . . A love of adventure and a poetic temperament have disguised the real character of the expedition in which Carvajal has engaged their services. If the country was rife for revolution, they would not have to explain the miscarriage of the late siege. The people would have risen en masse to welcome them as deliverers. . . . If the undisguised object of the foreign sympathizers be not to carve out of Mexican dominions a separate Republic, by conquest, for themselves, the issue of the last attempt might induce them to abandon Carvajal as an impostor." [7]

Meanwhile, Carvajal had changed his base to Camargo where he hoped to build up his strength before moving again. On November 21 Wheat wrote his mother: "The general is for the time being recruiting his forces. We may remain here two weeks; but shall then move towards the enemy who are very much afraid of us. . . . I am anxiously awaiting the arrival of some heavy pieces from the United States. . . . My pay is $200 a month and I can save something out of that." That Rob expected, or at least hoped for, great financial benefits from the revolution when it succeeded is evident from the following: "Tell Leo that if I win he shall go to Europe and see and hear all the great composers." [8]

Several days later Carvajal made an attack on Cerralvo, driving the government forces into the cathedral there. With the battle cry, "God and Liberty," the insurgents charged the cathedral. During the assault Wheat was slightly wounded in the arm. The government troops, escaping from the cathedral, took refuge in a stone house which had been built as an American quartermaster depot during the Mexican War.

This building was too strong for Carvajal to take, so he called off the attack. As he retired Federal cavalry took up the chase and soon the liberators of the oppressed were scurrying back across the Rio Grande to the American side.

For the next few months Carvajal's movements were

generally unknown; his "army" dispersed, some to indulge in guerilla activities, others to return home. Wheat, who remained in Texas, kept in contact with Carvajal, who plotted another "invasion." Rumors that the insurgents were about to move began to circulate in December, and early in February the word along the Rio Grande was that Carvajal would soon be in the field again.

It was not long before this became a reality. On February 20 Carvajal with a force variously estimated as between two hundred and five hundred men and a twelve-pound gun under Colonel Rob Wheat crossed the Rio Grande and advanced on Camargo. Near the town government troops under General Canales and Colonel Cruz were promptly engaged. When Colonel Cruz's cavalry charged, the insurgents broke and ran, except for about eighty men, who rallied around Wheat's twelve-pounder. Four times the Federal cavalry rushed Wheat's position and four times it was raked with a double load of canister as Wheat kept his gun blazing away. Finally, having suffered great losses, the Federals called off the attack at nightfall and withdrew, leaving Carvajal in possession of the field. Then occured a most extraordinary battle incident. Carvajal paraded his victorious troops on the field but he could muster barely a hundred effective men. The realization of how small their number was caused a sudden panic among the victors. They broke rank and made for the river, all crossing to the American side. At 10 P. M. the officers were thus compelled to leave the field and desert their cannon with which the victory had been won.[9]

Carvajal was able to rally the men on American soil and, reorganized, they crossed back into Mexico. But their newly found courage didn't last long and they disbanded and dispersed. Thus evaporated Carvajal's revolution, to Rob Wheat's great disappointment.

Rob did not immediately return to New Orleans. For three months he waited in Texas, hopeful that Carvajal would move again, but finally he accepted the inevitable. Writing

to his mother from Corpus Christi on May 25, 1852, Roberdeau said: "I saw Gen. Carvajal yesterday, he is down-
spirited but yet hopes. I shall not move again in the matter
unless I am certain of success." He was to leave the next
day for Austin where he would be "surrounded by friends
and admirers." He had to defer his visit to Chapel Hill
"until fall, if then." And then the frustrated young filibuster
opened his heart: "How soon this stormy life of mine will
last"—he meant to write "end"—"I cannot tell but I do so
look forward at times to a calm and peaceful home with a
sweet wife. I wish I could win Sallie Jones I would then cease
to roam and be a steady quiet lawyer." [10]

CHAPTER VIII

THE RELUCTANT LAWMAKER

I have just returned from Mexico," Roberdeau wrote Grandfather Wheat from New Orleans on July 23, 1852, " and have resumed the practice of law my profession and am trying very hard to be a sober, steady and peaceful citizen. I am much afraid that I should find it uphill work. I am essentially a soldier and from you I take the bent which has ruled my life. . . . I am exceedingly anxious to have Gen. Scott elected as then I think I can get an office which will in connection with my profession pay me well and allow me some little to lay up." [1]

Dr. Wheat was much pleased by the fact that Roberdeau had given up " filibusterism," as he called it. The minister wrote his old father: " I am almost sorry to see that he has not given up politics too, tho an occasional speech in public may help him at the bar." With evident, if reluctant, pride, Dr. Wheat continued, " The Rev. Mr. Leacock . . . wrote to me lately from Roberdeau's office in terms highly eulogistic of him, observing that even when he was ' playing the fool ' (alluding to his soldier life) he did it grandly and to some purpose." [2]

Roberdeau, far from giving up politics, entered enthusiastically into the 1852 presidential campaign. As an ardent Whig he campaigned vigorously for his old commander,

General Winfield Scott, who was opposed by another Mexican War general, Franklin Pierce. "I am stumping it all through the city," Wheat wrote his father. He appeared on the platform with some of the leading men of New Orleans. At a huge Whig mass meeting on Canal Street, Wheat's name was linked with those of Judah P. Benjamin, Randall Hunt and Christian Roselius, and other "distinguished speakers." Benjamin, Hunt and Roselius were among the greatest lawyers in the history of the New Orleans bar.

There was no question but that Roberdeau Wheat was making his mark in New Orleans. Ex-Governor Isaac Johnson presented him with a massive gold-headed cane, duly inscribed. He was chief marshal of a memorial funeral procession for Narciso Lopez on September 1, first anniversary of his execution. On this occasion a lady, unknown to him personally, sent Roberdeau a red, white and blue silk rosette, "as an humble tribute of her admiration of him . . . as a brave and gallant friend of human rights." [3]

Wheat didn't devote all his time to politics, however, and he wrote his father confidently: "I am progressing rapidly in my profession and hope ere long to be able to invite Uncle James to New Orleans and pay his expenses for one year. If my business increases I shall be able to support John Thomas this winter."

Naturally optimistic, Roberdeau always felt every venture he went into would be successful. He began to build air castles about the presidential election. "If Gen. Scott is elected our fortunes are made," he told his father. [4]

Roberdeau was so confident that "Old Fuss and Feathers" would be elected, he was unprepared for Pierce's overwhelming victory, 254 to 42, in the electoral college. Even Louisiana, a Whig stronghold, went with its six votes into the Pierce column. In New Orleans the vote was close, 5,300 for Pierce and 5,141 for Scott, but Pierce's majority in the state was 1,392 votes.

Two weeks after Pierce's election, Wheat was still

stunned by "that ill-fated day which crushed my political
fortunes in the bud." His keen disappointment was not disguised in a letter to his mother: "I am gradually recovering
from the stupefaction into which I was thrown by this unprecedented rout. I am a better Whig than ever now and shall
ever be so. Had I consulted my own interest I should have
turned Democrat and given as a reason my ill treatment under
the present administration."

Roberdeau then switched subjects: "I have progressed
no farther in my matrimonial campaign but I begin to believe
that when I seek a woman she will fly from me. I have 25
or 30 in this city who would jump to gain my hand." This
amazing statement, blurted out in the spirit of frustration,
indicates that Wheat's "matrimonial campaign" was directed
at a young lady outside of New Orleans. In all likelihood
that young lady was Miss Sallie Jones of North Carolina.

He put the letter aside, and when he picked up his pen
two days later to finish it his ego had been given a lift. He
had visited General Quitman the previous day and the conversation had turned to the Mexican War. "Gen. Quitman
. . . said that if I had been in command of Twigg's division
at the Garita de Belen that he would have entered the Plaza
that night. This was the greatest compliment I have ever
received. He says that I am the best natural soldier he ever
knew and said in the presence of a large company that if
he were in command of the Army of the Republic he would
place me at the Head of the Cavalry. I tell you this, because
I know it will please you." [5]

The Louisiana state election followed by only a few
weeks the presidential race and the Whigs, hoping to restore
their shattered political fortunes, sought a strong ticket. The
party leaders prevailed on Rob to run for the House of Representatives.

Wheat took time out from electioneering to serve as first
aide-de-camp to the grand marshal of a strange memorial
funeral parade honoring Daniel Webster, who had recently

died, and John C. Calhoun and Henry Clay, who had preceded him to the grave.

On election day, December 27, Roberdeau had tremendous success at the polls. Out of twenty-two candidates seeking the five representative posts, he was top man with 1,060 votes. "The election is over," he wrote his mother. "I awoke this morning the chosen candidate beating every Whig on the ticket . . . I intend to make myself . . . conversant with the wants of the people. I am I know a better soldier than any I can ever be a statesman." An incident in the election opened Roberdeau's old wound. "Will Cheatham is here," he wrote, "with $65,000 which he has won at cards. He spent $75 yesterday to secure my election. Whenever I see him I think of his beautiful sister. I would rather have her now were she a widow than any maid in the world. I love her still. Perhaps I may yet make her regret the refusal of my hand." Then Roberdeau revealed the frustrated state of his mind, in an amazing passage: "Miss M. Scott will be here in a few days and I may possibly marry her. I wish I could get Sallie Jones. I want some woman who will love me so much that she will in time teach me to love her." [6]

Roberdeau was making an honest effort to settle down but already he must have known this was impossible for him to do. His restlessness, stemming in part from his disappointments, is reflected in his letters. "I look forward to but little enjoyment at Baton Rouge. . . . Cousin Thomas has the best business in the city except Mr. Benjamin and Mr. Roselius. He has 4 lawyers employed in his office—*I am not one of them.* . . . Remember me to Lawyer Wheat and tell him as soon as I can pay office rent, etc. I will be pleased to have him as my partner under the title of Wheat and Brother. Please court Sallie Jones for me. I would rather have her now than any one I know."

Two weeks later, after he had taken his seat, Rob again indicated his boredom with his legislative assignment. "I look forward to a very dull and uninteresting session as the

Democrats have an enormous and overwhelming majority,"
he told his mother. "I shall advocate some few measures
with all my strength but with that exception I shall be a
quiet looker on. . . ." [7]

Wheat's fame as a filibuster preceded him to Baton
Rouge. Among the ladies that he met in the capital at least
one, Mrs. Clarissa E. L. Town, thought the meeting worth
recording in her diary. "I have heard he was a famous duelist,
having killed and wounded several persons." She added, "I
think he would be a good mark to shoot at for he is very
large—I fancy he would weigh 225 pounds." [8]

Wheat, indeed, took his legislative duties lightly. He
was absent from more sessions of the House of Representatives
than he attended, and his activities when he was on hand
were trifling. He was named to several committees, presented
a few petitions and urged suspension of the rules a number
of times. He introduced a handful of bills, one an inconse-
quential land bill, another to amend an act to prevent gambling
and a third which would tax insurance companies of New
Orleans for the benefit of the city's fire companies.

Strangely enough, three measures in which Wheat
should have had intense interest didn't attract him to the
House sessions when they were voted on. One of these was
a resolution concerning the *Susan Loud*, on which Wheat
had sailed in the Cárdenas expedition, and the *Georgiana*,
on which the Kentuckians had set out. Both vessels had been
seized by the Spanish and confiscated. Another resolution
was a memorial to Crittenden, Kerr and other Americans
who had lost their lives in Cuba in the final chapter of the
Lopez tragedy. The third was a resolution declaring "that
it is highly expedient that the island of Cuba ought to be
peacefully annexed to and form a part of the territory of
the United States." The resolution passed 35 to 16. [9]

Rob's twenty-seventh birthday was "handsomely cele-
brated." A gala affair, a grand dinner and ball for Governor
Hebert was held the night previous. Roberdeau gave a toast,

punning on Governor Hebert's name: "Now that war's a brewing (Bruin) thank God we have Herbert (a bear)." [10]

On April 29, several days before the legislature adjourned, Wheat left for New Orleans after trying in vain to get a Whig elected to the United States Senate. John Slidell, Democratic boss of New Orleans, was elected over Colonel T. G. Hunt, 70 to 37, to fill the vacancy created when Pierre Soulé was named minister to Spain. [11]

If Baton Rouge was dull and the legislature a bore, Roberdeau found more pleasant ways to occupy his time and thoughts. He fell "desperately in love with Miss Brown." Who was Miss Brown? Roberdeau gave no clue, no more than he did earlier regarding Miss M. Scott, whom he once contemplated marrying. Miss Brown may have been the daughter or sister of Representative J. N. Brown of Iberville Parish, fifteen miles down the river from Baton Rouge.

"She is not beautiful, but she is good," Wheat told his mother, "not brilliant but amiable, not witty but looks as if she would think her husband so even when others said he was dull and stupid." Roberdeau said that he had visited the family, spent the night and "actually grew bold enough, when she said good night to say 'May all bright angels bless and guard you.'" Miss Brown was a true member of the Church, Roberdeau said, and if he got her, he knew his Pa would love her. "When I have expressed a little doubt at some of sacred History, her gentle rebuke was that she would be miserable did she doubt a single iota. God bless her, her influence has already purified me much and will doubtless win me back to the paths of Pleasantness and Peace. I have not courted her yet but feel that I shall win her." [12]

Shortly thereafter Wheat left New Orleans for a family reunion at the home of his grandfather in Wheeling. With his departure, Miss Brown appears to have passed out of his life forever. The family visit concluded, Roberdeau probably returned to Chapel Hill with his parents. And there, he doubtless renewed his quest of Sallie Jones.

It is likely, too, that Roberdeau was on hand in North Carolina when his sister Josephine May married Francis E. Shober of Salisbury on July 12, but the next spring he was once again on a wild goose chase, this time to California.[18]

CHAPTER IX

THE EMISSARY OF LIBERTY

On March 14, 1854, Wheat penned a hasty note to his mother from Acapulco, Mexico:

> Dear Mother:
>
> I am thus far on my way to California. The steamer has just touched and I have only time to say I am well and in 8 days will be in San Francisco. Give my love to all and think of me as your bright emmisary [*sic*] in the cause of Liberty.
>
> Your devoted
Son Roberdeau [1]

Where in the region of California did the "cause of Liberty" need a "bright emmisary"? What oppressed people was Wheat going to liberate this time? The only logical explanation of Roberdeau's California junket is that he was on his way to join William Walker's filibustering expedition to Sonora.

Roberdeau had known Walker, two years his senior, in Nashville, where the filibuster's younger brother, James, was Wheat's college chum and classmate. Walker, born in 1824, was something of a prodigy, having been graduated from the University of Nashville at the age of fourteen. At nineteen, he received an M. D. degree from the University of Pennsylvania, after which he continued his medical studies in Europe for two years. He returned to Nashville with a facility in several languages and no desire whatever to practice medicine. Walker's restless spirit next turned to the study of law and he went to New Orleans where he was admitted to the bar. Journalism attracted Walker more than the law and in 1848 he put aside his second profession to enter a third. He became one of the editors of the *Crescent*. When Rob Wheat was engaged in the Lopez affair, ironically enough, Walker was writing articles denouncing the filibustering schemes against Cuba.

In 1850 Walker went to California and engaged in journalism in San Francisco for three years. Then the doctor, lawyer and editor once again changed professions. He became a soldier of fortune and a filibuster, bestowing upon himself the title of Colonel Walker. In mid-October, 1853, Walker and forty-five men sailed on the *Caroline* from San Francisco for Lower California. After capturing the Mexican governor at La Paz, Walker proclaimed the independent Republic of Lower California with himself as president. His first "presidential" decree announced to the world: "The Republic of Lower California is hereby declared free, sovereign, and independent, and all allegiance to the Republic of Mexico is forever renounced."

On January 18, 1854, "President" Walker issued four decrees, annexing Sonora to the Republic of Lower California, changing the name of the country to the Republic of Sonora, dividing it into the states of Sonora and Lower California and defining their boundaries. Walker, of course, assumed the presidency of the new state of Sonora.[2]

The comic-opera aspect of this business was accentuated by Walker's dead seriousness. "Santa Anna must feel obliged to the new president that he has not annexed any more of his territory than Sonora," wrote a San Francisco editor. "It would have been just as cheap and easy to have annexed the whole of Mexico at once, and would have saved the trouble of making future proclamations."[3]

There can be little doubt that Walker's fantastic scheme sent Roberdeau Wheat hurrying to California in the spring of 1854 as Liberty's "bright emmisary." Wheat arrived in San Francisco about March 23 to learn that Walker's affairs in Sonora were deteriorating rapidly. Brevet Major General John E. Wool, new commander of the Department of the Pacific, had arrived in San Francisco on February 14, 1854, with the determination to break up filibustering. Almost immediately he arrested Walker's California agents, thus halting recruitment of reinforcements for the Republic of Sonora. This kept Roberdeau from joining Walker, if he still entertained ideas of doing so.

Meanwhile, Walker's "army" was in rags and without food or ammunition. Desertions were numerous, yet, while the expedition disintegrated before his eyes, Walker continued to play the president and commander-in-chief in the constant skirmishes with Mexican troops which were beginning to close in on him. Finally, harassed by the Mexicans for days, Walker decided to make a break for American soil. But at the border Mexican troops blocked the way. Walker led a charge through the Mexicans and he and his men dashed across the border. Walker surrendered to the American authorities and on his parole agreed to go to San Francisco to answer the charge of violating the neutrality laws of the United States.[4]

Having satisfied himself that Walker's expedition was not for him, Roberdeau kept himself occupied during his more than four months' stay in San Francisco by joining the California Guard as an honorary lieutenant. This gave him a chance to keep his hand in military affairs and, of course, the members of the Guard were delighted to have an already well-known young soldier of fortune associated with the organization.

At this time agents for Juan Alvarez, who was plotting a Mexican revolution, were in San Francisco and it is most likely that Wheat's interest in the undertaking was aroused.

Perhaps Rob even met Colonel Ignacio Comonfort, Alvarez's chief collaborator, who came to San Francisco in June, 1854, to try to borrow money with which to finance the revolution.

Wheat, however, had a more immediate interest. In the spring of 1854 the California newspapers reprinted from Eastern journals rumors of the revival of the Cuban project, with General John A. Quitman as the leader of the invasion and Colonel Wheat as one of his staff officers. Wheat's departure for the East in midsummer lent strength to the rumors, and papers speculated that the Cuban expedition, far greater in size and equipment than Lopez's ill-starred forays, would shortly leave American shores.[5]

Before leaving San Francisco Wheat in all likelihood participated in the planning of William Walker's legal defense against the charge of violating the neutrality law. A friend of Walker's and a lawyer, Wheat was also a filibuster who had himself been charged with violating the same neutrality law.

Walker was arraigned in June and pleaded not guilty. He stated that his expedition, when it left the United States, was not organized on a military basis. This was the same argument used in the three mistrials of John Henderson in the Lopez affair. Accordingly, it is likely that Wheat suggested it to Walker. At any rate, it later proved the winning argument, for the jury took just eight minutes to acquit Walker of violating the neutrality laws of the United States.[6]

On August 1 Roberdeau sailed on the *Sonora* for Panama on the first leg of the long voyage to New York. The California Guard turned out in uniform, and with its two field pieces, to give their first lieutenant a sendoff. Before leaving the armory for the march to the wharf, Captain T. D. Johns, on behalf of the company, presented Wheat with "an elegant and serviceable saber." At the wharf the Guard fired a national salute in his honor. Describing the event, the San Francisco *Daily Herald* added: "Mr. Wheat was a prominent participant in the two Cuban expeditions, in the last of

which he held the rank of Colonel. His name is now frequently mentioned in the Eastern papers in connection with
the New Cuban movement, and from his allusions yesterday,
both on the occasion of the sword presentation and that of
bidding adieu to his comrades on the wharf, it seems that
the object of his return East is to participate in it."

Noting the full-dress ceremony at the wharf, the *Alta
California* said: "As we see Col. Wheat's name among the
list of candidates for 'martyrdom' in Cuba, we presume he
is on his way there."

The San Francisco *Chronicle* hoped that the enthusiastic
sendoff of Colonel Wheat by the California Guard was only
a gesture of friendship and not to be construed as an endorse-
ment of any scheme to snatch Cuba from Spain.

"Col. Wheat . . . it is generally understood here . . . has
gone to take part in the movement now on foot to renew
the attempt on that island," said the *Chronicle*. "It is legitimate, therefore, to consider him one of those who, under the
leadership of Gen. Quitman, intends to wed the 'Queen of
the Antilles' to his Excellency, Uncle Sam.

"We have no objection to an honorable and national
acquisition of Cuba. . . . But we do condemn every movement calculated to stain the national honor [with] a forcible
attempt at the seizure of Cuba. . . ." [7]

While Wheat was in California the Cuban project was
again set in motion. General Quitman made a trip to New
York, Philadelphia, Baltimore and Washington in 1853 to
arouse interest in the liberation of Cuba, a cause which was
near to his heart. Quitman considered the possession of Cuba
by the United States to be closely connected with the fortunes
of the South. He entered warmly into the enterprise, but
he determined to carefully avoid violating the laws of the
United States or existing treaties with Spain. To do this
Quitman planned to leave the United States before hostilities
broke out in Cuba but he did not intend to land on the island

until the Cubans had made a formal declaration of independence.[8]

Rob hoped that by the time he reached New York
Quitman would be ready to move against Cuba. Perhaps
on the journey of more than a month he thought often of
Cuba, where four years earlier he had launched his career
as a filibuster. The steamer to Panama took fifteen days
from San Francisco, including a stop at Acapulco. The tedious mule and river boat trip across the Isthmus, a matter of
sixty miles, took four to six days depending upon the weather.
It wasn't until the following year that the Panama Railroad
was opened, making the transit from shipside to shipside on
each ocean in a few hours. From Chagres to New York
consumed another twelve or fourteen days.[9]

Wheat arrived in New York early in September, 1854.
Before leaving for New Orleans he participated in a ceremony commemorating the anniversary of General Scott's
entrance into the city of Mexico. This celebration took place
on September 14 at the Prescott House, the hall being decor-
ated with American flags and captured Mexican standards.
The " regular " toasts were drunk, after which " several volunteer sentiments were proposed and the company separated
at an early hour."

Wheat responded to the third toast: " Winfield Scott—
our gallant leader and friend." After the " enthusiastic
applause" subsided, " Col. Wheat . . . eulogized Gen. Scott
as owing his elevated position to his sword alone." Roberdeau
also replied to the tenth toast, " Our companions in arms—
the ladies," after the Navy band finished playing " The Girl
I Left Behind Me." [10]

Wheat left New York near the end of September for
New Orleans from where, on October 13, he wrote General
Quitman of his plans " until you shall want me in Cuba."

" I received a long letter yesterday from Gen. Alvarez
writing me to emigrate to Guerero [sic] and work the silver
and gold mines as soon as he can drive Santa Anna out of

the country," wrote Wheat. " I met Gen. Comonfort and Ex-President Ceballos in New York and after an interview with them determined to go to Tamaulipas and join the Revolution there. I am on my way there now to encourage the Northern Army with assurances of the support and cooperation of Alvarez. I am very poor and worse than poor in debt. I intend to try to get money enough to pay my debts and to support me until you shall want me in Cuba. I hope you may be able to move this winter and I know that you will inform me in time for me to return from Mexico to join you."

Wheat's admiration for Quitman and his boyish adulation (slightly outdated, considering that Roberdeau was twenty-eight years of age) are evident in the closing lines of his letter: " I shall study hard and try to learn as much as I can so that I may be the more worthy of the position which you have promised me. I shall be ready at any moment to throw up any position, be it never [sic] so elevated, to obey your commands and to lead your Cavalry wherever you may point the way. Dear General, the height of my ambition is to lead a desperate charge, in your presence and then to receive your commendation."

But Wheat did not stay long in New Orleans, for on October 29 he addressed another letter to Quitman from Brownsville, Texas:

" I arrived here on the 20th of October," he wrote, " and found Gov. Garza and Capistran the two leaders in this revolution on this side of the river with 300 men. They fought handsomely at Victoria and also above Matamoros, were victorious in a field fight above Matamoros but were obliged to evacuate Victoria on account of the failure of their ammunition. The revolution is now in statu quo for the want of artillery, powder and the silver sinews of war. I am going up to see Carvajal in a day or two and shall then know definitely whether anything is soon to be done and if not I shall leave on the next steamer for New Orleans. . . . How

soon Dear General will you call me to your side to go with
you to the glorious work which you have espoused and which
I know you will perfect? God grant it may be soon." [11]

Wheat was impatient for action but he got no assurances
from his old friend, the perennial insurgent Carvajal, that
a campaign would be immediately forthcoming. Indeed,
Carvajal's revolution never did materialize, perhaps because
that worthy had too many other irons in the fire. He was
reportedly involved in the brewing Cuban expedition and,
at the same time, he had considerable interest in Juan Alvarez's
revolutionary movement against Santa Anna. In a short while
Carvajal forgot his own revolution and joined Alvarez.

Rob now had nothing to do until the Cuban venture
opened. But soon this, too, collapsed when the so-called
"friends of Cuba" failed at a critical moment to produce
the necessary funds to launch the expedition. With this disappointment Wheat decided to cast his lot with Juan Alvarez
in Mexico.

The sixty-three-year-old governor of the State of Guerrero
offered Wheat a brigadier generalship. Rob had informed
himself of the revolution in correspondence with Alvarez
himself and in conversations in New York with his associates,
Ignacio Comonfort and Juan Ceballos. So he accepted the
appointment, which was made on April 10, 1855, a day after
his twenty-ninth birthday.[12] With characteristic pride in his
new rank, Roberdeau saw to it that the passenger list of the
Sonora, which brought him from Panama to Acapulco, listed
him as "Gen. C. R. Wheat."

Shortly after landing Wheat went to Taxco to visit
Alvarez, whom he found to be "a noble, high toned, old
Patriot, surrounded by a people who worship him for his
goodness."

Santa Anna's propagandists, however, drew a different
picture of the old Indian:

"The phrenologists by means of comparative anatomy
have learned how to estimate and classify individuals of our

species. Alvarez resembles the orang-utang in his rough and
hairy hide, his attitude, vacillating between man and beast;
the owl in his melancholy habits and love of darkness; the
vulture in his insatiable rapacity; the domestic cat in his
ingratitude, dissimulation and cowardice; the tiger in his
unslakable thirst for blood; the panther, in short, in his constant hatred of our race and furious love of victims and
spoliations."

After visiting Alvarez Roberdeau wrote hopefully of the
success of the venture, as he always did. "Santa Anna is a
doomed man," he told his mother. "Our motto is 'Mueran
a tyranno' ('Death to the Tyrant') and is worn on every
man's hat. . . . State after state is pronouncing on the Alvarez
platform and in three months we will be in the capitol."

Wheat then touched on a familiar theme, the rescue of
the Mexican people from the thraldom of the Church.
"Alvarez told me that the Priests had ruined and blasted his
country. He says that he is opposed to a monopoly of religion.
This looks like wisdom."

That he was happy in his latest liberating operation
General Wheat left little room to doubt. "I am in fine health
and spirits," he wrote. "I am living with the agent of the
Mail Company. Have 6 Horses, 6 servants, a yacht, a row
boat, guns etc at my disposal at all times. Fresh and salt baths
oysters and all kinds of tropical fruits in the greatest profusion.
Pineapples and bananas are my favorites." [13]

Ten days later Wheat wrote again, touching on the
more practical aspects of being a revolutionist: "I . . . hope
ere long to have plenty of money. If the revolution succeeds
I shall have my pick and choice of lands. Gen. Alvarez
wants me to take a Hacienda near him. All will yet be
well and then I will buy a nice farm for Pa on the North river
near enough to the city for him to be able to drive a span
of throughbreds every day to New York and back."

Roberdeau touched on the religious festivals of the Mexicans and expressed surprise that "these poor ignorant people

take their religion with them into the ball-room and the race
course and into all their business. What a pity then it has
no better effect upon them." Rob revealed a new development regarding Sallie Jones: "One of the senoritas here
reminds me very much of Miss Sally Jones though not half
so beautiful and queenly. I hope I may one of these days
greet her as Sister Sallie. Ask J. T. about that." Wheat's
younger brother John Thomas apparently had joined Roberdeau in the quest of the young lady's hand.

At a Fourth of July celebration in which Roberdeau got
permission from General Alvarez to raise the American flag,
an incident occurred which is undoubtedly the basis for the
erroneous story which linked him and the Mexican general
La Vega at Resaca de la Palma in the Mexican War.

"Mr. Van Brunch gave a splendid dinner at which all
the officials were present," wrote Rob of the celebration.
"General Villareal asked me if I were at Churubusco. I
said yes after the battle. He then said I was your prisoner.
You were a captain of Dragoons. I recognized him immediately. He embraced me. For I had treated him very kindly
when a prisoner. Was it not a strange meeting? Then we
fought against each other and now side by side in the holy
cause of Liberty." The "holy cause" was making real
progress, Wheat confided. "Nearly every state has pronounced
against Santa Anna so that he has nothing left him but to
decamp." [14]

In August 1856 General Alvarez sent General Wheat
to New York on "special business," in all probability to
secure arms and ammunition. He was very busy, he wrote
his mother on August 14, but would try to pay the family
a visit before returning to Mexico in a month or two.

"I think Santa Anna is about to leave the country,"
he wrote, "and if he does not I will drive him out. General
Alvarez has given me the command of the column which
will march on the Capital. I shall have American Rifleman
and Artillerists and 4,000 Indians. Should we succeed,

Liberty civil and religious triumphs. I shall then be rich and powerful and then Dear Mother I will spend my days by your side, ministering to yours and Pa's wants. I will be happy yet." [15]

Two days before Wheat wrote this letter, Santa Anna abdicated and the first phase of Alvarez's revolution was over. When he returned to Mexico on October 26, Wheat found General Alvarez's affairs going splendidly, with the "noble old soldier" now president.

General Alvarez entered Mexico City on November 14 at the head of thirty thousand men. The old warrior's entry, Wheat recorded, drew "acclamations of the whole population." The capital made a gala fiesta of the occasion. The city was splendidly illuminated at night and twenty brass bands performed in the Plaza every evening. Wheat attended the grand banquet at the palace, a dazzling affair.

Roberdeau was in his element. And he was delighted with his quarters. "I am living in the Palace of Iturbide built 100 years," he wrote. "It is the most magnificent building I ever saw. It cost $1,000,000." [16]

For the next few months, Wheat lived in elegant inactivity. He wrote John Thomas, now practicing law in New Orleans, that he was getting "fat and lazy" on an assignment in Vera Cruz which involved no military duties. But his health was fine and he had a pearl fishery at Acapulco from which he expected big things. "I hope it is making money," he told John Thomas, "for I cannot get what is due me from this government. If I make some money, my Dear Brother, you shall have as much as you want and I will send Pa enough to make him perfectly comfortable the rest of his life. If I have even ordinary luck I shall be able to buy a farm near New York for Pa. . . . Should I get the funds, I will set you up there."

In June 1856 General Wheat was in Mexico City, still eager to get his hands on some money. "I am trying hard to make my arrangements to give you a visit in August,"

Wheat wrote his mother. "The Government owe me a great deal of money and as soon as I can get it I shall be off for Home. My monthly pay is $448 and yet it is with difficulty that I can make both ends meet. I could live better in New York on $200 than I do here on more than twice the amount. All the Generals of Mexico have heretofore been rich men and they are expected to live in a certain style. . . . The country is very rich but the Government is poor. A young lady is not called rich unless she has $500,000. I know three who are worth $3,000,000."

Wheat told his mother of the strained relations between Spain and Mexico and the strong possibility of war. "Should there be a war Cuba will then throw off the yoke of Spain and take her place among the Republics of the new world. Then and not until then will I be willing to hang up my sword upon a rusty hook." [17]

On July 7, 1856, General Wheat requested that he be retired from the Mexican army. Shortly thereafter he was on his way home. Dr. Wheat, writing from Chapel Hill on August 25 to his brother, said: "We have just heard through J. T. that R. passed through New Orleans on route to Washington with the new Postal Treaty with Mexico. He promised to visit us soon. J. T. says he is sanguine of success in his colonization scheme and his pearl fishery. He has 160 square leagues of land in Tamaulipas— think of that."

It would appear that this land acquisition took place shortly before Roberdeau left Mexico, for this is the first mention of it in existing family correspondence. Of course, that Roberdeau was confident of great success with his colonization is not surprising. He dreamed only grandiose dreams for everything he went into.

In North Carolina Dr. and Mrs. Wheat waited eagerly for Roberdeau's visit. "Roberdeau hasn't yet made his promised appearance," the rector wrote his sister on December 3. "We are looking for him daily." But the year ran out, and still no Roberdeau. Finally, on January 17, 1857, Dr.

Wheat, with a heavy heart, picked up his pen to address his sister again:

"Roberdeau, as you have probably seen in the papers, is gone to Nicaragua with relief to Walker. I have much need, my dear sister, of your faith and patience—so wayward has been the life of my darling boy! And, yet, when he writes that he is prompted by piety and personal friendship towards Walker and his family (his brother was his college 'chum') and that the enterprise is sanctioned by some of the most patriotic and sagacious statemen of the South, I cannot entirely condemn him, or, indeed, withhold my sympathy and good wishes. Of course, you understand, that above all and before all things else, I desire to see him a sober-minded, settled Christian man. I much fear that he is very far from being such an one; that was what was present to my mind when I spoke of him as 'wayward.'" [18]

CHAPTER X

TO THE AID OF GENERAL WALKER

For a quarter of a century before William Walker arrived in Nicaragua, revolution was the normal state of affairs. The two rival factions went by high-sounding names of Liberals, or Democrats, and Legitimists, or Aristocrats, but for all practical purposes the names were meaningless. "These may once have stood for what each professed to advocate, but by 1850 they had degenerated into 'ins' and 'outs.'"

Sectionalism entered the revolutionary picture, too, for Granada, the largest city, was the Legitimist stronghold and dominated the southern half of the country, while its rival, Leon, was the Liberal headquarters and controlled the politics of the north. And so the seat of government fluctuated between Leon and Granada, depending upon which party for the moment was victorious.

William Walker was induced late in 1854 to recruit an expedition in San Francisco to support the Liberals, who were in revolt against the Legitimist government. But when the contract arrived, Walker realized that participation on his part would violate the neutrality laws of the United States. He suggested that a "colonization grant" be issued to him and when one was forthcoming, providing for the introduction in Nicaragua of three hundred colonists, who were to have the privilege of bearing arms, Walker decided to move.

On May 4, 1855, Walker sailed from San Francisco with fifty-eight men, later known as the Immortals. After a rough voyage he landed in northern Nicaragua at Realejo. Walker was warmly welcomed by the Liberals, whose revolution was just about petering out. He was commissioned a colonel and his men were called the American Phalanx.

Ever since the California Gold Rush of 1849, Nicaragua had been one of the short cuts to the Pacific for travelers from the United States. Cornelius Vanderbilt and his Accessory Transit Company had a monopoly for steam navigation on the waters of Nicaragua. By using steamers on the San Juan River, which emptied into the Atlantic, and Lake Nicaragua, it was possible to cross all but twelve miles of Nicaragua by water. The land leg of the journey, on the Pacific side, was made first by muleback over trails and later by comfortable carriages pulled by four mules over a macadamized road.

It was Walker's intention to secure control of points along the Transit route as a means of inducing tourists to become "colonists." His idea, quite independent of the Liberals, was to Americanize the country and to take charge of things himself.

The "Grey-eyed Man of Destiny," as Walker liked to be called, was soon playing off both Nicaraguan factions against each other as a preliminary to seizing power. In June 1856 he "legalized" his control of the country with an "election" in which he was overwhelmingly named President of Nicaragua.

At first the American press considered Walker merely an agent for Vanderbilt's Accessory Transit Company. This was not true but there was a definite relationship between the corporation and the rise and fall of the filibusters.

A coalition of Central American states—Honduras, Guatemala, El Salvador and Costa Rica—was established to oppose Walker. The coalition recognized Patricias Rivas as the provisional president of Nicaragua and supplied him with troops with which to take the field against the filibuster.

Vanderbilt, according to rumor, supplied arms to the anti-Walker forces.

When Walker's affairs deteriorated, he hurriedly dispatched agents to the United States to recruit more "colonists." William L. Cazneau of Texas contracted to introduce a thousand able-bodied colonists of good character into Nicaragua within twelve months. These the Nicaraguan government would establish in settlements of not less than fifty families with each settler to receive eighty acres of land.

But the threat of war by the Central American coalition against Walker was sufficient to dissuade bona fide colonists from going to Nicaragua. Whatever recruits were rounded up were primarily motivated by the spirit of adventure. Walker suffered reverses in the field and the coalition forces occupied various parts of the country. Outnumbered, Walker needed reinforcements badly.[1]

Such was the situation late in 1856, when Roberdeau Wheat decided to go to Walker's assistance. Leo Wheat says Walker had previously offered General Wheat a high position when the Nicaraguan venture looked promising. Wheat declined the offer at the time, but "true to his characteristic self-sacrifice for the good of others, he hastened to their relief in the hour of adversity."[2]

Wheat sailed from New York late in December on the *James Adger* for Greytown, or San Juan del Norte, as it was also called. He had on board with him about forty recruits for Walker. Colonel Frank Anderson and Colonel C. W. Doubleday, who were also going to join the "Grey-eyed Man of Destiny," were also on board.

On January 9, 1857, the *James Adger* reached Greytown, where General Wheat and his companions soon learned that Walker's forces under General Henningsen had been compelled after a determined defense to evacuate Granada. Moreover, the Central American coalition had forced Walker to withdraw troops from various points along the Transit route.

"The enemy," wrote Colonel Doubleday, "now had

possession of the lake and river steamers and the various points of defense on that line, so that our way between Greytown and Rivas, where we had hoped to effect a junction with Walker, was beset by the armed posts and garrisons of the enemy, who also had the steamers." [3]

Sizable reinforcements for Walker arrived about this time in Greytown. Colonel S. A. Lockridge, who had gone to New Orleans for recruits, landed with more than two hundred men and he promptly purchased a small, open-decked river steamer, the only available craft, which had been condemned because of its defective machinery.

While the steamer was being repaired the filibusters were moved to a sand spit at the mouth of the San Juan River known as Puntas Arenas to make them inaccessible to British naval officers who had attempted to discourage them and detach them from Walker's cause. The British said Walker was keeping up a hopeless war for personal aggrandizement and that he was opposed by a host of enemies in the field and by the sentiment of the world. To this sort of talk some of the men lent willing ears. They had been recruited in the slums and on the docks of New Orleans and when the British offered them a free trip home many were ready to accept.

The British gunboat *Cossack* brought a broadside to bear on Lockridge's camp from close range and Captain Cockburn came ashore. Backed by the authority of his guns, aimed at the camp, Cockburn ordered Colonel Lockridge to parade his men on the beach, for he wanted every British subject there. There was nothing to do but submit, galling though it was, and about twenty men came forward to accept the British offer of free transportation to the United States.

All the while, Wheat was in a rage. The humiliation of the incident was aggravated by his chronic hatred of Englishmen. Colonel Doubleday has given a vivid account of Wheat's conduct:

"Gen. Wheat, hoping to fasten a quarrel on Cockburn

pointed me out to him as a 'British subject' for I had been
born in England. The witless Briton, thinking to make a
convert of me, actually offered me his protection.

"I am afraid my language was very bad to him, for
Wheat tried suavely to convince him that he ought to resent
it in a manner customary among gentlemen. As a last inducement he offered to take my place if Cockburn had an scruples
about matching his rank with that of a Nicaraguan officer;
he, Wheat, claiming no rank other than that of an American
gentleman, and as such, the equal of anyone. Capt. Cockburn,
continuing to disregard the invitation to a personal settlement,
Wheat told him, much to the amusement of the grinning
sailors who manned his boat, that he was sorry to see an
English tar take refuge in his rank at the expense of his
courage." [4]

Wheat was very popular with the filibusters, and the
men respected him as a soldier and as a leader. His willing-
ness to take the same risks to which he exposed them, his
bravery under fire and his firmness tempered with justice,
in the matter of discipline, combined to endear him to his
men. One of them related later: "On moving off on our
expedition, three cheers were given for Walker, three for Col.
Lockridge, and three times three for Gen. Wheat, who was a
great favorite with us." [5] His taunting of Captain Cockburn
must have been the subject of conversation around the campfires for several days.

Several days later the rickety little steamer was ready
and the filibusters "quickly steamed away from the vicinity
of their too powerful tormentors." Several hours of traveling
up the San Juan brought the vessel to the mouth of the
Sarapiqui River, at Hipp's Point, which was guarded by a
fort over which flew the Costa Rican flag.

When the steamer approached within musket-range of
the fort, it was suddenly greeted by "a fusillade of bullets,
which, whistling about us, notified us . . . of the intentions
of the garrison." The filibusters landed downstream, on the

opposite side from the fort. Here the Costa Ricans had established an earthwork which could be supported by the fire from the fort.

Under prodding from Anderson and Doubleday, Colonel Lockridge attacked the earthwork, which was carried after stubborn resistance. The filibusters' losses were trifling but

WHEAT IN
NICARAGUA

JAN. — APRIL 1857

they faced a sterner job in reducing the fort across the river. This had to be done in order to ascend the river safely.

Several small brass pieces had been captured at the earthwork, and for these, Wheat busied himself devising " a kind of chain-shot composed of melted leaden balls connected by short chains." When all was ready, Wheat set up his

battery across from the fort and at midnight Anderson and
Doubleday crossed the river in a steamer and landed the men
a couple of miles below the fort.

Shortly before daybreak the filibusters reached the clear-
ing in front of the fort. The trees which had been cut down
to eliminate cover for an attacking force had not been removed
and they offered good protection as long as the men stayed
close to them.

Wheat waited patiently for the signal to begin blasting
away with his captured pieces. It came at daylight, when
the filibusters opened up on the fort from behind their cover
of logs.

" The firing for about an hour was really very sharp,
and the casualties frequent on our side," wrote Doubleday,
" for, whenever a head or arm was exposed in the act of
firing, the rain of bullets was pretty sure to find it." When
the enemy fire slackened off, the filibusters charged the fort,
only to discover that the surviving members of the garrison
had taken to the woods, leaving a large number of dead.
" This showed that Wheat's artillery and our fire combined
had rendered the place untenable."

Not long after the capture of Fort Sarapiqui Colonel
H. T. Titus, one of the Kansas " Border Ruffians," arrived
with a company of a hundred strapping men from the Middle
West. While the filibusters were making plans to push
upstream to capture Fort Castillo, Titus asked for the honor
of attacking the fort with his company alone.

" Titus, without opposition, took possession of the batteries
and a lake steamer, the Scott, and then summoned the fort
to surrender. They replied, requesting 24 hours in which to
convey a message. . . . Titus . . . had the mortification, before
his truce had expired, of seeing the fort reinforced . . . so
that he had barely time to cut his two steamers adrift and
get from under their guns, leaving the passage of the river
far more formidable than before."

This blunder caused a lot of grumbling and insubordination in the camp, and desertions were numerous, especially among Titus's Kansans, who despite their fine appearance, were wholly lacking in discipline. They made rafts and floated down the river in the middle of the night.

By now Wheat, Doubleday, Anderson and other officers were rather disgusted with the inefficiency of Colonel Lockridge and in a council of war it was decided that the only way they could get through to Walker would be to take passage to Panama, cross the Isthmus and then sail to San Juan del Sur. But just at this time Captain Marcellus French, with a company of Texas Rangers, 135 strong, arrived by chartered boat. This encouraged the filibusters to believe that they could force a passage past Fort Castillo. But after landing and making a reconnaissance of the fort, Wheat and the other officers unanimously agreed that its capture without artillery was impracticable. Inasmuch as the river was equally well guarded, the filibusters decided to abandon the attempt of passing up the river with their fragile steamers.

Anderson, Doubleday, Wheat and several other officers decided to take the Texans aboard the *Scott* and steam for Greytown to join Walker via Panama, "leaving the mass of the troops, now utterly worthless, to be managed by Lockridge as he might see fit."

Because it seemed prudent to make a reconnaissance of Fort Sarapiqui before attempting to pass that point, the *Scott's* nose was grounded in a sand bank and a landing party went ashore.

From the hurricane deck Rob Wheat watched the men winding in and out of the trees. Suddenly there came a terrible explosion. "The engineer had pumped cold water into the superheated cylinder, and the boiler had burst, tearing the entire front of the boat into fragments," wrote Doubleday, who was in the pilot house on the upper deck when the blast came.

Wheat was thrown into the water amidst the debris of the shattered vessel. When he came to the surface, he realized he was uninjured. He saw about him many injured men struggling in the water amidst burning timber. Reaching for the nearest victim of the blast, Rob swam ashore with him and then returned to the water to help rescue others.

Doubleday, meanwhile had been hurled into the water " bruised and mangled from contact with the splinters and the debris of the wreck. . . . I struck on what proved to be the debris about the disrupted cylinder on the lower deck. I was plunged into the steam and scalding water . . . utterly unable to take a single step away from the dangerous proximity of steam and fire." Piteous cries of the burning and wounded pierced the air, men calling for help or begging to be put out of their misery. Flames sprang up in all directions. Suddenly, there came a terrified cry: " The powder! "

About three tons of powder were piled on the upper deck, covered by tarpaulins, but the tarpaulins were now ablaze. Panic seized the men who were unhurt and they made a dash for the safety of the woods. " But the voices of Anderson and honest Bob Wheat were raised for volunteers, and leading the way, they scrambled up the wreck and tore the flaming canvas away."

Once the threat of the fire reaching the powder was removed, Wheat and Anderson renewed the work of rescuing the victims and ministering to their wounds. They went to Doubleday's aid, lifting him tenderly from the wreckage and at his request laid him in the cool water of the river to reduce his excruciating pain. They discovered that the explosion had killed twenty men and injured many more.[6]

It was a dejected expedition that made it way back to Greytown where Wheat and others learned that they had missed the *Tennessee*, bound for Panama, by only two hours. Roberdeau abandoned any hope now of reaching Walker, whose situation was worsening daily. When the British naval commander offered to transport the filibusters to Aspinwall from where they could get passage to the United States, he accepted the invitation. On April 20 Wheat, Doubleday and

several other officers, and a large number of filibusters sailed
from Aspinwall on the *Illinois*, arriving in New York on
April 29.

"The returned volunteers from the San Juan River,"
commented the New York *Tribune* the next day, "attributed
the failure of their expedition to the inexperience of Col.
Lockridge, and consequent unfitness to take command of the
force; that had Gen. Wheat been intrusted with the command, they would have promptly pushed their way up the
river and captured Fort Castillo before the Costa Ricans
could possibly have obtained reinforcements, inasmuch as
the fort was then defended by about 30 men." [7]

Three days after Wheat and the filibusters reached New
York, William Walker temporarily abandoned his dream.
On May 1, 1857, he surrendered to United States Naval
Commander Charles H. Davis.

Wheat lingered but little in New York before traveling
to North Carolina to visit his family. He was at Chapel Hill
as late as June 12, for on that day his sister, Selina Seay,
wrote her mother: "Kiss . . . Bro. Roberdeau (who may have
a namesake . . . by the time you read this)." [8]

There is nothing to suggest that Wheat concerned himself at all in Walker's plotting during the summer and fall
of 1857 to return to the country of which he still called
himself "President." Roberdeau had made up his mind
that any further expeditions to Nicaragua were not for him.

CHAPTER XI

WHEAT'S ACCELERATING CANNON

Roberdeau Wheat hated writing letters. From the Mexican War he had written his parents: "I will give you a full description of Mexico and the Mexicans in my next—that is when I get home for you know I could never write. I'd rather talk."

Years later he wrote his brother John Thomas from Mexico: "You know my antipathy to writing . . . and this will account for my short uninteresting letters."

John Thomas had more than his fill of the one-way correspondence with Roberdeau and when his letter arrived he sent it on to their parents.

"I remit you the long expected and eminently interesting letter from brother, that has been promised as an answer to about a dozen from me," he wrote.

"It will no doubt be interesting to you, who loving so much for anything from him, for my own part, I am *done*, as it is perfectly useless to attempt keeping up a correspondence with him, and besides, they are somewhat of a tax, the last letter took the only ten cents I had in the world to pay the postage on . . ." [1]

For the eighteen months following Wheat's return from Nicaragua, there are very few letters of his in existence. This indicates that Roberdeau not only had an antipathy to letter writing in general but that he wrote even more infrequently when he was in the United States than when he was off filibustering. But on his Nicaraguan adventure he seems to have written not at all.

Because of this scarcity of letters it is difficult to follow Wheat's movements after his return from Nicaragua. That he spent part of the summer of 1857 with his parents at Chapel Hill seems likely. That he didn't concern himself seriously with William Walker's expedition which sailed from Mobile on November 14 is equally likely.

At Christmas Roberdeau wrote his parents from New York that he was seeking the help of influential friends in Washington to get an appointment in the United States Army. He urged his parents, then visiting in Washington, to call on Governor Floyd and Governor Brown. "Both have been very kind to me and I hope through their mediation to secure a colonelcy in one of the new regiments," stated Roberdeau. "I would like you also to call on Gen'l Quitman for you know he is my military father and on Gen'l and Mrs. Cazeneau for they have been so kind that no one can thank them but you." [2]

On December 27 William Walker, his latest expedition having been smashed by United States Naval forces, arrived under parole in New York aboard the *Northern Light* to present himself to the United States Marshal. Wheat, acting as his counsel along with Thomas F. Meagher and Malcolm Campbell, accompanied Walker when he surrendered the next morning.

Greeley's *Tribune*, which had bitterly attacked Walker, his motives and his methods, disposed of the "Grey-eyed Man of Destiny" with a few words which left no room for doubt as to old Horace's opinion of the man:

"With this event, Walker's career as a filibuster leader is probably ended; though we must say that such an end by no means does justice to the cruel, sanguinary and ruffianly character which he has exhibited throughout. His oppor-

tunities have been limited but it would be difficult to find
in history a more heartless and inhuman villain." [3]

Mrs. Wheat, as one of the heirs of General Roberdeau,
was very much interested at this time in a family claim against
the government for reimbursement of funds advanced during
the Revolutionary War. She enlisted the help of Roberdeau,
who promised: "When I go on again, I will exert myself
to the utmost for the Roberdeau claim."

But Roberdeau soon became engrossed in another project
and he never did get around to working up the Roberdeau
claim. Early in 1858 he became associated with James R.
Haskell, a New York inventor of armaments and ordnance,
in the development of what was called an "accelerating
cannon."

In 1854 Haskell had completed the first steel breech-
loading rifled cannon in the United States. He sold twenty-
five of them to the Mexican government. It is quite possible
that Wheat may have negotiated this deal when General Juan
Alvarez sent him to New York in August, 1855, presumably
to get munitions.

It was in 1855 that Haskell became associated with Azel
S. Lyman, who first proposed applying successive charges of
powder to increase the velocity of a projectile. Haskell at
once began experiments on a multi-charge gun, a project to
which he devoted the better part of his life and $300,000. [4]

In August 1858 Roberdeau Wheat wrote Secretary of
War John B. Floyd about a cannon, but either illness or
pressure of business prevented Floyd from immediately
answering his young friend. So Wheat, on September 28,
wrote again to Floyd:

"Dear Governor: I wrote you a letter on the 11th ult
and have as yet received no answer. I know how very much
you are engaged and am loth now to annoy you and would
not but for the fact that I am prepared to exhibit my cannon
and am anxious to get the verdict of a board of officers. If

you can see fit to order a board to examine it at West Point
(as it is now there) I shall be most happy."

This letter proposes several questions:

Did Wheat actually invent a multicharge gun? Did
he only have an idea which he took to Haskell, an arms
expert, to develop? Or was he just Haskell's "front" because
of his connections and friendship with the "right" people
in Washington?

Roberdeau didn't hesitate to refer to the gun as "my
cannon" and it was mentioned in official correspondence as
"Wheat's accelerating cannon" but one wonders where and
how he became an ordnance expert. Certainly his artillery
tour in the Mexican War, his experience in charge of Carvajal's "artillery" and later with Álvarez and Walker did not
qualify him as an inventor of a cannon, however proficient
he may have been as an artillerist.

Moreover, it is known that Haskell had been working on
a multicharge gun for three years before Wheat came into
the picture. The inescapable conclusion is that the personable
young man, a close friend of the Secretary of War, and now
badly in need of a job, was only the salesman in the Wheat-
Haskell partnership.

When Secretary Floyd received Wheat's second letter,
he penciled on the back: "Do this. J. B. F" And so a board
of three officers was set up "for the trial of Mr. Wheat's
cannon." [5]

On January 2, 1859—Roberdeau dated it 1858 by mistake—he sent New Year's greetings to his mother from Philadelphia where he stopped for the night en route to Virginia.
"I am on my way to Old Point Comfort near Norfolk where
my cannon is to be tested this week," he explained.

One may suspect from Roberdeau's next letter that
already he was itching to be somewhere else, although the
tests of "his cannon" were encouraging.

His mother had written that John Thomas was suffering
from the effects of yellow fever. "I wish I were in Mexico

that I might have him with me in that genial climate," he wrote Mrs. Wheat. "Gen'l Alvarez has again invited me to return to the Army with the same grade I had when I left. Mexico has a strange fascination for me. . . . I am and have ever been a favorite in that country. They give me rank and pay while my own country will not."

Mrs. Wheat might well have paused at this point in reading Rob's letter to shake her head prophetically. She had cause to know in her heart of hearts that her restless son, as soon as he lost interest in "his cannon," would pack himself off again to Mexico.

But Roberdeau had high hopes for his gun. "I have concluded the experiments with my cannon at Point Comfort," he added, "beating the greatest government ranges more than one hundred percent. The large gun at West Point Foundry will be finished in about 5 weeks and then we will triumph."[6]

Wheat's optimism was somewhat excessive. The official report on the firing stated "it was the intention of the *Board* to have conducted a Series of experiments to ascertain how much of this *increased range* was due to the Accelerators. The *Board* does not deem that the experiments have been as yet sufficiently numerous to warrant it in expressing an opinion upon the merits of the plan."

On May 28, 1859, Wheat wrote Colonel William H. Drinkard, acting Secretary of War during the illness of John B. Floyd, that his accelerating cannon was completed and the shells for it would be ready in early June. "I am exceedingly anxious that the cannon shall be examined at Cold Springs," he wrote. "It is an entirely new invention, requiring a great many experiments in shot and shell and on that account should be as near the foundry as possible. I shall leave for the South in a few days, but Mr. Haskell . . . will advise you when the cannon will be ready for a Board to examine it."

Brevet Colonel Benjamin Huger, a top ordnance officer and later a Confederate major general, was ordered to visit the West Point Foundry at Cold Spring, New York, and inspect Wheat's accelerating cannon.

Haskell had set June 9 for the inspection of the gun, but on that date Wheat, who apparently had delayed his trip South, wrote Colonel Huger asking for a postponement of "the examination of our rifle cannon," because Mr. Haskell "has been unavoidably prevented from finishing the shells."

Huger, however, did not receive the letter until after he had accomplished his mission. His official report of Wheat's accelerating cannon was brief, concise and clear: "The gun is of a special pattern and is designed to give increased range to the projectile, by the discharge of the powder contained in two chambers made in the projecting metal on the underside of the gun; which additional charges are to be fired by the flame of the principal charge. The principal charge and the projectile are inserted by the breech—and the breech is closed by a screw. This breech pin is attached by a hinge, so as to be turned out of the way while inserting the charge. The 'Accelerators' open into the core near the trunnions and are charged through two openings on the top of the gun, which are stopped by a ground plug or stopper, secured by a screw." Then followed technical data on the bore and the rifling of the gun and the fact that the weight of the finished gun was 13,877 pounds.

The cannon was shipped to Fort Monroe, Virginia, where tests were being conducted with rifled guns submitted by several other parties.

Captain A. B. Dyer, post commander, wrote the Chief of Ordnance on September 17, 1859: "The rifled cannon presented for trial by Genl Wheat has been fired a few times. . . . The shells all appear to have been defective and the firing was not good in accuracy or range. In consequence of the very long ranges which were obtained here last winter from a small gun of Genl Wheat's the Board recommended that *ten* shells like those which gave the long ranges should be made for Genl Wheat's cannon. . . ."

Wheat's restless nature demanded action and no matter how enthusiastically he threw himself into a project, if it didn't move, his enthusiasm cooled and he was ready to divert his time and energies in other directions. The "triumph" which he had predicted for "my cannon" was too slow in coming and his interest in the gun had definitely flagged by the fall of 1859. Wheat's declining interest underlines the likelihood that his part in the partnership with Haskell was that of contact man and not of inventor.

From this time on, Haskell carried on all the correspondence with the War Department and the Chief of Ordnance, a correspondence that extended well into 1861. Such references in Haskell's letters as "this cannon was made under my supervision" and "I had the honor to superintend the construction of an accelerating cannon," support the theory that Wheat had nothing to do with inventing, designing and manufacturing the gun that bore his name.

Less than two months before the battle of Manassas, Haskell asked for authority to rebore the gun and to make fifty shells, a few at a time so that he could adjust them to the gun. "I am confident," he wrote, "if my request is granted that I can have a gun ready for service within four weeks that will have a greater range than any gun now in service." [7]

It would have been ironic, indeed, if anything had come of Haskell's request and "Wheat's Cannon" had been fired by Union artillerists against Major Wheat and the Louisiana Tigers at Stone Bridge across Bull Run on July 21, 1861.

Before Inventor James R. Haskell passes out of the life of Roberdeau Wheat, a brief quotation from a sketch of his life is not inappropriate: "It was only with extreme difficulty that the inventor was able to finally overcome the opposition which he encountered in official and military circles. The plans for the Haskell multi-charge gun were, however, finally approved by the bureau of ordnance, and in April, 1891, the secretary of war appropriated $55,000 for the construction of a gun for experimental purposes. . . . Mr. Haskell subsequently built several of his multi-charge guns, and they showed remarkable results in velocity and penetration. The government paid him $100,000 for his invention, but later developments in the science of gunmaking prevented its practical application." [8]

With the accelerating cannon off his mind, Wheat returned to Mexico to associate himself with Juan Alvarez. From Acapulco, on November 27, 1859, Roberdeau wrote his mother that he was in splendid health " and take so much exercise that I am losing my fat very fast." He then reverted to a familiar theme of his, one which he knew would be popular with his father. " Tell Pa that freedom in religion has been proclaimed in our state organization and that Genl Alvarez told me yesterday that he wanted to see all religions represented in this state. So you see that I am an integral part of a great movement. Do not imagine that my life has been so far spent in vain. Grant good may yet spring from my humble efforts."

A month later Wheat complained to his mother that he had received no mail from home. He wrote hastily to assure her that he had not been shot as she may have feared from reading a piece in the New York *Herald* which stated that General Alvarez and an American had been taken and the American shot. " The general taken was not our general," wrote Roberdeau, " and I am safe."

Roberdeau frequently spoke of the ignorance of the Mexicans in religious matters. " I saw 30,000 people on their knees in Pueblo," he once wrote. " There are 52 churches in Pueblo and not as many Christians. They are good Catholics but not good Christians." However, he began to show more and more interest in the religious festivals of the people. There is evidence, too, that he himself was turning back to the religious practices of his youth.

On his thirty-fourth birthday, April 9, 1860, Wheat
wrote his mother: "I bow in humble obeisance on this my
natal day. I am, thank God, in good health. . . . Death stalks
boldly around me. The yellow fever is raging here. . . . There
is a custom in this country to name a child after the Saint
upon whose day he is born and many here think that the
C in my name stands for Cleopas that disciple who spoke
to Jesus not knowing who he was. I have just read the
Gospel for Easter Monday, from the little Prayer Book you
gave me in 1854. It has a gilt cross upon the back and
surprises Mexicans much, as they know that I am not a
Catholic (Roman)." [9]

The day finally came when Wheat had had his fill
of Mexico. Whether disgusted with the continuing round
of revolutions or whether, as Leo Wheat asserts, "being now
in the fullest flush of a matured manhood, he could not be
content with a life of inglorious ease," [10] Roberdeau returned
to the United States.

On July 18 he arrived in New Orleans on the *Virginia
Antoinette* to the surprise of his brother, John Thomas, who
hastened to write their parents "the good tidings that Bro. R
is now here . . . having, I believe, abandoned Mexico for
good, but of this he will tell you himself, for as soon as he
returns from the ship, whither he has gone for his baggage,
he will append a postscript to this."

Roberdeau's postscript was brief, but meaningful: "My
dear Ma: I reached here yesterday after a tedious voyage
of 12 days from Vera Cruz. I shall not return to Mexico
again, as a Mexican. Should I ever go again it will be with
my own countrymen." [11]

CHAPTER XII

THE GENERAL'S LUCK

The terrific emotional spree was over," wrote Carl Sandburg. "Strong men hugged each other, wept, laughed, and shrieked in each other's faces through tears." [1]

It was May 18, 1860, and the Chairman of the Republican Convention, the balloting over, had just announced: "Abraham Lincoln, of Illinois, is selected as your candidate for President of the United States."

When word of Lincoln's nomination at Chicago reached the South, there was no such jubilation. Some men began to talk openly about secession if the Republicans won the election.

The Democrats had been split wide open ever since their convention in Charleston in April, when in a fight over Stephen A. Douglas, forty-five delegates from the Southern states walked out. The Democrats adjourned the convention to reconvene in June in Baltimore, at which time Douglas was nominated as the Democratic candidate.

In the meantime, the remnants of the Whigs and Know-Nothings had joined to form the Constitutional Union Party and had nominated John Bell of Tennessee, former Whig Congressman and Senator.

Southern Democrats, those who had walked out at Charleston and those who bolted later at Baltimore when

Douglas seemed certain to get the nomination, now joined
forces. In a convention at Charleston they nominated the
Vice-President of the United States, John C. Breckinridge,
as their candidate for the Presidency.

Such, briefly, was the political situation when Roberdeau
Wheat arrived in New Orleans in mid-July.

"What is Roberdeau going to do?" inquired Dr. Wheat
of his wife. "Does he say, in his letters to you?"

Roberdeau did say what he was going to do. He was
going to get back into politics. This upset Mrs. Wheat. She
wrote Leo, now studying in Germany:

"News from your brothers is that both are stumping
the state of Louisiana for the new president, Rob for Breckinridge—J. Thos. for Bell—this makes me often tremble for
fear of conflict between brothers. I rely, however, upon their
good sense and feeling and manly sentiment as children of
the same parents." [2]

One wonders why Wheat, a pronounced Whig in earlier
days, did not support the Whig candidate, Bell, as did his
younger brother, and such old Whig associates as Randall
and Carlton Hunt, Harry T. Hays and I. G. Seymour. With
the latter pair he would soon be again closely associated in
the Confederate army. It is possible that Roberdeau still bore
resentment to the Whigs for their attitude toward the filibusters years earlier.

Perhaps Wheat felt kindly towards President Buchanan,
who was supporting Breckinridge, because of his real interest
in the acquisition of Cuba and for his more tolerant attitude
towards the filibusters. Perhaps a clue lies in a sentence
Wheat's father had written Roberdeau's uncle before the
1856 election: "I am going to vote for Buchanan ... because
he is a Filibuster!!!" [3] At any rate, Wheat's support of
Breckinridge did not prevent his old constituents from arrang-
ing a large dinner in his honor.

Roberdeau didn't keep his mind on electioneering entirely; he was soon intrigued by the news from Sicily where

Garibaldi and his Thousand had landed in May. It did not take long for Wheat to convince himself that he should go to Italy and enlist his ever-ready sword in the cause of the Red Shirts.

A flowery newspaper story of the 1890's said: "Wheat . . . hearing . . . the rifle blasts of Garibaldi's carbonari piercing the quiet air of sunny Italy, . . . crossed the ocean for a chance to polish up his liberating sword once more." Leo Wheat says that Roberdeau had met Garibaldi in New York, and later received "an earnest invitation to join him in Italy." When did Wheat meet Garibaldi in New York? The Italian liberator lived there from about July 30, 1850, to sometime in 1851. Although no evidence has been discovered to verify Leo's statement, Roberdeau could have visited New York after the Cárdenas expedition, probably just before returning to New Orleans in October 1850, after a visit to his parents in North Carolina. And he could have met Garibaldi if he made such a visit. Moreover, since this is something Leo could have known first hand, his account may be tentatively accepted.

Leo summed up Roberdeau's Italian adventure in this manner:

"General Wheat . . . was received by [Garibaldi] in most flattering terms. . . . Promptly accepting the staff appointment that was tendered to him, General Wheat engaged once more in active service; and in the several engagements which quickly followed, his dash and gallant courage were the frequent theme of the army correspondents of the British press. Besides the high rank which Gen. Wheat bore upon Garibaldi's staff—that of a general officer—he was also the confidential friend of his commander, and was present when Garibaldi crowned Victor Emmanuel with a laurel wreath, as King of Italy." [4]

Whatever the motive, whether an old friendship with Garibaldi, the "earnest invitation" of the old Red Shirt leader, the desire "to polish up his liberating sword once more," or his eternal craving for military action, Roberdeau dropped politicking for Breckinridge and hastened to New York to sail for England.

The New York *Herald* of September 9 recorded his departure: "Gen. Wheat, late of the liberal army in Mexico, sailed in the *Vanderbilt* yesterday with the intention of joining Garibaldi at Naples. It is understood that Gen. Wheat is backed financially on his undertaking by Mr. Samuel Brannon, a wealthy gentleman of California."

Upon arrival in England Wheat "joined a party of congenial spirits going to Italy," sailing on the *Emperor* on October 1 for Naples. A British correspondent, describing the departure of the "Garibaldian excursionists" as this British Legion was sometimes called, had words of praise for "General Wheat . . . going out as a private. Truly a noble specimen of your countrymen, with a form like an expanded and mature Heenan, and a head like some fine classic model of antiquity. He appeared to me to be framed on the noblest scale of humanity, and to combine gentleness and simplicity of character with intelligence, manliness and vigor. I felt proud . . . to see such a sample of American sympathy with Italian Independence, fraternizing with this British expedition." [5]

As usual, Wheat didn't tell his family in advance that he was going to Italy. On October 2, at which time Rob was already at sea with the British Legion, Dr. Wheat, now living in Little Rock, Arkansas, wrote Leo in Germany:

"Your Brother R is gone to join Garibaldi in Italy. He did not apprise us of his designs. We learned his movements from the newspapers." [6]

Roberdeau wrote his mother from England telling her what the newspapers had already told her. He wrote again, briefly, from Gibraltar on October 7: "Thus far am I safely through. I am in fine health and spirits. . . . We had divine service on board last Sunday and I with my Prayer Book was in my place and what would I not given for you and

Pa to have heard the Creed as it was then said by the whole Regiment—every head bowing and many knees bent at the name of Jesus Christ."

That their firstborn son, whose waywardness they had feared, was thinking of religion gratified his parents. Mrs. Wheat expressed such a thought in a letter to Leo: "What have I to comfort me, if you or Roberdeau fall victims to Death in a foreign land—only let me feel assured you are God's own and this alone would give me reason." [7]

On October 14 the *Emperor*, accompanied by the *Melazzo*, entered the harbor of Naples, but the 650 members of the British Legion which the two vessels carried did not disembark until the following morning.

Wheat's love of military fanfare and all the trappings of glory must have found satisfaction in the reception the Neopolitans gave the British volunteers. The *Illustrated London News* gave its readers a lively description of the scene:

> The National Guard, carrying an English flag, went out to meet them, with music playing. Ten thousand people accompanied them, carrying nosegays and garlands of flowers. Everybody had a nosegay in his hand, and, if he carried a rifle, another in the muzzle of it. . . . Then the march through the Toledo began. The whole town was there; all the windows were lined with ladies, waving handkerchiefs, strewing flowers, and shouting vivas. The military bands, posted here and there, struck up the National Anthem while the Legion passed them. The shower of nosegays and single flowers was so dense at some points that it darkened the air like a shower of rain. Ladies and gentlemen, everybody of note in the town, went up to the volunteers to shake hands with them, and to express to them the gratitude of Italy. . . . The scene evidently took these young men by surprise; most of them hardly knew what to do under the embraces of the people, and kept on shaking hands, right and

left, and smiling with a funny expression of bewilderment. At last they hit upon crying "hurrah" and waving their rifles over their heads. . . .[8]

Having arrived in Naples in mid-October, Wheat could have participated in Garibaldi's passage of the Volturno on October 26; in the bombardment of Capua on November 1; in the siege of Gaeta; and in Victor Emmanuel's entry into Naples on November 7.

Just how much action Wheat saw is a matter for speculation. Mrs. Wheat wrote Leo that "the papers state [Roberdeau] has been in one battle," but on the other hand, Leo's sister, Selina, wrote him that "Bro. R. . . . was too late for the fighting." A newspaper sketch written in the 1890's, doubtless based upon Leo Wheat's accounts, declared: "Garibaldi gave him all the chance he wanted, and he went through battle and skirmish displaying the magnificent courage, the rare horsemanship and the personal chivalry of the cavalier. He was close to Garibaldi and in his confidence and the enthusiastic Latins called him the 'American Murat.'"[9]

The day before Victor Emmanuel entered Naples the American people elected Abraham Lincoln President of the United States, thereby setting into motion the engine of disunion throughout the South. Although a minority leader in the popular vote, Lincoln piled up 180 electoral votes, with Wheat's man, Breckinridge, a distant second with 72 votes.

Wheat's brief stay in the United States between his arrival from Mexico and departure for Italy had been sufficient for him to know that civil war was a distinct possibility if Lincoln's election broke up the Union.

And so, when the news reached him, after less than two months with Garibaldi, Wheat started for home, his taste for action and desire for glory on the field of battle still unsatisfied.

Mrs. Wheat wrote Leo on November 18: "I hope before

this you have been able to confer with your Brother Roberdeau, who is in Italy. . . . You would not even try to go to him, I am sure, it would be like finding a meteor—but you must write to him under the care of Genl. Garibaldi." [10] But by the time Leo received this letter, Roberdeau was on his way home.

Wheat traveled to England by way of Paris where, while walking one day in the Bois de Boulogne with a fellow officer, he encountered the Empress Eugénie. Wheat and his friend, turning the corner in a shaded avenue, suddenly came face to face with the Empress. "His friend, from the impulse of his national sentiment that no one may presume to come unannounced, and without previous permission into the presence of royalty, turned instantly and beat a hasty retreat." But not so General Wheat, says Leo, who relates the story. He stood his ground, made a "reverent salutation . . . by expressive look and gesture." And the lovely Eugénie promptly responded, acknowledging it by "a bright smile and a gracious inclination of the hand." Leo concludes his account of this incident with an eulogy of his brother: "That exchange of grave, sweet courtesies would make a pretty picture, for General Wheat was a man of as noble and commanding presence as she of queenly grace and beauty. Over six feet in height and finely formed, he had a dignified carriage and a polished ease of manner and address."

While in Paris Roberdeau was seized with a violent illness which delayed his journey, and after he returned to the United States he was again ill for three weeks. Relaying this information to Leo, Mrs. Wheat added: "Oh, how has God spared his precious life it may be it is for some noble purpose."

Roberdeau had written his mother from London on January 15, 1861, and a little more than a month later, on February 18, Mrs. Wheat wrote Leo that "We are hoping to hear of Robs arrival in his own country every day. We need him here [Little Rock]. . . . We are at the mercy of the militia. We are hoping if Roberdeau comes he may be put in command."

When Wheat reached the United States he called on his old commander, General Winfield Scott, who urged him to fight with the Union, "promising his influence to procure for him an eligible position in the Federal army." But General Wheat declined, "for he felt the call of a still higher and holier duty—and he obeyed—which was to share in the fortune of his own people and kindred and family." [11]

Before leaving New York for Montgomery Roberdeau wrote his brother John Thomas on March 10, stating he was "ready, willing and anxious to enter the campaign." He sent love to all his friends, "particularly to Pattina Brown. I have a strange presentiment concerning her." Was this the Miss Brown, "not beautiful but good" with whom Roberdeau fell in love when he was in the Louisiana Legislature in 1853?

Roberdeau continued: "I am now a cold water man will you not join me. I will not even drink cider for fear I may fall into temptation. For my sake refuse to drink the next time you are asked and drink nothing stronger than water until we meet. I do not ask this because I think you intemperate; but because you may become so."

News of Wheat's forsaking of strong drink drifted back to his family. Several months later, Selina Seay wrote her parents: "Mr. Decatur Hill, who is one of Col. Gee's cavalry soon to be in Little Rock was telling me yesterday of [Roberdeau]. . . . Mr. Hill also said the Genl. was a *teetotaler*, is that so?" [12]

Meanwhile, Wheat had offered himself for duty to the Confederate government in Montgomery. But once again it was a question of the General being too late. All the choice command positions had been given out. Leo Wheat asserts Roberdeau was turned down because he was a Whig. Roberdeau's first inclination, says Leo, was to go to Pensacola where John Thomas was in command of a battery. "I will go and be a private in my brother's company," he said. "I fear he

knows nothing of military tactics. I will teach him." Instead,
Wheat went to New Orleans, where General Twiggs, under
whom he had served for a while in the Mexican War, urged
him to assist in recruiting Louisiana troops.

Among the first persons Roberdeau saw when he reached
New Orleans early in April were his and John Thomas'
friends, Colonel and Mrs. Frank Webb, who had a plantation
at Killona, about thirty miles up the Mississippi from New
Orleans on the west bank.

When she returned to Killona Mrs. Webb wrote Mrs.
Wheat on April 10 about her sons: "The Gen. arrived the
morning I left much to my delight. He is looking better
than I ever saw him, not too fleshy but much handsomer as
on acct. of it. J. Thos. is well and an enthusiastic 'soldier
boy'!"[13]

P. G. T. Beauregard had not yet fired the shot at Fort
Sumter which opened the Civil War. But the lines were
drawn. South Carolina, which seceded on December 20,
1860, had started the march of the slave states out of the
Union. By January 11, 1861, Mississippi, Florida and Ala-
bama had seceded. Georgia followed eight days later and
on January 26, Louisiana got into line. When, on February
1, Texas left the Union, the cotton states, seven in all, had
declared themselves sovereign and independent states, their
connection with the Federal Union dissolved. Meeting in
Montgomery in February, delegates of these seven states had
formed the Confederate States of America and elected Jefferson Davis of Mississippi as President.

At 4:30 o'clock on the morning of April 12, Confederate
batteries opened fire on Fort Sumter. President Lincoln called
for 75,000 volunteers. This was the decisive factor in the
withdrawal of Virginia, North Carolina, Arkansas and Tennessee from the Union to join the Confederate States.

On Roberdeau's thirty-fifth birthday his father sat down
in his Little Rock rectory and wrote him a long letter. "The
return of this anniversary opens the roof of the Family Temple

of Love," began Dr. Wheat, in his best pulpit manner. "And from the great Fountain of Life and Beneficence enkindled anew the undying Vestal flame upon the Altar consecrated to our First Born." Having mixed his salutary metaphor, the good man lapsed into simpler language and one may read between the lines the hopes and fears and frustrations the rector had experienced during the previous fifteen years.

"God bless you, my dear Son!" he continued. "I had a rush of fond memories of your infancy and boyhood and early youth! And, although I cannot but wish that you had stayed home and helped me in the happy ministry which I love more and more every day and hour of my life; yet, I firmly believe that all your wanderings and disappointments will not be without precious residue; and I fondly hope and most devoutly pray that your future life may be the wiser and the happier for all that you have learned from your eventful Past."

Then Dr. Wheat touched upon a matter that must have grieved him and Mrs. Wheat repeatedly down the years—Roberdeau's silence on his movements until after he had undertaken them. "I do wish you would write oftener," he said, "and more fully of your personal matters. You have not truer more sympathizing, safer friends and advisers than your loving Ma and Pa. Depend upon it my dear Son, it is prima facie against any enterprise upon which you are asked to embark, if you cannot ask our approbation of it. . . . We cannot but highly approve of your seeking service in the Army of Confederate States. I am afraid you were too late in applying for any prominent position. But in such a cause and at such a time, I wouldn't have you refuse anything that may be offered."

The same day that Dr. Wheat addressed this letter to Roberdeau, April 9, Mrs. Wheat took up her pen to write to Leo in Germany:

"This is dear Brothers Birthday—and I feel very tender to him and you all today. Thirty five years ago I seemed to begin to live myself. It is time our dear one had done something for himself—God grant he may be wise and seek his Salvation. It would establish him in this life and he would prepare himself for the next aright. . . . I pray he may get a place in the Southern Army, he is a candidate, but he was late to offer. How has he trifled away his life, seeking riches in a day, and squandering his pennies because they were not pounds and borrowing. The veriest slavery is such debts as his." [14]

CHAPTER XIII

MAJOR WHEAT'S BATTALION

We understand that our friend, Gen. C. R. Wheat, is about raising a company of Volunteers, to serve in the Army of Louisiana," commented the New Orleans *Crescent* on April 12, 1861.

"His headquarters are at 64 St. Charles St., where we advise all friends of a glorious cause to repair and enlist. They will have a brave and experienced soldier for a leader, in whom all reliance and confidence may be placed."

The colonel of filibusters and general in the armies of Juan Alvarez, William Walker and Garibaldi wanted immediate action when the fighting started. General Wheat was perfectly willing to go out as a company commander if that was the only way he could get action.

He was feverishly busy. When not enlisting men for his company, which he called the Old Dominion Guards after his native state, Virginia, he made frequent speeches at various military meetings. He addressed a gathering of Virginians who met at the St. Charles Hotel to pass a resolution endorsing Virginia's secession from the Union. He attended the meeting of the Perritt Guards and made " a few happy remarks." [1] This company was made up of gamblers and it was facetiously remarked " to be admitted one must be able to cut, shuffle, and deal on the point of a bayonet."

One of the first companies organized in New Orleans was the Tiger Rifles, who rallied around Captain Alex White, veteran of the Mexican War who later served five years in the United States Navy. Most of the recruits were young Irishmen, some natives of New Orleans, others newly arrived in the city.

From the beginning, the reputation of the Tiger Rifles was not good. Kate Stone, on Brokenburn plantation in north Louisiana, recorded in her diary: "My brother told us much of the soldiers he saw in New Orleans: the Zouaves, with their gay, Turkish trousers and jackets and odd drill; the Tiger Rifles, recruited from the very dregs of the City and commanded by a man who has served a term in the penitentiary. . . ." [2]

Captain White had indeed been in the penitentiary for pistol-clubbing a passenger on a steamboat. General Dick Taylor, in whose brigade the Tigers later fought, wrote of him: "The Captain . . . enjoying the luxury of many aliases, called himself White, perhaps out of respect for the purity of the patriotic garb lately assumed." [3]

Nevertheless, the Tiger Rifles were a spirited, daredevil company, rakish in the picturesque new Zouave uniforms. A wealthy citizen, A. Keene Richards, was so taken with the Tiger spirit, that at his own expense he outfitted the Tiger Rifles. Their uniform consisted of a scarlet skull cap with long tassel, red shirts and open brown jackets and baggy trousers of blue and white striped bed ticking, tucked into white leggings.

The Tigers, apparently, didn't feel they were sufficiently decorative, so they painted pictures or mottoes on their hats. Typical slogans were: "Lincoln's Life or a Tiger's Death," "Tiger by Nature," "Tiger During the War," "Tiger on the Leap," "Tiger in Search of a Black Republican," "Tiger Bound for the Happy Land," and "Tiger in Search of Abe." [4]

By April 23 the Tiger Rifles' roll was full. Overtures having been made to General Wheat to organize a battalion,

the Tiger Rifles helped Roberdeau fill out the Old Dominion
Guards. On that date the *Daily Delta* carried an announce-
ment that "Gen. C. R. Wheat, with reference to raising a
battalion, invites such of our friends and citizens generally,
as feel an interest in the cause, to call at . . . No. 29 Front
Levee street, where they will find the material for the first
battalion in the States, and one that will make its mark when
called upon."

Shortly after this a third company, the Walker Guards,
commanded by Captain Robert A. Harris, asked to be a part
of Wheat's proposed battalion. It included on its rolls many
men who had followed William Walker to Nicaragua.

When the battalion began to shape up, Wheat turned
the command of the Old Dominion Guards over to Captain
Obed P. Miller, who led it throughout the battalion's existence.

By now volunteers swarmed all over New Orleans, drilling in the streets, in the parks, in warehouses and on the
docks. The Adjutant General of Louisiana commandeered
the Metairie race track, named it Camp Walker in honor
of the Confederate Secretary of War, Leroy Pope Walker,
and ordered the various New Orleans companies to encamp
there. By May 4 there were twenty-five companies at Camp
Walker, among them the Old Dominion Guards with ninety-
one men; the Tiger Rifles with ninety-seven men; and the
Walker Guards with eighty men.[5]

For many of the recruits, Camp Walker proved a hard-
ship. As one Louisiana volunteer, W. H. Tunnard, recorded:

> In the early part of May upwards of 3,000 troops
> were present, and still rapidly arriving. It was somewhat
> different affair from holiday soldiering at home. The
> enforcement of strict and rigid military discipline, the
> daily compulsory drill, guard mounting and duty, caused
> many a high toned and independent spirit to rebel against
> restrictions upon personal liberty. Yet duties imposed

were bravely, and at last cheerfully, discharged. It was a spectacle both strange and new to see young men, reared amid the luxuries and comforts of home, whose fair faces and white hands had never been soiled by contact with work, doing soldier duty, bending over the campfire, preparing meals or boiling coffee, tears streaming from their eyes, caused by villainous smoke from these same campfires, carrying wood and water, and when the day's duties were completed, lying down on a board or the bare ground with knapsack or billet of wood for a pillow and a single blanket for a covering.

Most of Rob Wheat's recruits, gathered from the levees and alleys of New Orleans, could hardly be said to have missed at Camp Walker " the luxuries and comforts of home." At Camp Walker bad blood arose between the Tiger Rifles and another New Orleans unit, the Louisiana Independent Rangers. The latter accused the Tigers of stealing and the Tigers got angry, probably because the accusation was true.[6]

On May 15 the Old Dominion Guards, the Tiger Rifles and Walker Guards were in camp at Camp Moore, in the piney woods across Lake Pontchartrain, about eighty miles by rail from New Orleans. The camp was well shaded, cool, pleasant and healthy. But everyone grumbled, officers as well as men, at their inability to go to the city. All kinds of excuses or reasons were offered—business in New Orleans, family illness, disastrous fires which had made loved ones homeless. " I have never heard of so many people being sick in the city at any one time (except in fever season) before, as is reported here in one day," wrote a correspondent for the *Daily Delta*. " At a fire in the city a short time since, almost fifty here had their friends rendered houseless by the devouring element. Anything in the world for an excuse to get to town." [7]

Shortly after Wheat and his men reached Camp Moore two more companies were assigned to him, the Rough and

Ready Rangers, commanded by Captain H. Chaffin and the
Delta Rangers, led by Captain Henry Clay Gardner. On
May 22 Roberdeau wrote his father: "I have five companies
encamped. I was elected Major of the 19th by a unanimous
vote."

Major Wheat was anxious to be off for Virginia. In
vain did General Twiggs urge Rob to wait for a larger command. The old general pointed out that Rob's battalion
could easily be expanded into a regiment which would have
entitled Wheat to a colonelcy.

Wheat shook his head. "I fight not for rank, General,"
he replied. "It is for my country—it is for Virginia that I go."

On May 25 Governor Moore issued Wheat's commission
as Major. On June 5 the five companies under his command
were organized as the First Special Battalion which the next
day was mustered into the Confederate service.[8]

Wheat's men were as anxious as he was to get to "the
seat of war" in Virginia. They and other troops, bored by
the tedium of life at Camp Moore, began to grumble at the
delay in moving to the front. The irksome monotony of
drilling and guard duty was relieved by poker playing "and
frequent trips to the sutler's store to indulge in convivial
fellowship." Officers could buy all the wines and liquors
they desired, but enlisted men were required to present a
written order signed by a company officer. "The enlisted
men secured the signatures of captains when they could do so,
but to save time and chances of being met by a refusal, most
frequently forged the name of their officers," stated a veteran
of Camp Moore. "The average soldier, whether wearing
the shoulder straps of an officer or the plain, unadorned
jacket of a private will indulge, to a greater or less extent,
in ardent spirits when it is to be had, and it is generally to
be had."

Wheat's Special Battalion was doubtless as thirsty as any
unit at Camp Moore. From the reputation it rapidly built
up after its arrival in Virginia, one is even justified in assuming

that they were the guzzling champions of the camp. But even with this title to defend, they were impatient to move. At last, Wheat's Battalion was alerted for transit to Virginia and all was astir in their section of the camp. Wives, mothers, sisters, relatives and friends arrived to help the men pack for the trip. Wheat, of course, was constantly occupied during these last days. "The major was very busy," recorded Clara Solomon, daughter of the battalion sutler, in her diary, " but he had no feminine hands to share or lessen his toil." [9]

Three days before Wheat's Battalion left, Rob lost Captain Chaffin's Rough and Ready Rangers, which were disbanded after failing to fill their roll. In their place Major Wheat received the Catahoula Guerrillas, commanded by Captain J. W. Buhoup.[10] Not many weeks later Captain Buhoup and his men were to save Wheat's life on the field of Manassas.

On June 13 Major Wheat loaded his battalion, about 450 strong, on a train at Camp Moore and the journey to Virginia got under way. The route Wheat's Battalion followed took them through Jackson, Granada and Corinth, Mississippi, thence to Chattanooga, Knoxville, Bristol and Lynchburg.

Wheat's Battalion was greeted with enthusiasm all along the way, "ovations and entertainments" taking place at the different stations. Pretty girls passed "bouquets and billet-doux" to handsome officers. And at one stop, Major Wheat was presented with a delicious cake. These were "sources of pleasurable entertainment recurring all the way."

But the Battalion had a disagreeable experience in Chattanooga, which, one of Rob's officers complained to the *Daily Delta*, "is the only place on the route where we have been charged anything." So put out was the Battalion by the ill-treatment, "it was with great difficulty that our men were restrained from acts of destruction and violence."

The incident developed when the men were forced to pay ten dollars for wood with which to cook their supper. "A company passing here a day or two ago since paid ten cents apiece for washing themselves," wrote the officer, " I paid 50 cents for a cup of coffee. Our men, after cooking, gathered the remaining wood and consumed it in a bonfire, with three times three groans for the hospitable people of Chattanooga."

Major Wheat remained in Lynchburg only long enough to be supplied with ammunition and equipment. On June 19 he was issued 10,000 musket ball cartridges, 5,050 rifle ball cartridges, 76 knapsacks and 50 haversacks. Then Wheat's Battalion moved on to Manassas Junction, probably reaching there the next day. The *Daily Delta* of June 22 commented on Wheat's Battalion: " We learn ere this they are at Manassas, or in the vicinity and will be among the first in the great battle to be fought."

From Manassas Wheat's Battalion was sent forward to Centreville to join the command of Colonel Philip St. George Cocke, who stationed the Louisianians at Frying Pan Church. On July 3 Roberdeau wrote his mother that he was " within 8 miles of Fairfax Court House and have been in this country ten days." So by June 24 or 25, Wheat's Battalion was in line, facing the avenue of approach for Federal troops sallying forth from the defenses of Washington. " I occupy the most advanced post on the left of the army . . ." Roberdeau told his mother.[11]

The first members of Wheat's Battalion to engage the enemy was a small detachment of Tiger Rifles under Captain White. At Seneca Dam, on the Potomac, on June 28, " they had a nice little skirmish, killing three of the enemy and my loss was one man shot in the leg (both bones broken)." Another casualty in this skirmish with Major Everett's Union command was " Henry Wheat's mare, ridden by one of my officers, Mr. McCausland."

Roberdeau wrote about Virginia relatives he had seen, Robert Wheat, Henry Wheat, their families and his dashing young cousin, " the approved and accomplished officer of Dragoons, whose praise is on every one's tongue—George

Baxter. He is a splendid fellow and I am very proud of him. His name is the synonym of courage."

Several weeks before Wheat arrived in Virginia, Bishop Leonidas Polk, devoted friend of Rob's family and namesake and godfather of Leo Wheat, had been commissioned a major general in the Confederacy. Bishop Polk, a West Pointer who left the army for the pulpit, had gone to Richmond to supervise the welfare of the Louisiana troops and President Davis had prevailed upon him to accept a commission and engage himself in the defense of the Mississippi River.

"What!" exclaimed a friend of the Bishop when he heard the news. "You, a Bishop, throw off the gown for the sword?"

"I buckle the sword over the gown," replied Polk.

Roberdeau concluded his letter by referring to Bishop Polk's appointment. The few words must have both startled and delighted his mother and father:

"Bishop Polk Brigadier General 1861. General Wheat Bishop 1871. Who knows but what it may be so." [12]

Dr. and Mrs. Wheat must have assured themselves that Roberdeau had turned back to religion; indeed, not just turning his thoughts in that direction, but actually entertaining the idea of entering the ministry. They must have been overjoyed by these lines from their eldest son.

On the Fourth of July Roberdeau heard the guns firing in Washington in celebration of the day, so near was the Battalion to the Federal capital. The Confederate troops, in the unseasonably cool July, were chilled by the sudden cold wave. "It was so cold day before yesterday [July 2] that I had to wear an overcoat all day," wrote Wheat to a friend. But the discomforts of war were hardly noticeable at this time. "We have everything that is good to eat and plenty of it . . . cherries and blackberries which I have every day in large quantities."

Rumors, common to all armies in all times, were numerous. "We think we will be ordered to attack Alexandria in a few days," Wheat confided to his friend. This attack never came off.

It was evident, however, that soon real action would break out. "The ball will open on this line in a few days, if not hours," wrote Lieutenant William W. Blackford to his wife on July 10. "Of that you can tell more in Lynchburg than I can down here. . . . A wagon passed by with four women in it belonging to Col. Wheat's 'Louisiana Tigers,' all dressed up as men. I presume they are vivandieres from New Orleans. They are disgusting looking creatures who have followed the camp. They are being moved back to a safer place in anticipation of an attack." [13]

Besides Wheat's Battalion, the Confederate troops at Frying Pan Church included Colonel J. B. E. Sloan's Fourth South Carolina Regiment and a troop of 180 mounted men, all under the command of Colonel Nathan G. Evans, whom West Point comrades had called "Shanks."

At nightfall on July 12 a wild rumor circulated rapidly through Evans' force that it was surrounded by twenty thousand Yankees and the only chance of escape was to cut its way through them and strike out, each man for himself, for Manassas Junction, where General Beauregard was with the main Confederate army. J. W. Reid, a private in the South Carolina Regiment, described the tense situation in a letter home. "Our officers told us that if we failed in this we would all be cut to pieces or captured," he wrote. "We were ordered . . . to prepare for action. Provided an attack should be made in 10 minutes all was ready. Each man drew 45 rounds of cartridges, and had everything in wagons ready for an emergency." Daylight dispelled the state of alarm, for a picket sent forward to study the situation returned with the information that the nearest Yankee troops were in Alexandria.

Several days later orders came from Beauregard for Colonel Cocke to abandon his advanced position and retire across Bull Run. On July 17 Cocke took up positions at or near Stone Bridge.[14]

To Wheat's Battalion, Colonel Cocke assigned the extreme left of the Confederate line on the high ground overlooking Bull Run.

CHAPTER XIV

THE FIRST HOUR AT MANASSAS

It was inevitable that the first big battle of the Civil War would be fought in Virginia. This was evident to both sides, once the Confederate capital had been moved from Montgomery to Richmond. But it was not inevitable that it should be fought on a steaming dusty Sunday in July.

Jefferson Davis intended from the beginning that the South should fight a defensive war. This would sit well in England and France, which Davis hoped to woo to the side of the Confederacy. Moreover, in July 1861 the Confederacy had neither the men, nor organization, nor plan to attack Washington and invade the North.

President Lincoln, for his part, was determined to carry the war to the South, but neither he nor General Scott, who commanded the United States Army, wanted to go off half-cocked.

But the press, the public and the politicians in the North clamored for action. "On to Richmond!" was on everyone's lips. Calls for "sudden, bold, forward, determined war" rang out in the Senate and House.

Old Fuss and Feathers argued for delay until a fighting force adequate to crush the rebellion could be trained. He pointed out to Lincoln that soon the time of the three-months volunteers would be up and not much service could be expected from them. Scott wanted to wait until the 400,000 men the President had asked Congress to authorize "for making this contest a short and decisive one," were ready for action. Then a massive blow could be directed against the Confederacy in a short intensive campaign which could not but be successful.

Under heavy pressure on all sides Lincoln began to desert his original position. The day he sent his message to Congress, Horace Greeley's New York *Tribune*, for the ninth day in succession, screamed: "Forward to Richmond! Forward to Richmond! The Rebel Congress must not be allowed to meet there on the 20th of July! By that date the place must be held by the National Army." This stirring cry, which fell on ready ears, was written by the paper's Washington correspondent, Fitz-Henry Warren. It appeared first in the *Tribune* on June 26 and Greeley repeated it daily through July 6.[1]

The radicals in Congress joined in the pressure on the President, demanding aggressive action by ordering McDowell's army to invade Virginia. These politicians were suspicious of the continued inactivity of the Federal troops, a fact which they attributed to Southern sympathies among the generals. The radicals doubted whether General Scott, himself a Virginian, had any real desire to whip the rebels.

Brigadier General Irvin McDowell, who made a quick jump from Major to the command of the Union army, protested that he should not be forced to "organize and discipline and march and fight all at the same time," a view with which General Scott heartily agreed.

The pressure on the President mounted until at last he ordered Scott to put the Union army into motion, with Beauregard's force of 22,000 at Manassas as the primary target and Richmond as its goal.

The hero of Sumter had six brigades based at Manassas, with advanced detachments at Centreville, Fairfax Court House and Germantown, and at various crossroads between Bull Run and the Potomac.

In addition to Beauregard's main army, General Joseph E. Johnston with 11,000 men was in the Shenandoah Valley where he opposed a Federal force of 18,000 under Major General Robert Patterson in the neighborhood of Martinsburg. At Aquia Creek, thirty miles to the south, protecting the road from Washington to Richmond, there were about 3,000 Confederate troops. At Leesburg, north of Manassas and near the Potomac, another small Confederate force was posted.

McDowell's Union army around Washington numbered about 50,000, approximately twice the number Beauregard could call upon. The Union plan of campaign was a sound one. McDowell, with 35,000 men, would attack Beauregard at Manassas while Patterson, with a numerical superiority of three to two over Joe Johnston, kept the Confederate force in the Valley so occupied as to prevent Johnston from reinforcing Beauregard.

From spies in Washington, Beauregard learned on July 16 that McDowell had received his marching orders. He hastily called in his advance forces and set up a defense line behind Bull Run from the Stone Bridge, over which the Warrenton Turnpike passed, to Union Mills, a stretch of about nine miles.

"Shanks" Evans, of Colonel Cocke's brigade, was assigned the job of defending the Stone Bridge with Wheat's Battalion and the Fourth South Carolina Regiment, a total of fifteen companies. Evans held the extreme left of Beauregard's line and Wheat's Louisianians were on the extreme left of Evans' force.

The reluctant McDowell began his march on Manassas on July 16, as Beauregard had been advised. Heat, dust, thirst and the weight of heavy equipment combined to slow the advance and considerable straggling soon developed.

To make matters worse, the line of march was cluttered by the carriages and wagons filled with Congressmen and fashionable Washingtonians who had ridden out to see the show. There were repeated halts and it took McDowell all day to cover six miles. It wasn't until noon on July 18 that the Federal army reached Centreville.

Beauregard, on the seventeenth, had wired Davis that his outposts had been driven in by the enemy and he asked for reinforcements at the earliest possible moment.

"Beauregard is attacked," Adjutant General Samuel Cooper wired Joe Johnston at Winchester. "To strike the enemy a decisive blow a junction of all your effective force will be needed."

Johnston, leaving a small force and J. E. B. Stuart's cavalry in front of Patterson to demonstrate, immediately marched to join Beauregard. In Washington, Scott, impatient that Patterson had reported no victories over Johnston, telegraphed him on July 18:

"I have certainly been expecting you to beat the enemy. If not, to hear that you had felt him strongly, or, at least, had occupied him by threats and demonstrations. You have been at least his equal, and, I suppose, superior in numbers. Has he not stolen a march and sent reinforcements towards Manassas Junction?"

Patterson sent an immediate and emphatic reply: ". . . The enemy has stolen no march upon me. I have kept him actively employed, and by threats and reconnaissances in force caused him to be re-inforced. . . ." [2]

Before the old general—at seventy, he had returned to duty after retirement from the army—realized Johnston was no longer on his front in force, the two Confederate armies were uniting on the plains of Manassas.

On the same day that Johnston began his march to join Beauregard, McDowell sent Tyler's division to feel out the Confederates' defense. In a sharp engagement at Blackburn's Ford on Bull Run, Brigadier General James Longstreet's Confederates threw the Union troops into confusion and they retired hurriedly up the road to Centreville, their setback casting gloom into McDowell's camp.

Meanwhile, reinforcements were pouring in on Beauregard. Johnston's Valley troops began arriving by train on the nineteenth and President Davis rushed other troops, newly arrived in Richmond, to Manassas Junction.

Beauregard decided he was now strong enough to attack McDowell, his old West Point classmate, at Centreville. But Beauregard was no longer in command, for Joe Johnston outranked him. Accordingly, Beauregard submitted his plan to Johnston, who approved it. The Confederates would converge on Centreville by a number of roads from their Bull Run line and strike McDowell's left flank heavily.

By coincidence McDowell's plan of attack also involved a powerful blow at his enemy's left. Two diversionary attacks were to be made, one to contain Confederate forces at Blackburn's Ford; the second was to be a demonstration in front of Stone Bridge. The main Union force, by a wide circuitous march, was to cross Bull Run at Sudley Ford and catch the Confederates in the rear.

Faulty staff work, with a delay in delivering the battle orders, prevented Beauregard's attack from getting underway before heavy cannonading at Stone Bridge announced that McDowell was attacking the Confederate left.

It was just before daylight on July 21 that General Tyler's first cannon shot screamed harmlessly over Evans' position at Stone Bridge. Soon a frightful cannonading commenced, much more noisy than damaging, to which Evans, with his two outmanned guns, did not reply.

Major Wheat, on orders from Evans, formed his command to the left of the Stone Bridge and he sent forward the Tiger Rifles under Captain White to deploy as skirmishers in the woods near Bull Run. The Tigers, accordingly, opened the fight for the Confederates. Wheat himself, "with characteristic daring and restlessness," as Beauregard later reported, crossed Bull Run at Red House Ford, about a mile upstream from the Stone Bridge. Encountering some Union scouts on

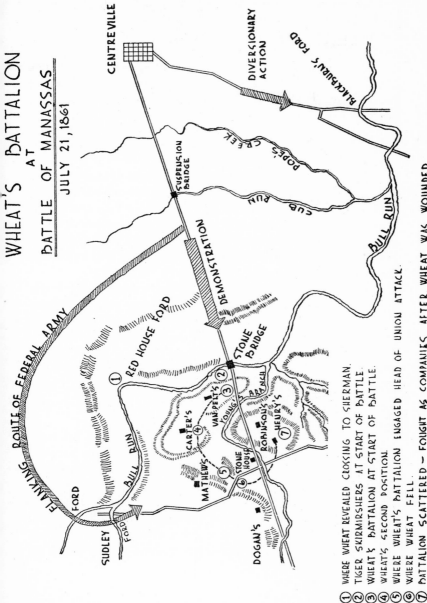

WHEAT'S BATTALION
AT
BATTLE OF MANASSAS
JULY 21, 1861

CENTREVILLE

DIVERSIONARY ACTION

BLACKBURN'S FORD

POPE'S CREEK

SUSPENSION BRIDGE

CUB RUN

BULL RUN

DEMONSTRATION

RED HOUSE FORD

STONE BRIDGE

FLANKING ROUTE OF FEDERAL ARMY

BULL RUN

SUDLEY FORD

FORD

FORD

MATTHEW'S

CARTER'S

VAN PELT'S

YOUNG'S BRANCH

STONE HOUSE

ROBINSON'S

HENRY'S

DOGAN'S

① WHERE WHEAT REVEALED CROSSING TO SHERMAN.
② TIGER SKIRMISHERS AT START OF BATTLE.
③ WHEAT'S BATTALION AT START OF BATTLE.
④ WHEAT'S SECOND POSITION.
⑤ WHERE WHEAT'S BATTALION ENGAGED HEAD OF UNION ATTACK.
⑥ WHERE WHEAT FELL.
⑦ BATTALION SCATTERED — FOUGHT AS COMPANIES AFTER WHEAT WAS WOUNDED.

the far bank, he shouted "taunting defiance" at the Yankees and then wheeled his horse and recrossed the stream.

This bit of bravado by Major Wheat was a costly mistake, for it revealed to Brigadier General William T. Sherman a place for crossing Bull Run. In his memoirs Sherman said: "Early in the day, when reconnoitering the ground, I had seen a horseman descend from a bluff in our front, cross the stream and show himself in the open field on this side; and, inferring that we could cross over at the same point, I sent forward a company of skirmishers, and followed with the whole brigade."[3]

Meanwhile Tyler's cannons were still booming at Stone Bridge, but it soon became apparent to Evans that the Union force on his front was not pushing the attack with vigor.

Seven miles away at a Confederate signal station on Wilcoxen Hill, young Captain Alexander surveyed the field with his glasses when suddenly his eye was caught by flashes in the distance. In an instant he recognized them as the reflection of the morning sun from a brass field piece. Soon he was able to pick up the glittering of bayonets and rifle barrels.

"It was about 8:45 and I had discovered McDowell's turning column, the head of which, at this hour, was just arriving at Sudley, eight miles away," wrote Alexander. Quickly Alexander signalled Evans by wigwag: "Look out for your left; you are turned." As a courier rushed up to Evans with Alexander's message, another courier from the picket at Sudley Ford reported a large Federal force was crossing Bull Run at that point.[4]

Evans, impressed by the report from two different sources, acted with great boldness. He sent orders to Major Wheat, then at the Carter House with the bulk of his command, to advance as skirmishers, covering Evans' entire front. Then Evans, leaving four companies to defend Stone Bridge, took the rest of his command, about six companies of infantry, one troop of cavalry and the two-pounders, and marched off to join Major Wheat and the Louisiana Tigers at the Carter House.[5]

Wheat, meanwhile, had deployed Captain Buhoup's Catahoula Guerrillas as skirmishers in the direction of Sudley Ford to meet the Union advance. The rest of his command he moved into position on the extreme right of the new battle line. "Having reached this position," he reported to Evans later, "I moved by the left flank to an open field, a wood being on my left. From this covert, to my utter surprise, I received a volley of musketry which unfortunately came from our own troops, mistaking us for the enemy, killing three and wounding several of my men." [6]

Captain Hawthorn's company of Sloan's Fourth South Carolina Regiment, in the excitement of their first battle, had fired on Wheat's men from the woods and the Louisianians quickly fired back at them. Wheat, immediately sizing up the situation, called out to his men not to return the fire. Those near enough to hear his command obeyed but the more distant did not.

By now it was about 9:45 A. M. and at almost the moment that the South Carolinians and Louisianians were shooting at each other, Burnside's brigade emerged from the woods, paralleling the Sudley-Manassas road. Wheat's Battalion quickly engaged the Union skirmishers. "The enemy in front opened upon us with musketry, grape, cannister, round shot and shells," Wheat reported. "I immediately charged upon the enemy and drove him from his position. As he sallied again, in a few minutes, I charged him a second and a third time successfully."

Beauregard noted in his report that "the enemy, soon galled and staggered by the fire and pressed by the determination with which Wheat handled his battalion . . . hastened up three other regiments." [7]

Wheat sent word to Evans to rush reinforcements as he now found himself "in the face of a very large force—some ten or twelve thousand in number." He ordered his men to seek the cover of the hills, but through a mistake some of the battalion crossed an open field and suffered heavily from the Federal fire. "Advancing from the woods with a portion of my command, I reached some hay-stacks under cover of which I was enabled to damage the enemy very much," reported Wheat. "While in the act of bringing up the rest of my command to this position, I was put hors de combat by a Minie ball passing through my body."

Major Wheat had dismounted, and holding the bridle of his horse with one hand, with the other he had waved his sword aloft to urge on his men. His gigantic frame was a conspicuous mark, and he was struck down by a rifled ball which passed through his body, from side to side, piercing one of his lungs.

When he fell, Wheat was forty or fifty yards west of the Sudley-Manassas road, near the first bend, a quarter of a mile north of Warrenton Turnpike.[8]

Thinking their leader killed, Wheat's Battalion began to lose its organization but the various companies continued to fight under their respective captains. Captain Buhoup, crossing the field where Wheat had fallen, came across the Major on the ground, bleeding profusely from his wound.

He rallied his men around Wheat, and in the face of the advancing Federals, the Catahoula Guerrillas made a litter out of muskets and placing Wheat on it, carried him to safety. They were exposed to intense fire as they carried their bleeding commander through lanes of wounded and dead. At almost every step a soldier would drop, his musket falling from his hands. "Lay me down, boys," protested Wheat. "You must save yourselves." Buhoup and his men refused to desert Roberdeau.

A mounted officer rode into the woods. Captain Buhoup, assuming he was a Confederate, asked for his horse to carry Major Wheat to the hospital. The horseman wheeled, galloped back out of the woods, and a moment later the place was riddled with shot.[9]

Austin Eastman, color bearer of the Old Dominion Guards threw the battle-torn company flag, pierced with fifteen or more bullet holes, over the wounded commander.

Wheat, in his report to Evans, took note of this: " By the judicious management of Capt. Buhoup I was borne from the field under the persistent fire of the foe who seemed very unwilling to spare the wounded."

While their major was taken in an apparently dying condition to a field hospital on the Manassas road, half a mile above the New Market crossroads, the Battalion, without a field officer to hold it together, fought bravely as companies throughout the day in the face of an enemy far outnumbering them.[10]

Evans' brave band of 1,100 rifles, having stemmed the Federal advance for more than an hour despite the enemy's tremendous superiority, was now sorely pressed. " Never, perhaps in the history of modern warfare was there so unequal a contest," wrote Colonel Cocke in his report. "With his small but heroic numbers, Major Evans advanced to fight the head of a column of 25,000 men. . . . For more than an hour the contest was maintained without assistance, the other troops of my command being held to their positions by the strong demonstrations in their front." [11]

From far across the Confederate lines, near McLean's Ford on Bull Run, marched the brigades of Bee and Bartow to Evans' assistance. They made a gallant fight on the hills north of the Warrenton Turnpike, but the Union pressure was overwhelming. To make matters worse, Sherman's command, having crossed Bull Run by the ford Major Wheat's impulsive recklessness had revealed in the morning, now struck the hard-pressed Confederates on their right flank.

This was too much for the Confederates and, about noon, they broke ranks and fled in disorder across Young's Branch and the Warrenton Turnpike. As they scurried up Henry Hill, General Bee, valiantly trying to rally his men, pinned a name on Brigadier General Thomas J. Jackson which will last as long as history lasts. "Look!" he shouted, pointing with his sword to Jackson's troops in line just below the brow of the hill, "there is Jackson standing like a stone wall! Rally behind the Virginians!"

By now it was 1 P. M., and for an hour there was a lull in the fighting while the Union forces, having crossed the valley of Young's Branch, regrouped for a final victorious assault on the Confederate position.

Generals Johnston and Beauregard, having by now realized that this was the main Union effort and that the battle of Manassas was not being fought as Beauregard planned it, ordered up Confederate brigades from the fords farther down Bull Run.

These reinforcements, forming on either side of Jackson, were in line when McDowell reopened his attack about 2 P. M. For more than an hour the battle ebbed and flowed in furious fighting, always at close range and sometimes hand-to-hand. Then Jeb Stuart first immobilized, and then captured, the advanced batteries of Ricketts and Griffin and the tide of battle began to turn in favor of the Confederates.

As more Southern reinforcements came up the field, the last of Johnston's troops from the Valley under Kirby Smith, and Jubal Early's brigade from McLean's Ford, Beauregard switched from defense to attack. The whole Confederate line, the rebel yell on their lips for the first time, moved forward to the charge. The Union line wavered, fell back, broke. The rout of McDowell's army was underway.

Meanwhile the Tiger Rifles of Wheat's Battalion were busy. Captain White's horse was shot from under him and he was thought to be killed. A number of Tigers were dead or dying. Lieutenant Tom Adrian fell from a rifle ball through his thigh. Seeing the Tigers' temporary confusion at this turn of events, the New York Fire Zouaves let out a cheer.

From where he was lying on the ground, Lieutenant Adrian, "than whom a braver man never wore hair," shouted:

"Tigers, go in once more, go in my sons, I'll be great

gloriously God d——d if the s—s of b——s can ever whip the Tigers."

"Our blood was on fire," wrote First Sergeant Robert Ritchie to a friend. " Life was valueless, the boys fired one volley, then rushed upon the foe with clubbed rifles beating down their guard; they then closed upon them with their knives. . . . I have been in battle several times before, but such fighting never was done, I do believe as was done for the next half hour; it did not seem as though men were fighting, it was devils mingling in the conflict, cursing, yelling, cutting, shrieking."

Just then, behind them, the Tigers heard a great shout: " Hurrah for the Tiger Rifles, charge for the Tigers and for Louisiana! "

It was Colonel Harry Hays' Seventh Louisiana Infantry of Jubal A. Early's brigade, just come upon the battlefield in time to prove a decisive factor. Although the Seventh Louisiana had marched eight or nine miles at the double, it charged the Federals with a vengeance. That broke the spirit of the Fire Zouaves. The New Yorkers fled, " throwing down their arms, equipment, clothing and everything." [12]

The Tigers were not yet through. An English observer commended the way " these heroic soldiers sustained every shock with unwavering courage, and on more than one occasion dropped their rifles, and rushed among the enemy with long bowie knives." Wheat's impetuosity had revealed to Sherman a place to cross Bull Run early in the morning. The Tigers, however, with their leader believed to be dying, evened the score late in the day. " The Tiger Rifles pitched into Sherman's battery, when they were retiring, and took two pieces and gave them to us—a good present," wrote John W. Wilcox of the Washington Artillery to a friend in New Orleans. The English observer accounts, at least in part, for the enthusiasm with which the Tigers went at Sherman's force: " As the majority of Wheat's command were Louisiana

Irish, they robbed the dead of their whiskey, and were in high spirits when ordered to assail Sherman and Keyes." [13]

Meanwhile, surgeons at the field hospital had examined Major Wheat. They shook their heads hopelessly when they saw the extent of his wound. They warned him that the wound would prove fatal.

"I don't feel like dying yet," replied Wheat, cheerfully.

"But there is no instance on record of recovery from such a wound," said one of the doctors.

"Well, then," responded Wheat with determination, "I will put my case on record." [14]

That Roberdeau hovered between life and death for several days is evidenced by dispatches from Virginia to the New Orleans papers:

"Major Wheat's condition . . . is critical."

"Major Robert Wheat is shot through the body. His recovery is doubtful."

"Major Wheat . . . is still living. It is now believed he will recover."

"Major Wheat is better this morning. He will undoubtedly recover." [15]

Word was sent at once to Wheat's family that he was in a critical condition. Dr. and Mrs. Wheat set out at once for Manassas; so did John Thomas, who was stationed at Pensacola. But the first member of the family to reach his side was Rob's brother-in-law, Francis Shober, who hurried up from North Carolina.

Arriving at Manassas on July 25, he found Rob "still improving and . . . evidently rallying very rapidly." In a long letter to his wife, Rob's sister, Joe May, he confessed his relief at finding him "so much improved." Shober's description of Wheat's wound is doubtless the most accurate of all: "His wound is through and through the chest, immediately under and a little in front of the armpits—one of his lungs is perforated and he suffers great pain in throwing off the matter from it." Rob had no fever, his appetite was good and he talked a great deal when the doctors let him. He was comfortably established in Major Cabell's cottage near the railroad station and was well nursed by his men. " His life seems to be a charmed one and he is full of vitality and strength still."

Shober told his wife of his walks around the entrenchments " looking . . . at the wilderness of guns taken from the enemy." Suddenly he encountered " Beauregard with a brilliant staff, all splendidly mounted." Beauregard examined Sherman's guns and inspected other points and then " the whole party halted at Rob's quarters and called in to see him. Rob presented me to Beauregard, and I was charmed with his graceful easy manner. He spoke a few words of the most soothing and tender character to Rob, and when he went away, it seemed as if the influence of his presence had left a charm in the room." Beauregard's visit had an electric effect on Wheat, Shober told his wife, " and he has been in good spirits ever since." [16]

Wheat received a steady flow of visitors, mostly fellow officers and the men of his battalion, who idolized their major. One day, before he was considered convalescent, Wheat saw one of his Tigers peering into the room, an expression of great anxiety on his face. Wheat called to the man to come in and as the Tiger advanced, the wounded man, struggling to raise his right hand, said: " Come here my royal Bengal, and let me shake your paw." The nurse came up at this moment and the Tiger had to content himself by warmly embracing Wheat's hand.[17]

Major Potter of the New York Scott Life Guard, captured in the battle, came to see Rob as soon as he arrived at Manassas Junction. They were old friends, and when he heard of Wheat's wound he asked permission to visit him. " It was quite an incident in the fortunes of this war," Francis Shober told his wife.

When Major Potter was leaving Rob instructed his orderly to give him some underclothes and money, for he

would need both in his Richmond prison. When Rob's father
and mother arrived, Mrs. Wheat immediately took charge
of nursing her son back to health. A native of Virginia, Mrs.
Wheat was "righteously indignant at the invasion and dese-
cration of the soil of her own loved native State." And when
she heard of Rob's gifts to the Yankee officer, she expressed
her disapproval in Major Potter's presence.

Rob reproved her gently: "Why, my dear mother, Potter
is as conscientious in this war as we are," he said. "And
if our places were changed, he would do as much for me,
wouldn't you, Potter?" [18]

It must have been gratifying to the wounded commander
of the Louisiana Tigers to learn that early reports of the
destruction of his command were exaggerated. One story had
it that only twenty-six Tiger Rifles had escaped death or
wounds; another that the battalion was so badly cut up that
barely a hundred out of four hundred escaped death or
wounds; another that the Old Dominion Guards lost half
their number in wounded. The official casualties for Wheat's
Battalion, however, were as follows: Killed, eight; wounded,
five officers and thirty-three men; missing, two. Total: forty-
eight.[19]

Everyone who visited Wheat praised his gallantry and
the bravery of his battalion. General Beauregard had sent
word from the battlefield that "for this day's work, you and
your battalion shall never be forgotten by me," and he doubtless repeated this in person when he called on Roberdeau.

The general feeling at Manassas Junction was that
Roberdeau would be promoted to the command of a regiment
or even a brigade.

"Wheat, I'd give a thousand dollars to stand in your
shoes today," said a friend.

"Give the captain my shoes," Rob told his orderly.[20]

The official reports took due cognizance of Wheat's
valor in that first bitter hour at Manassas and of the reckless
heroism of his men. Beauregard noted "the desperate odds

A Louisiana Tiger

(Courtesy National Archives)

The Tiger Rifles, the only Zouave company in Wheat's Battalion, gave
their name and character to the unit. Their uniform consisted of a scarlet
skullcap, red shirt, open brown jacket and baggy Turkish trousers of blue
and white bed ticking, tucked into white leggings.

WHEAT'S BATTLE FLAG AT MANASSAS   (*Courtesy Thomas Harrison*)

This flag, preserved in the Confederate Memorial Hall in New Orleans, was the standard of the Old Dominion Guards. It was chosen by lot before the battle to be the Battalion Battle Flag. When Wheat fell, the flag was wrapped around his body as he was carried from the field. It is riddled with bullet holes and the bloodstains are still discernible.

against which Evans and his men had maintained their stand with almost matchless tenacity" and he commended the "dauntless courage and imperturbable coolness" of Evans, Wheat and Colonel Sloan of the Fourth South Carolina. And he made special reference to "Major Wheat, than whom no one displayed more brilliant courage."

In a Napoleonic flourish Beauregard added: "But in the desperate, unequal contest, to which these brave gentlemen were for a time necessarily exposed the behavior of officers and men was worthy of the highest admiration, and assuredly hereafter all those present may proudly say, 'We were of that band who fought the first hour of the Battle of Manassas.'"

Colonel Philip St. George Cocke called attention to "the skillful and heroic struggle of Evans on my left, after he had been turned and taken in flank by overwhelming numbers. . . . Where so many have acted well their parts it would appear almost invidious to mention the names of any. Nevertheless, I deem it proper to state that conduct of Majors Evans and Wheat is above all praise."

General Nathan G. Evans—he is variously called Major and Colonel in the reports, but he was made a brigadier after Manassas—not only praised Wheat's bravery, but he gives a clue as to just how important a part Rob Wheat played in saving the Confederate army from destruction.

"I would call the attention of the general commanding to the heroic conduct of Major Robert [sic] Wheat, of the Louisiana Volunteers, who fell, gallantly leading his men in a charge," reported Evans. "I am also much indebted to him for his great experience and excellent advice." [21]

Few, if indeed any, officers in either the Union or Confederate armies at Manassas had as much combat experience as Rob Wheat. For after the Mexican War, there was little to do in the regular army except to chase Indians in the West. And while most of the regular army officers were doing that, Wheat was fighting in Cuba, on the Rio Grande, in Mexico,

Nicaragua and Italy. In what particular way was Rob's admitted experience useful to Evans? And what "excellent advice" could Wheat have given his commanding officer?

Evans had one mission, to defend the Stone Bridge. Did he arrive at the conclusion that Tyler's attack at the bridge was merely a demonstration? Or did Wheat, drawing on his experience, point out to Evans that the Yankee effort lacked purpose and the reality of a genuine attack? It is probable that Wheat's experience rather than Evans' intuition prompted the latter to recognize that Tyler was not making the main Union push.

When Evans received Captain Alexander's message that his left was turned, he made the bold decision to leave Stone Bridge virtually unguarded, and to move most of his command to meet McDowell's thousands, now pouring across Sudley Ford.

If Evans made that decision on his own judgment, there was no need for him to single out Major Wheat's "excellent advice." On the other hand, if Wheat inspired the daring move, which possibly saved Beauregard's army from disaster, then Evans had reason to acknowledge his debt to Major Wheat.

This view was held by Alexander, who flashed the signal to Stone Bridge that McDowell had turned the Confederate left. Years later in his brilliant *Military Memoirs of a Confederate*, Alexander concluded that Wheat was responsible for the bold maneuver: "He doubtless advised Evans in his movement to the left." [22]

If this is correct, then one fact stands out boldly from the bitter struggle of "the first hour of the Battle of Manassas," namely: Major Rob Wheat not only fought with great personal valor until felled by a ball, but he proposed the daring move which blunted McDowell's spearhead and gained time for Beauregard to regroup his forces and escape defeat.

CHAPTER XV

ALL QUIET ON THE POTOMAC

Major Wheat was well enough on July 31 to put his signature on a pay voucher and to draw from his friend Major Cabell, Quartermaster of the army, the amount of $275, his pay for one month and twenty-five days in the Confederate army.[1]

The next day Rob was able to dictate his report on the battle, but apparently it was never delivered to General Evans. "When all behaved so well," he reported, "I forbear to make invidious distinctions and contenting myself with commending my entire command to your favorable consideration, I beg leave to name particularly Maj. Atkins, a distinguished Irish soldier, who as a volunteer Adjutant, not only rendered me valuable assistance, but with a small detachment captured three pieces of artillery and took three officers prisoners. Mr. Early, now Captain Early, also, as a volunteer Adjutant, bore himself bravely and did good service. My Adjutant, Lieut. Dickinson was wounded while gallantly carrying my orders through a heavy fire of musketry. Capt. Miller of Company (E), Lieutenants Adrian and Casey were wounded while leading their men in the thickest of the fight." [2]

Lieutenant Dickinson, who was shot in the thigh, was responsible to a degree for some of the wild stories that circulated about Wheat's Battalion being all but wiped out. The Richmond *Enquirer* quoted him to the effect that "out of 400, which constituted that command, there were not more

than 100 that escaped death or wounds." Captain Miller
suffered the breaking of a small leg bone. Lieutenant Adrian
was wounded in the thigh and Lieutenant Casey suffered two
wounds. He was "shot in the foot, and when lying on the
field stabbed through the thigh by a Yankee officer, whom
he killed." [3]

Major Atkins, whom Wheat identified as a "distinguished Irish soldier," was Robert Goring Atkins of County
Cork, son of an Anglican rector. He and Wheat had met
in Garibaldi's camp in Italy and had become fast friends.
Arriving in Virginia before Manassas he had attached himself
to Wheat as a volunteer aid. After the battle Atkins wrote
Wheat, seeking a permanent assignment in the command.
"If, however, your list of officers is made up already and
that I must be debarred the pleasure of following to another
field the fortunes of Gen. Wheat—much as I love your character and esteem yourself—I regard my own too highly to
remain in inglorious ease," he wrote. He asked Wheat to
recommend him to President Davis if he could not place him
in the Tigers. In September the Irishman was elected captain
of Company E of Wheat's Battalion. [4]

On August 3, two weeks after the battle, Wheat had
mended so well he was moved to Culpeper, thirty miles below
Manassas Junction, for his convalescence. This he spent in
the home of James Barbour, an old friend of Roberdeau's
family.

They had frequent talks together and Roberdeau told
him of his various experiences under arms and the hopes and
aspirations which had guided his life. Barbour was much
taken with Wheat and he, along with many others, felt that
Roberdeau should be promoted for his heroism at Manassas.
After Wheat had been in Barbour's home for a week or ten
days, the latter decided to take a hand in Rob's affairs. Barbour
wrote a letter, presumably to Governor John Letcher of Virginia, on August 12:

Dear Sir:

Major Roberdeau Wheat who was severely wounded in the battle . . . at Manassas . . . will be ready for active service in a week or two. As he is a native of our state . . . it is appropriate to present to you . . . the past career of this remarkable man. . . . An intense ambition for military distinction has been the controlling influence in his life and has made his life a career of rich and bold adventure. . . . He was educated at the Military High School under Rev'd now Colo W. N. Pendleton. He served through the Mexican War under Scott as Captain of Cavalry. He commanded a Louisiana regiment in Lopez' expedition against Cuba. He was for 10 years—[two years is closer to the truth]—a brigadier general in the Mexican Service.

He held an artillery command in Walker's Nicaraguan expedition. He was with Garibaldi in Italy being volunteer aid to Avezano second in command to Garibaldi. He raised a battalion in New Orleans and came to Manassas . . . where it was his fortune to open the last battle. . . . In the thick of this fight he received a wound which was at the time considered mortal. . . . A man only 35 years of age of his intellect courage and energy has vast capacity for public service in these strange wild scenes that surround us. He is a man of fine abilities and good education. . . . A chance for noticeable service is all that he asks. He has earned promotion by his skill his courage and his blood. . . . President Davis General Beauregard and the Secretary of War know him and can suggest more in his favor than I have said if attention be called to his case. The rank which he now holds is not sufficient to offer him much opportunity for the distinction for which he yearns. Promotion is sought not for the honor which it confers but for what it may enable him to win. I am sure that it cannot be necessary to say more to enlist you in his interest.

Very Respy and Truly

" Jas. Barbour [5]

This remarkable letter could not have set forth Wheat's claim and eagerness for promotion any better had Rob written it himself.

While Wheat was mending at Culpeper the battalion was commanded by Captain Robert A. Harris of Company A, the Walker Guards. With the reorganization of the Confederate army after Manassas, Wheat's Battalion was assigned to the Eighth brigade along with four Louisiana regiments, the Sixth under Colonel Isaac G. Seymour; the Seventh under Colonel Harry Hays; the Eighth under Colonel Henry Kelly; and the Ninth under Colonel Dick Taylor, son of President Zachary Taylor and brother-in-law to President Davis through the latter's first marriage.

In temporary command of this Louisiana Brigade was Colonel Seymour, New Orleans newspaper editor and an Indian fighter and veteran of the Mexican War, " a man of culture and refinement, respected of all," whose " high spirit . . . though past middle age," brought him into the Confederacy.[6]

However, General William H. T. Walker of Georgia was named commander of the Louisiana Brigade. After a brief period which Walker spent judiciously in training the Louisianians, he was assigned to lead a Georgia brigade.

Colonel Dick Taylor, on sick leave at Fauquier Springs, Virginia, learned on the eve of reporting back to his regiment that he had been promoted to brigadier general and placed in command of the Louisiana Brigade. " This promotion seriously embarrassed me," he said. " Of the four colonels whose regiments constituted the brigade, I was the junior in commission, and the other three had been present and ' won their spurs ' at the recent battle, so far the only important

one of the war. Besides, my friendship for President Davis
. . . would justify the opinion that my promotion was due
to favoritism."

Taylor protested this to Davis, but the latter would not
rescind his order. Instead, he wrote letters " to soothe the
feelings of these officers with a tenderness and delicacy of
touch worthy of a woman's hand, and so effectually as to
secure me their hearty support." [7]

When Major Wheat returned to his battalion he found
his old friend of Mexican War days as his commander. He
also found that the Louisiana Tigers in his absence had
enriched the legend which had already grown around them—
the legend that made them known as the toughest, roughest,
meanest fighters in the army.

Shortly after the battle Captain Alex White of the Tiger
Rifles engaged in a duel with Captain George McCausland,
one of Major General Dick Ewell's aides. Captain McCausland, it appears, made some disparaging remarks about the
Tigers and when these reached White's ears he immediately
issued a challenge. McCausland selected rifles as the weapons.
At the first fire, McCausland was " bored through just above
the hips, and died in great agony." [8]

In Lynchburg, on August 10, some Tigers staged a little
riot which landed them in jail. Tigers and other New Orleans
soldiers brawled among themselves but in such a way as to
disturb the peace of the town and put in jeopardy the safety
of the citizens. "We witnessed no exhibition of legitimate
authority, either civil or military, to preserve the peace," commented the Lynchburg *Virginian*, "and felt that ours was
the condition of people at the mercy of a drunken soldiery
who could with impunity riot in the public thoroughfare. . . .
It is a shame for the community to be left at the mercy of
armed men, influenced by passion and mean whiskey."
Eventually, however, an armed posse of Lynchburg citizens
restored order in the streets by arresting the Tigers and putting
them in prison. [9]

Perhaps this and other tales about the Tigers induced Major Wheat to speed up his convalescence. Still feeling the effects of his wound, but able to get around, Wheat and his father called on President Davis to pay their respects. Mr. Davis urged Wheat to return home with his father and " keep quiet until entirely well."

" I shall keep quiet, Mr. President," Rob replied, " as long as yourself and the army do, but no longer."

But Wheat apparently didn't keep quiet very long. Too much needless activity caused his wound to break open and he was compelled to rest again. Wheat went to Alleghany Springs, where for some days he was quite ill. Wheat's sutler, S. P. Solomon, wrote his daughter Clara in New Orleans that Rob's imprudence was endangering his life. " The wound may kill him yet," he wrote, " and if it does through spreeing, it will *serve him right*." [10]

However, Wheat mended rapidly and he was able to rejoin his battalion at Manassas on September 14. One of his men, in a letter to the New Orleans *Crescent* described Rob's " homecoming" in a manner which reveals how his men idolized him:

" Major Wheat is with us again, but looking badly. He came back Saturday. It would have done anyone good to have seen the boys on Friday evening. We came in from a hard drill of about three hours and were cooking something to eat when Lieutenant Cagle told us that Major Wheat was coming. We fell in ranks, and with the rest of the battalion went to meet him, singing and shouting. We marched about two miles, only to be disappointed, for the Major had stopped on the road, too weak to come farther. There are not many officers who could get such a reception as he did on Saturday. We went out again, and escorted him in, and he then made us a speech."

Although Rob was able, and certainly eager, to be on active duty again, he still felt the effects of his wound. Five weeks later he wrote his mother: "My health is improving but I do not think I can stand a severe Winter." [11]

Wheat soon discovered that the Tigers were now much better equipped than when they had left home. They had "India-rubber coats and splendid blankets, besides hats, shoes, pants, pistols, swords and some money and jewels, saved by them from the wreck and waste of the enemy's flight." [12]

General Johnston's army was still based at Manassas but he had pushed his line forward again. Wheat's Battalion encamped at Camp Reserve near Fairfax Court House in September and October and later at Camp Carondelet near Centreville.

Nothing, of course, was happening. The South, elated at the rout of McDowell, was plainly overconfident. Many of the soldiers took off for home without leave, confident that one Confederate could lick six Yankees and equally confident that the Yankees, realizing this, would do no more shooting.

The North, much sobered by the defeat at Manassas, settled down to raising and training the large army that General Scott had wanted before venturing on the road to Richmond.

Many Confederate officers grumbled at the inactivity, especially as discipline was becoming something of a problem. In addition, the Confederate camps were swept with sickness which greatly reduced the effective strength of Joe Johnston's army. "Our cause of inaction, I think, has been our weakness," wrote one officer. "The army now in front of Washington is only 40,000; on paper it is 65,000, but sickness has reduced it to about 40,000 effective men."

Dick Taylor's Louisiana Brigade was particularly hard hit. He stated that "the men were scourged with mumps, whooping-cough, and measles." Major Wheat's Tigers contributed many to the hospital list. In August 1861, of 421 officers and men in the battalion, 239 were on the sick rolls. In September the number of Wheat's men treated dropped to 179 and in October the total was further reduced to 134. With cool weather there was a sharp drop in the ailing and only 49 Tigers went on sick call in November and 68 in December.[13]

Boredom was to be expected under such circumstances but there were occasional diversions such as Professor Lowe's balloon, from which the Yankees made aerial observations of the Rebel lines. One day, the Washington Artillery of New Orleans elevated a gun and fired at Lowe's gas bag—the first anti-aircraft shot in history. The Confederates camouflaged logs, making them look like cannons to fool the aerial observers into believing the Southern army was more strongly supported by artillery than it actually was.[14]

For many, especially the thirsty souls in Wheat's Battalion, and more specifically the Tiger Rifles, the only relief from boredom during this "phoney war," was to get drunk, start a fight with another unit or throw a brawl within the bosom of the family. More than once the Louisiana Tigers exercised their option on all three methods.

Liquor was forbidden in the camps and the railroads and express companies were under strict orders that no intoxicants were to be transported to the army. "However, much whiskey found its way there," said Captain Jim Nisbet of the Twenty-first Georgia regiment. "Taylor's Louisiana Brigade, of our Division, being mostly city or river men, 'knew the ropes,' and could get it from Richmond."

It was during this quiet on the Potomac that the Tigers built up their already considerable reputation for meanness. A dozen of them tried in vain to beat up a whole company of the Twenty-first Georgia for stealing their whiskey. The only satisfaction they got was some bashed heads.

This did nothing to abate their cussedness, the evil report of which soon spread quickly over the Confederate cantonment. Many a soldier went out of his way to avoid the Tigers' camp, but few were as frank about their fear of

these "tigers . . . in human form" as was W. A. McClendon,
a young Alabamian.

"I was actually afraid of them," he confessed, "afraid
I would meet them somewhere and that they would do me
like they did Tom Lane of my company; knock me down and
stamp me half to death." [15]

There was no shortage of food during this period. For
instance, for the three-day period October 19–21, 1861,
Wheat's Battalion, then 412 strong, received the following
rations:

> 1,030 pounds of fresh beef.
> 300 pounds of bacon.
> 7 barrels of flour.
> 123½ pounds of rice.
> 150 pounds of sugar.
> 15½ pounds of candles.
> 49½ pounds of soap.
> 105 pounds of salt.
> 2 barrels of potatoes.
> 82½ pounds of coffee.[16]

The officers fared well, too, during the long period of
inactivity. As Colonel Frederick Augustus Skinner of the
First Virginia Regiment later put it: "If war has its horrors,
it is not without its compensations. Among the pleasantest
memoirs of my old age are those connected with the first year
of our great Civil War . . . when we had plenty to eat, plenty
to drink, plenty to wear . . . and we did our best to live up
the comfortable precept of . . . 'Eat, drink and be merry.'"

Anyone waging a "phoney war" on that basis was sure
to attract the interest and attention of Major Wheat of the
Louisiana Tigers, and it is not surprising to find his name
on Colonel Skinner's list of the "noted gourmets" in the
Confederate army. Skinner recorded his affection for "that
accomplished soldier of fortune, Bob Wheat of the Louisiana
Tigers," and his other gourmet friends, Major Louis Cabell,

quartermaster, and Colonel J. B. Walton of the Washington Artillery.

"We bon-vivants and educated gourmets, next to our military duties, devoted ourselves to the 'flesh pots,'" said Skinner, "and displayed no little ingenuity and skill in concocting culinary surprises for each other in the way of good breakfasts and succulent suppers."

Skinner handed the palm to Colonel Walton, fairly drooling in his old age over "the memories of the magnificent hospitality of the Washington Artillery's mess table." But after paying "grateful tribute to the gastronomic superiority" of Colonel Walton, Skinner turned to the culinary contests between Wheat and himself:

"The first striking success in which he scored a maximum of points was achieved by the accomplished Major Wheat with an entirely new dish which he pompously called 'cabeza de buey al ranchero,' which was nothing more than the head of ox, horn, hide and all baked under the ashes like a sweet potato."

Colonel Skinner first got wind of this fantastic dish from his chaplain, an intimate friend of Wheat's who reported that Rob was preparing a strange surprise for breakfast. Skinner rode over to Wheat's camp to witness the process. Wheat grumbled at the chaplain's indiscretion in letting his secret out when Skinner explained his reason for the visit. Rob pointed to a corner of his tent where there rested on the ground a freshly severed head of a large ox, so cut from the carcass as to leave adhering to it a flap of the skin. This was neatly skewered over the raw part of the neck.

Leading Skinner behind his tent Wheat showed him a circular, well-lined hole in the ground filled with blazing logs. The fire, explained Wheat, was to be kept in full blast until tattoo sounded when it would be allowed to burn itself out. Then the ox head, just as it was, would be thrown in and the pit filled up. In the morning the ox head would be dug up and dressed for the table.

Skinner hurried to Wheat's quarters early the next morning to watch the operation which he described. " The head,
when dug up and brought into the tent covered with ashes
and dirt, was, I think, about as repulsive an object as my eyes
ever beheld, but giving out a most appetizing odor. The dirt
and ashes were brushed off and the skin and horns speedily
and skillfully removed, and lo! a metamorphosis occurred like
that of a repulsive caterpillar when it escapes from the chrys-
alis in the shape of a gaily colored butterfly. We had before
us a dish as grateful to the eye as it was to the nostrils, and
one which might have tempted the sternest anchorite to
break his vows."

Major Wheat's guests acknowledged a " gastronomic
triumph " for their host with his novel dish and paid him
the sincerest of all compliments " by devouring the whole
and sighing for more."

Colonel Skinner thought for several weeks as to how he
might match Major Wheat's performance. Then one day
early in October the area was suddenly visited by a flight of
small birds, a species with which Skinner was not familiar.

Some of the Colonel's men went hunting, and he was
able to secure six dozen of the little birds, each of which he
stuffed with a plump York River oyster. " My supper that
night was a great culinary triumph," he stated, " and Wheat
himself confessed with an honest frankness, inspired by his
third tumbler, that my ortolans en caisse exceed his cabeza
de buey, because more delicate and refined." [17]

When Wheat wasn't vying with Colonel Skinner of the
First Virginia in the preparation of exotic dishes, he participated in social gatherings at the various headquarters, but
especially those of the Washington Artillery.

The organization, commanded by Wheat's old New
Orleans friend, Colonel Walton, had provided itself with a
very cosy headquarters, having had a frame house transported
from the outposts and fitted up with a fireplace large enough
to roast an ox whole. And during the dreary winter nights

of 1861 there gathered around this cheerful hearth Captain Willie Allan, quartermaster of the First Virginia, Major Bob Wheat of the Louisiana Tigers and other kindred spirits.

The gathering sparkled with wit, song and anecdote. William Owen of the Washington Artillery recalled that each member of the coterie had a specialty: Allan with " Sally in Our Alley" and the " Prisoner's Lament"; Rosser with "Dragoon Bold"; Garnett with "The Captain With His Whiskers" and " The Soldier's Dream "; Brewer with " Maryland, My Maryland! "; and Moore with Irish song and story.

" ' Old Bob Wheat ' would contribute a roaring chorus, and would at intervals prognosticate the future life—' when, on the high battlements of Heaven, George Washington would be officer of the day, and Bob Wheat officer of the guard.' "

On one particular bitter day, with snow half a foot deep, Wheat and Major Cabell rode up to the Washington Artillery headquarters. As they dismounted, comfortable observers within saw through the windows a pair of new boots, tied together and flung over Wheat's saddle. The visitors were welcomed to the blazing log fire. In a few moments, after they had thawed out, Wheat addressed Walton: " I have a treat for you. Please ask your servant to bring in those boots that hang on my horse."

The boots, obviously heavier than they should have been, were brought in.

" Have you any glasses? " asked Wheat. " If so have them filled with snow."

Then to the surprise of Colonel Walton and his staff, Wheat drew from each boot a bottle of champagne. " Pop went the corks," said Owen, " and the sparkling fluid was poured into the snow-filled glasses. It was delicious—the best champagne, we thought then, we had ever tasted. . . . It is safe to say that there never was such a sociable and agreeable set of officers and men assembled together as those of the army that fought at Manassas." [18]

One young officer who attended some of the social gatherings was not too impressed with the calibre of the oratory. "At some of the dinners," wrote Tom Goree to his sister, "we had speeches from Genls Johnston—Beauregard—Smith—Van Dorn—Bonham and others—all of who can fight much better than they speak."

About this time, Major Wheat and General Joe Johnston allegedly threw "a grand drunk." The charge was made by Colonel L. B. Northrop, former Confederate commissary general, who had few friends other than President Davis. The President retained Northrop in office despite complaints from all directions.

Sometime in 1870, when Davis was gathering ammunition for his feud with General Johnston, Northrop wrote him: "Johnston . . . had a disgraceful debauch with Colonel Wheat at Manassas the soldiers got the liquor and it was a grand drunk."

In the absence of other evidence one might be inclined to challenge the credibility of Colonel Northrop, who seemed perfectly willing to play the part of "hatchet man" for Mr. Davis. There is, however, evidence from a completely reputable source that Wheat did stage a memorable dinner in the Tigers' camp near Centreville and that General Joe Johnston attended and that the cup was freely passed around.

Major David French Boyd of the Ninth Louisiana Regiment, who years later became president of Louisiana State University, gives a graphic picture of the affair and the amusing incidents connected with it. He wrote:

> Wheat gave what was known as "The Tiger Dinner" to many of his friends, including the leading officers of the army. Gens. Joe Johnston, Gustavus Smith, Ewell, Jubal Early, Earl van Dorn and others of high rank were present. Beauregard and Dick Taylor, our brigade commander, suspecting what might occur, prudently excused themselves. A more brilliant set of clever

men, military or civilian, perhaps never sat around a
board during the war.

Wheat was the prince of hosts and entertained
royally. He had a superb dinner for his distinguished
guests within his large marquee, and gave a more plebian
feast to his Tigers on the outside. But all were filled
with plenty and good cheer. The choicest of liquors and
wines were served within the tent; the Tigers stole all
they wanted from the outside, and all were happy. A
fine band enlivened the occasion with its sweetest strains.
And while the major and his guests within were toasting
and responding, reviving old memories and dreaming of
glorious careers, the Tigers were having their fun, too,
on the outside. To the music of the band, mounted on
the horses of the generals—two big Tigers on Joe Johnston's big bay—they rode around and around, circus
fashion, and ran races up and down the road as long as
they were sober enough to stick on.

About 2 o'clock in the morning Wheat had his
guests well hors de combat, and the commander was
hauled to his headquarters in an ambulance—maybe his
horse was too tired!

What if McClellan, only a few short miles away,
had marched on us that morning! I fear wary 'Old Joe'
might for once have been caught a-napping.[19]

Late in November some irresponsible conduct by some
of the Tigers took Major Wheat's mind off feasting. Dis-
orders after tattoo resulted in the arrest of several Tigers who
were confined in the brigade guardhouse. A group of other
Tigers led by two reckless youngsters, Dennis Cochrane and
Mike O'Brien, tried to force the guard and free the prisoners.
In the melee the officer of the guard was struck and man-
handled.

When the attempt failed, Cochrane and O'Brien were
arrested and put into irons. A courtmartial was assembled

the next day, November 29, and the two Tigers were found guilty of violating the ninth article of war. Their sentence: " To be shot to death, at such time and place, and in such manner as the commanding general may designate."

Wheat pleaded for their lives, begging that some other severe punishment be imposed. He was told that the maintenance of discipline demanded their execution. One of the men had risked his life to help rescue Wheat at Manassas. Wheat was overwhelmed with grief and chagrin that he could do nothing for this brave fellow. He was mortified and crushed that he could not save the pair from the firing squad.

General Dick Taylor of the Louisiana Brigade ordered that the two Tigers were to be shot by a firing squad made up from their own company, the Tiger Rifles. Major Wheat begged Taylor not to impose this sad duty upon his men and other battalion officers joined in the plea. In vain did Wheat point out that the Tigers might refuse to fire on their own comrades.

" I insisted for the sake of the example," wrote Taylor in *Destruction and Reconstruction*, " and pointed out the serious consequence of disobedience by their men." Although General Taylor gives the impression that the offense, trial, sentence and execution all occurred within twenty-four hours, the fact is that the two hapless Tigers were not shot until December 9.

The execution took place in a field on the Murtaugh place on the Blackburn Ford road between Centreville and Cub Run. It was witnessed by thousands of the troops, some in formation, some from vantage points atop houses or in the trees of the surrounding hills.

It was a bright, sunny December day. The three brigades of Taylor, Trimble and Elzey formed three sides of a square, facing inward. In the center of the square were two white stakes, ten feet apart.

A covered wagon, escorted by two companies with fixed bayonets and loaded muskets, slowly moved into the square

and halted by the two stakes. The condemned men got out
and their coffins were removed from the wagon and placed
near the stakes. Each Tiger was attended by a Catholic priest,
in vestments, whose consolations the two young Irishmen
eagerly received.

The two men were clad in the picturesque uniform of
their company, the scarlet fez or skull cap, light brown jacket,
open in the front, showing the red shirt, large Turkish trousers
of white and blue stripes, full and fastened just below the
knees, white leggings and shoes.

When they were in position and the wagon had retired,
the left-hand corner of the square opened and two sections
of Tiger Rifles in full uniform marched slowly down the
center, arms shouldered. The twenty-four men halted, each
section opposite a man and a coffin, at a distance of ten paces.
Twelve of the guns were loaded and twelve held blanks, the
firing squad not knowing which were which.

The sentence was read. The two Tigers knelt down each
in front of a stake and their hands were tied behind their
backs and then to the stakes. A blindfold was then placed
over their eyes. One of the men made a slight resistance, but
when one of the priests spoke to him he became quiet.

"The silence was oppressive," recalled an eye witness.
"Not a breath was heard in the vast concourse."

Captain Alex White of the Tigers gave the command:
"Ready! Aim! Fire!" As if from one gun, the volley sounded
in the crisp air. The condemned "sprang forward and fell
over, the one on his face, the other on his side."

Wheat was excused from the execution by General
Taylor. When the shots which ended the lives of the two
young Tigers rang out he waited in his tent, sobbing like a
broken-hearted woman. He loved his rough and tough men
and they loved him, and his helplessness in their behalf
crushed him.

Scarcely had the men slumped to the ground than from
the crowd there rushed a Tiger, who ran to one of the men

and held the lifeless body in his arms. It was Dennis Cochrane's brother Daniel. "It was heart-rending to see the poor brother's agony," reported the Richmond *Dispatch*. "The death of the criminal was borne with stolidity, but the simple sight of such heartfelt, brotherly grief moistened every eye."

Among the heavy-hearted who trudged back to camp afterwards was Sergeant Z. Lee Gilmer of the Eighteenth Virginia Volunteers. When he got to his tent he took up his diary and inscribed the following:

> Today I witnessed the most effecting [sic] sight and heart rendering [sic] affair that has transpired during the campaign. It was the public execution of Denis Cochrane and Mik O'brian (2 of the New Orleans Tigers). . . . They met their fate without a sigh, without a murmur. They neither feared God, man nor the Devil. . . . These two men I think are the first that have been shot and I hope the last. My idea of this decision is that the men are now going into winter quarters and to prevent them slipping off home, for they thought they would have to make an example of some one and they concluded this the best time and it fell to these poor Tigers to share such an unfortunate lot. Yet perhaps they deserved it for they are the lowest scrapings of the Mississippi and New Orleans and fear not even death itself. Court Martials are always formed entirely of officers. Never have a single Private.[20]

The execution was, indeed, the first in the Army of Northern Virginia and it, contended Dick Taylor, with " punishment, so closely following offense, produced a marked effect."

Tom Lane, the Alabamian who had been beaten up and stomped upon by the Tigers, was the victim of a grisly practical joke shortly after the execution.

When Lane was on guard duty at night, one of his

outfit got a Tiger uniform and crawled to the part of the sentry
line Lane occupied.

As Lane walked along the practical joker moaned " a
resurrected Tiger." Peering through the darkness, the sentry
thought he spied the form of a man with striped pants, the
Zouave trade-mark of the Tiger Rifles. As he hesitated, the
jokester groaned again, " a resurrected Tiger," using an Irish
brogue.

This time Lane understood. Without a moment's hesi-
tation he left his post on the run and dashed for his tent.
Yelling for the corporal of the guard, Lane explained that
he had seen " one of them Tigers that had been resurrected."

By this time the practical joker had everyone in his
quarters in on the joke. " It was so funny that the officers
took no steps towards punishing Tom for leaving his post,"
recalled W. A. McClendon. " Always after that when the
boys would see anything streaked and stripped [sic] they
would holler out, ' Tom Lane, here's your Tiger.' " 21

Almost six months had now passed since Manassas and,
despite the general opinion of Rob Wheat's friends that he
would be promoted, he was still a major.

That Wheat was piqued because the much-discussed
promotion hadn't come through is very evident from his letter
dated January 20, 1862, to General Samuel Cooper, Adjutant
and Inspector General:

Sir:

> Having received communications from your office and
> elsewhere, from time to time, addressed to me as " Maj,"
> " Lt Col," and " Col," and being desirous of knowing
> *what* my *Rank* really is, have the goodness to enlighten
> me accordingly and oblige,
>
>   Very Respt yrs obt svt
>   C. R. Wheat
>   Commanding 1st Specl Batt
>   La Vol.22

Wheat, of course, had no doubt but that he was still a major, but he could not overlook the opportunity which erroneously addressed letters from headquarters offered to remind Richmond that he had not been promoted.

CHAPTER XVI

IN THE VALLEY WITH STONEWALL

Spring came to Virginia in 1862 with all possible weather abominations. The winter, which had been bitter, returned with renewed energy for a last fling. The encamped Confederates found themselves at war with snow, ice, rain, and mud, if not with the Yankees. The latter, meanwhile, had not wasted time during the dreary winter months. After the shock of Manassas had been absorbed by the North, Lincoln had retired General Scott, and McDowell had been replaced by George B. McClellan, whose success in West Virginia had made him the Union's new and much-needed hero.

It was evident to Major Wheat and the other Confederate officers, as they made the rounds from one hospitable headquarters to another, that with the coming of spring the war would be resumed in earnest. Would General Joe Johnston take the offensive? Was an attack on Washington contemplated? The invasion of Maryland and Pennsylvania? Or would the Confederates wait on the line of Bull Run for McClellan to move on Richmond? February had not run its course before the Confederate army found out, and McClellan probably got the information shortly thereafter.

On February 20 General Johnston was in Richmond, summoned by President Davis to confer "on a subject in which secrecy was so important that he could not venture . . . to commit it to paper, and the mail." Johnston joined Davis

at a cabinet meeting and was told that the subject under
discussion was the advisability of " withdrawing the army to
a less exposed position." Johnston argued that the condition
of the roads made retirement impossible at that time but
that when winter was over, " the withdrawal of the army
from Centreville would be necessary before McClellan's invasion." The meeting ended with no orders to Johnston but
with his understanding that the army would fall back as soon
as the movement was practicable.

Despite the strict secrecy with which President Davis
had clothed the conference, Johnston was startled to meet
on his way to his hotel an officer, newly arrived in Richmond,
who asked him if he had any news on the proposed withdrawal
of the army from its present position.

" On my way back to Centreville next day," wrote
Johnston, " I met an acquaintance . . . too deaf to hear conversation not intended for his ear, who gave me the same information that he had heard, he said, the evening before.

" This extraordinary proof of the indiscretion of the
members of the cabinet, or some one of them, might have
taught the danger of intrusting to that body any design the
success of which depended upon secrecy." [1]

There can be little doubt that the " secret " of the
proposed Confederate pull-back from Centreville and the line
of Bull Run leaked all the way to Washington. But the
Virginia roads were in miserable condition for horses pulling
heavy field pieces with loaded caissons and ammunition wagons
as well as for the foot soldiers, and they presented no better
avenues of attack for McClellan than routes of retreat for
Joe Johnston.

The winter which Rob Wheat had feared he could not
stand did not prove too taxing on him. In December he was
" not so well," but early in February Rob was " in high
health." [2] When the order came on March 8 to fall back to
the Rappahannock, Major Wheat was his old self again and
eager for action.

Johnston's plan was to concentrate his army near Orange Court House. This would put him in easy reach of both Fredericksburg and Richmond, either of which he could move to rapidly if McClellan appeared suddenly in force at the other place.

Dick Taylor relates that " the movement was executed with the quiet precision characteristic of Johnston, unrivaled as a master of logistics." General Taylor himself contributed greatly to this " quiet precision " by the manner in which he led his brigade on the march. Moreover, Taylor's conduct on the retreat from Bull Run to the Rappahannock not only endeared him to his troops but established the superb morale for which the Louisiana Brigade was soon to be famous.

The road was a wretched one, rough and mud-rutted. Frequently the route, which led east of the railroad from Manassas to Orange, was crossed by swollen streams which added to the difficulties of the march. Here, indeed, was a severe test of the marching capacity of the Confederate army.

Dick Taylor devoted himself to correcting straggling, " the vice of the Southern armies," and as he worked patiently with his Louisianians, Major Wheat observed his brigade commander's leadership, courage and military skill. Taylor called frequent halts to let the stragglers close up. Often he rode to the rear of the column and gave a weary soldier a lift on his horse, a practice Rob and the other brigade officers soon imitated. He instructed them on the care of their feet, the fitting of shoes, the healing of abrasions. It wasn't long before it became a disgrace in the Louisiana brigade for a man to fall out of ranks.[3]

Major Wheat worked as hard with his battalion as did the general with the brigade. When Taylor and his Louisianians crossed the mountains in Ewell's Division to join Stonewall Jackson in the Shenandoah Valley, the Louisiana Tigers were among the most mobile of Old Jack's " foot cavalry."

With Johnston dropping back from Bull Run, it was

necessary for Stonewall Jackson, who was in the Valley with less than four thousand men, to fall back from Winchester in order to maintain lines of communication with the main army. Already "Old Jack" was up to his tricks of occupying the attention of Union forces two or three times the size of his own and preventing reinforcements from going to McClellan.

Major General Dick Ewell, whose command consisted of the brigades of Taylor, Brigadier Generals Isaac R. Trimble and Arnold Elzey, took charge of the entire division for the first time at the Rappahannock, where the command went into camp on the south shore.

Although the bulk of Johnston's army had passed the Rapidan, Ewell was left to guard the Rappahannock. Finally, orders came to drop back to Gordonsville, but instead of finding Johnston there, Ewell found orders to reinforce Jackson in the Valley. Johnston had already marched to the Peninsula to oppose McClellan's advance up the tongue of land between the James and York rivers.

It was about this time that Rob heard of the death of his brother John Thomas, who fell at Shiloh on April 6. He had great affection for "J. T." and in the days when he believed that the law was his calling, he had entertained ideas of a partnership with him. But in the activity of the movement from the Rappahannock to the banks of the Shenandoah, Wheat had little time to brood over his brother's death, and the same was true when the Tigers marched and fought up and down the Valley with Stonewall Jackson.

Ewell's division passed through Swift Run Gap on April 30 and went into camp at Conrad's Store on the south fork of the Shenandoah River. While on picket duty early in May, Wheat's Tigers ambushed a large Union force—the obviously exaggerated newspaper account says it was three regiments. Holding their fire until the right moment, the Tigers sent "a well directed volley . . . into the enemy's ranks which threw them into confusion." [4]

Orders came on May 18 to Taylor to join Jackson at New Market. He struck out at dawn the next day on a road which crossed the foothills of Massanutten Mountain, reaching the Valley Turnpike by way of the little German village of Keazletown. ". . . Lovely weather, a fairish road and men in high health and spirits," got the Louisiana Brigade off to an auspicious start in the Valley of Virginia.

Taylor sent ahead a mounted officer to inform Jackson of his approach and to pick a camp for the Louisianians. Taylor's description of the arrival of the brigade at Jackson's camp is an admirable one:

"Over three thousand strong, neat in fresh clothing of gray with white gaiters, bands playing at the head of their regiments, not a straggler, but every man in his place, stepping jauntily as on parade, though it had marched twenty miles and more, in open column with arms at 'right shoulder shift,' and rays of the declining sun flaming on polished bayonets, the brigade moved down the broad, smooth pike, and wheeled on to its camping ground. Jackson's men, by thousands, had gathered on either side of the road to see us pass. Indeed, it was a martial sight, and no man with a spark of sacred fire in his heart but would have striven hard to prove worthy of such a command."

After seeing to camp details General Taylor sought out Stonewall Jackson, whom he had never met. A figure sitting on the top rail of a fence, sucking a lemon, was pointed out to him. Taylor, as he approached, discerned "a pair of cavalry boots covering feet of gigantic size, a mangy cap with visor drawn low, a heavy dark beard, and weary eyes."

Taylor saluted, giving his name and rank. Jackson sucked on the lemon contemplatively and then asked in a low gentle voice the road and distance marched by the Louisiana Brigade.

"Keazletown road, six and twenty miles," replied Taylor.

"You seem to have no stragglers," commented Jackson.

"Never allow straggling," was Taylor's response.

"You must teach my people; they straggle badly."

Taylor bowed, and as he did so, the regimental band of
Colonel Henry Kelly's Eighth Louisiana struck up a waltz
and the men, Cajuns from the Bayou Teche country, began
to dance.

"Thoughtless fellows for serious work," said the lemon-
sucker. He was soon to change his mind about the gay
Louisianians.

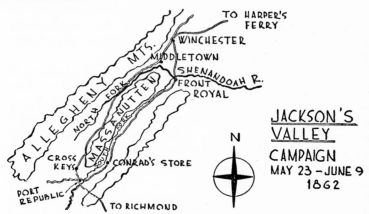

From the very beginning of their service under Jackson,
Rob Wheat and his Tigers idolized "Old Jack." Kyd Douglas,
Stonewall's young aide, made it very clear that they regarded
Jackson with a superstitious reverence. "No two men could
be more unlike than 'Old Jack' and Bob Wheat," said
Douglas, "but the latter's affection for his General was akin
to devotion. I never passed his command that he did not
stop me and ask how 'The Old General' was, sometimes half
a dozen times a day, and generally adding, 'God Bless him!'" [5]

Indeed, at first glance, one would be hard put to find
two more contrary personalities than Stonewall Jackson and
Rob Wheat. One was taciturn and ascetic; the other jovial
and convivial. One possessed none of the social graces; the
other had them all. One kept to his own counsels; the other
shared his confidences with a host of friends.

But beyond these seemingly irreconcilable differences
in taste and temperament there were several substantial bases
upon which mutual respect could be built. Both Jackson
and Wheat loved a good fight and neither ever asked his
troops to undertake a hazardous mission without himself being
in the forefront.

And there was something else, too. Wheat, in whom the
spirit of religion was stirring again, could not fail to be impressed by Jackson's religious fervor. Jackson's silent prayers,
as he sat for hours before the camp fire, had in a lesser degree
their parallel in Major Wheat's daily reading from a little
prayer book, *Day and Night Watches*, which his mother had
given him. His daily prayer ration, Rob called it.

Jackson, on his part, didn't have long to wait to learn
what manner of fighters Wheat's Tigers and the other Louisianians were. Dawn of May 21 was breaking when the army
started its northward march up the Valley, with Taylor's fast-
stepping Louisiana Brigade at the head of the column. Turning to the east, Jackson crossed over Massanutten Gap to
Luray, where the army camped for the night.

On the morning of May 22 Jackson, riding with Taylor's
Louisiana Brigade, led the way northward toward Front Royal,
the object of his march, over a road which passed between the
south fork of the Shenandoah and the western base of the
Blue Ridge. That night the army camped with the leading
elements only ten miles from Front Royal.

Jackson planned the next day's battle carefully. He knew
that he could take Front Royal with no trouble, for with high
ground looking down upon the town from every side it was
indefensible. But what Jackson sought was to surprise Front
Royal and capture it so rapidly that the small garrison could
not escape, or sound a warning or receive support.

Jackson's plan was simple. His cavalry would cross the
Shenandoah, cut the telegraph to Strasburg and seize the
Manassas Gap Railroad between Front Royal and Strasburg.
This would sever the lines of escape for the Federals, who

must either surrender or retreat to Winchester. His infantry, meanwhile, would be diverted from the main road to one to the east and it would approach the town from the south.⁶

His plans made, Jackson gave the order to march. The First Maryland Regiment was in the lead, followed by Taylor's Brigade, with Bob Wheat's Tigers in its van. Shortly past noon, as they approached a wood which extended from the river to the mountains, Jackson was called to the rear. A moment later a breathless young woman came running out of the woods. It was Belle Boyd, the Confederate spy. She told Taylor that Jackson's troops were close to Front Royal, that the town was full of Yankees, but that they had no idea of the nearness of Jackson, believing him to be west of Massanutten.

Taylor, impressed with Belle Boyd's information, ordered his brigade forward at the double. Hardly had they stepped up the march than Jackson galloped up and ordered Taylor to deploy his leading regiment as skirmishers on both sides of the road.

Wheat's Tigers and the First Maryland were sent wide to the right over a rough trail across the hills. The rugged path led them into a road which descended into the village from the mountains to the east.

Jackson achieved complete surprise. The first news the Federals had of his approach was the volley Wheat's Battalion and the Marylanders fired into the Yankee pickets about a mile from Front Royal, shattering the quiet of an oppressively hot afternoon.

"Very soon," recorded Kyd Douglas, "the First Maryland Infantry and Major Roberdeau Wheat's Louisiana battalion were rushing down the hill into the town. . . . It took very little time to get into Front Royal and clean it out."

Most of the Union garrison ran at the first alarm, but a few rallied and formed into line. Some climbed into the dome of the Court House, some into the upper windows of the hospital and made some show of resistance.

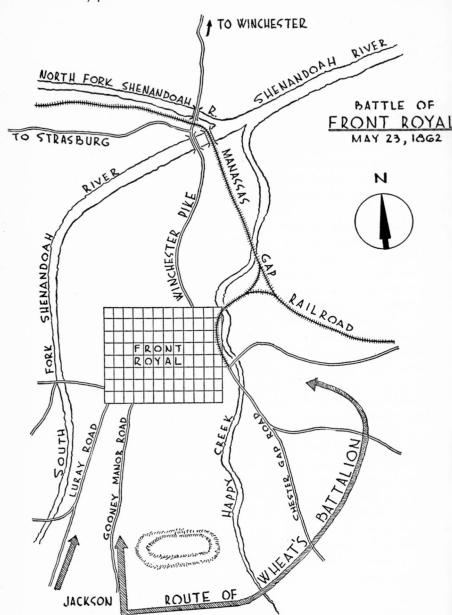

TO WINCHESTER

NORTH FORK SHENANDOAH R.

SHENANDOAH RIVER

BATTLE OF
FRONT ROYAL
MAY 23, 1862

N

TO STRASBURG

RIVER

MANASSAS

GAP

RAILROAD

WINCHESTER PIKE

FRONT
ROYAL

SHENANDOAH

SOUTH FORK

LURAY ROAD

GOONEY MANOR ROAD

HAPPY CREEK

CHESTER GAP ROAD

WHEAT'S BATTALION

JACKSON

ROUTE OF

The Sixth Louisiana had followed Wheat's Battalion and the Maryland regiment into Front Royal from the east and now came the other three of Taylor's regiments, the Seventh, Eighth and Ninth Louisiana, through the fields and woods to the south and west of the town.

This was too much for the Yankees, for, says an eye-witness, "firing one volley they wheeled about—every man for himself they scampered out of town like a flock of sheep. . . ." Reaching the hill north of the town—opposite the direction from which Jackson's men were pouring into Front Royal—they halted and formed a line in support of a Union battery that had been posted there.

Colonel J. R. Kenly, a comrade of Wheat in Mexico, put up a valiant defense until almost dusk, but, outnumbered and outflanked, he was forced to abandon his position and retreat in the direction of Winchester. His men, the Yankee First Maryland Regiment, tried to fire the bridge but Taylor's Louisianians rushed over in time to save it and the pursuing Confederates poured across.

Colonel Thomas G. Flournoy's Sixth Virginia Cavalry, in a vicious charge at Cedarville, rounded up the Yankees after Kenly had fallen severely wounded. Of a force of 1,063 men, 904 were killed, wounded or missing. Huge masses of guns and supplies fell into Jackson's possession. Jackson's casualties totalled less than 50; the Tigers lost one man, with six others wounded.

Major Wheat was flushed with pride over the way his Tigers had behaved at Front Royal, but the joy that victory brought was dampened by word that his young cousin, Captain George Baxter, had fallen in Flournoy's victorious charge. Wheat rode at once to the scene, but the youngster was dead by the time Rob reached his side. His cousin's death following so soon on the news of John Thomas' fall at Shiloh made a profound impression on Wheat.

General Dick Taylor was quick to praise Wheat's Battalion and the rest of the Louisiana Brigade for the day's work. "Major Wheat performed his part in gallant style," reported Taylor, "charging through the town and drawing up his command on the banks of the Shenandoah in a position sheltered from the enemy's shells." Although Jackson, who visited Taylor's campfire after the battle to tell him he would move with him in the morning, said nothing, Taylor interpreted Stonewall's silence as "approval of the conduct of the brigade," and he wrote: "I fancied he looked at me kindly."

Sometime before marching the next day, a group of Tigers "played a most amusing prank on the Yankees." In their hasty flight of the previous day the Federals had left behind, in addition to arms and commissary supplies, a large number of uniforms.

"The Tigers doffed their uniforms and donned the Yankee blue," a Front Royal girl confided to her diary. "Then they got on the cars and steamed off to Markham where the news of the fall of Front Royal had not arrived and the Federal troops of course took them to be some of their own men and coming out of quarters at the invitation of the Tigers a number of them concluded to 'take a ride up the road a little way.' The hospitable Rebels not only extended the ride to Front Royal but also gave them lodging and board there. . . ." 7

With Jackson leading the way the Louisiana Brigade, together with a section of the Rockbridge artillery and a small body of cavalry, struck out in the morning for the Valley Turnpike. Major Wheat's Tigers were assigned to accompany the guns and these sturdy marchers trotted along with the horse and artillery at Jackson's heels. After several hours of marching Wheat's men were some distance in advance of the rest of the Louisiana Brigade.

On the march Jackson received word from scouts that General Banks was leaving his prepared positions at Strasburg, and he felt certain that the Union general was retiring northward to Winchester. When Jackson met the Valley Turnpike at the village of Middletown, he saw the Union cavalry on

Camp Carondolet
January 20th 1862

Genl. Saml. Cooper
  Adjt & Inspector Genl.
    Confederate States Army.
      Richmond
        Va.

          Sir.
            Having
received communications from your
Office and elsewhere, from time
to time, addressed to me as
"Maj." "Lt Col", and "Col", and being
desirous of knowing what my
Rank really is, have the goodness to enlighten me accordingly,
and oblige

                Very Respt yr obt Srvt
                  C. R. Wheat
                Commdg 1st Spec.l Batt
                    La Vol.

"WHAT AM I?"
(Courtesy National Archives)

CHATHAM ROBERDEAU WHEAT
SON OF REV. J. T. AND SELENA PATTEN WHEAT
BORN ALEXANDRIA, VA. APRIL 9TH 1826
SOLDIER OF FREEDOM
COLONEL IN U. S. ARMY IN MEXICO
UNDER GENERAL SCOTT, 1847
COMMISSIONED COLONEL BY JUNTA
IN CUBAN WAR WITH SPAIN
CHAMPION OF ITALIAN LIBERTY,
AND GENERAL UNDER GARIBALDI
MEMBER OF BAR AND LEGISLATURE OF LOUISIANA, 1848
MAJOR CONFEDERATE STATES ARMY
ORGANIZED AND COMMANDED BATTALION
"LOUISIANA TIGERS"
DISTINGUISHED AND WOUNDED IN BATTLE
1ST MANASSAS JULY 21, 1861
KILLED AT THE HEAD OF HIS TROOPS,
BATTLE GAINES' MILL JUNE 27, 1862
UNUSUAL FOR PERSONALITY, WIT, ELOQUENCE AND GENIUS
ERECTED 1933 BY AN ADMIRER OF VALOR

WHEAT'S TOMBSTONE,
HOLLYWOOD CEMETERY, RICHMOND, VA.
(*Courtesy James Holland and Columbia Studios*)

From 1863 until 1933, Roberdeau Wheat slept in an unmarked grave in Richmond's Hollywood Cemetery. "An admirer of valor" raised this handsome stone in his memory in 1933. The inscription has two errors: Wheat was not a colonel during the Mexican War and he was in the Louisiana legislature in 1853, not 1848.

the road. Jackson ordered the artillery to gallop forward,
unlimber at short range and fire into the horsemen. "This
was done with perfect success, and the detachment scattered,"
wrote Jackson's preacher-adjutant, Dr. Dabney, "which was
a novel instance of a charge effected by field artillery."

From the village, Jackson saw moving toward him in a
cloud of dust on the Valley Turnpike, a large column of
Yankees. "Two of our guns were posted about one hundred
and fifty yards from the road, and the Tigers strung along
behind a stone fence on the roadside," remembered one of
Stonewall's old cannoneers. "Everything was in readiness
when the enemy came in sight. They wavered for a time,
some trying to pass around, but, being pushed from behind
there was no alternative. Most of them tried to run the
gauntlet; few, however, got through."

Jackson rode up to witness an amazing scene. "The
road," he said later, "was literally obstructed with the mingled
and confused mass of struggling and dying horses and riders."
A Union officer in the engagement noted "the bodies of
men and horses so piled up that it was impossible to proceed." [8]

This was the signal for the Tigers. They swarmed over
the stone fence upon the startled enemy, capturing numerous
prisoners and many supply wagons.

Meanwhile, at the first volley Dick Taylor had put the
Louisiana Brigade into the double and they arrived in time
to round up more Yankees trying to escape the village. As
for the Tigers, they were now busy in a phase of warfare in
which they were skilled specialists. "The gentle Tigers were
looting right merrily, diving in and out of wagons with the
activity of rabbits in a warren," said Taylor. "But this occu-
pation was abandoned on my approach, and in a moment
they were in line, looking as solemn and virtuous as deacons
at a funeral." [9]

As soon as he could reorganize the brigade Taylor turned
south for a brief engagement with some Federal artillery
which showed itself on high ground about the Valley Turn-

pike. After an exchange of shots, the Yankees fled westward. Taylor then marched northward to rejoin Jackson, with the Tigers overtaking their leader and his small mounted force at dusk.

BATTLE OF WINCHESTER
MAY 25, 1862

They marched until past midnight when Taylor, noting other Confederate units moving on the Valley Turnpike from Front Royal, drew his men off the road for a much-needed rest. The Louisianians all but dropped in their tracks. As usual, Jackson didn't let the sun get much ahead of

him the next morning. With the first light of day on May 25,
Stonewall began to march. His tired and hungry "foot
cavalry" roused themselves from an all-too-brief sleep as the
word passed rapidly down the line that "Old Jack" was
moving again. When Taylor's Brigade marched to within
two miles of Winchester, Jackson had already launched his
attack on the town, with Ewell coming up the Front Royal
road, pressing the Federal left. Against the Federal center,
to the left of the Valley Turnpike, Jackson had sent his
Stonewall Brigade. The Yankees held a strong position on
high ground overlooking Jackson's approach and deadly rounds
from Yankee guns were blasting Stonewall's batteries. To
make matters worse, Federal infantry had taken shelter behind
a stone wall from which it delivered intense musket fire into
the Confederate ranks.

It was at this stage of the battle that Jackson sent for
Taylor. Pointing to the ridge, Jackson wasted no words:
"You must take it." Kyd Douglas recorded a slightly more
"elaborate" conversation: Jackson: "General, can your
Brigade charge a battery?" Taylor: "It can try." Jackson:
"Very good. It must do it then. Move it forward."

While his command was moving up, Taylor wheeled his
horse to the left to study the terrain. He saw before him
Abraham's Creek, which flowed at the base of the ridge his
men would have to assault. He noticed that "the ascent . . .
was steep, though nowhere abrupt." He noted, too, at one
point "a broad, shallow, trough-like depression."

Taylor ordered Rob Wheat's Tigers to the extreme left
and the regiments of the Louisiana Brigade formed on Wheat's
right in a long line to the south. As they marched through
the depression, the Federal fire became hot. Some men fell,
and many began to duck their heads.

"What the hell are you dodging for," shouted Taylor.
"If there is any more of it, you will be halted under fire
for an hour."

Jackson, riding at Taylor's side, looked at him reproachfully. Placing his hand on Taylor's shoulder "Old Jack" said softly: "I am afraid you are a wicked fellow." And then Stonewall rode back to the Valley Turnpike to direct the battle.

When Taylor moved up the ridge at 7:30 A. M., it was a sight that thrilled the men of Jackson's Valley army.

"The enemy poured grape and musketry into Taylor's line as soon as it came into sight," recalled one of Stonewall's troopers. "Gen. Taylor rode in front of his brigade, drawn sword in hand, occasionally turning his horse, at other times merely turning in his saddle to see that his line was up. They marched up the hill in perfect order, not firing a shot! About half way . . . he gave in a loud and commanding voice . . . the order to charge!"

Taylor later recalled that while he was leading the brigade up the ridge, his attention became fixed on a bluebird which flew across the Louisiana line with a worm in its mouth. His own account of the advance is a brilliant one: "Progress was not stayed. . . . Closing the many gaps made by the fierce fire, steadied the rather by it, and preserving an alignment that would have been creditable on parade, the brigade, with cadence step and eyes on the foe, swept grandly over copse and ledge and fence, to crown the heights from which the enemy had melted away."

Taylor's men set up a shout, and Jackson, to the surprise of all, waved his cap in the air and let out a wild yell or two himself. Pausing to shout a command—"Order forward the whole line, the battle's won"—Jackson exclaimed, "Very good! Now let's holler."

Taylor encountered Jackson on the edge of town. Stonewall paused but a moment to grasp Taylor's hand which the latter said was "worth a thousand words from another."

In his report General Taylor had special word for Rob Wheat and the Tigers: "Major Wheat, with a part of his battalion, detached on the left, rendered valuable service in assisting to repel the attempt of the enemy's cavalry to charge our line." [10]

It may be assumed that having performed that task, Rob and his Tigers were yelling as loud as any one when Taylor's men swarmed over the crest of the hill and set out after the retreating Yankees. But serious pursuit was impossible for Jackson's tired infantry, and Stonewall looked in vain for his cavalry. "Never was there such a chance for cavalry!" he cried. "Oh, that my cavalry were in place." But "Maryland" Steuart, in command of the cavalry, wouldn't move until his orders came from Ewell, his immediate commander. By the time he got the orders through channels it was too late. Banks had crossed the Potomac.

The rout of Banks threw Washington into a panic. Wild stories that Stonewall Jackson and 40,000 men were about to invade Maryland were believed. Even Secretary of War Stanton concluded that "the enemy in great force are marching on Washington."

As Jackson collected the captured arms, ammunition and supplies left behind by Banks in his hurried departure, he received word that Frémont on one side of the Valley and McDowell coming up from Fredericksburg, threatened his escape route.

With 16,000 men, more or less, Jackson was now opposed in the Valley by a combined force of 62,000. Shields with 10,000 men was on his left and Frémont with 15,000 troops was on his right. These were his immediate opponents.

On Friday, May 30, "Jackson was in front of Harper's Ferry, which place is fifty miles from Strasburg; Fremont was at Moorefield, thirty-eight miles from Strasburg, with his advance ten miles on the way to the latter place; Shields was not more than twenty miles from Strasburg, for his advance entered Front Royal, which is but twelve miles distant, before mid-day on Friday; while McDowell was following with two divisions within supporting distance. Yet by Sunday night Jackson had marched a distance of between fifty and sixty miles, though encumbered with prisoners and captured stores, had reached Strasburg before either of his adversaries, and had passed safely between their armies, while he held Fremont at bay with a show of force, and blinded and bewildered McDowell by the rapidity of his movements."

Thus wrote Lieutenant Colonel William Allan of Jackson's remarkable evasion of the Federal trap set to bag him. Jackson's distinguished British biographer, Colonel Henderson, points out that within fourteen days, "the Army of the Valley had marched one hundred and seventy miles, had routed a force of 12,500 men, had threatened the North with invasion, had drawn off McDowell from Fredericksburg, had seized the hospitals and supply depots at Front Royal, Winchester and Martinsburg, and finally, although surrounded on three sides by 60,000 men had brought off a huge convoy without losing a single wagon." [11]

Colonel Henderson noted the important part Taylor's Louisiana Brigade played in Jackson's Valley campaign. And Major David F. Boyd, of the Ninth Louisiana, is authority for the statement that "all through that terrible work of less than 30 days, with its long, fatiguing marches and seven battles . . . Wheat was a leading figure in Taylor's Louisiana Brigade."

But the fighting wasn't over for Rob Wheat and the Tigers; there was still work to be done by the Louisiana Brigade before Jackson could slip off to join Lee on the Chickahominy.

On June 6 Jackson's main force was at Port Republic, where he controlled the only bridge still intact over the south fork of the Shenandoah. Thus he lay between Frémont and Shields, in possession of their only means of junction. As usual his plan was simple. He would meet Frémont north of the river first and dispose of him. Then he would turn to engage Shields south of the river. After routing both Union armies he would take off for the Chickahominy and his rendezvous with Lee.

That day, at Harrisonburg, there was both amusement and sorrow when the dashing Turner Ashby ambushed Sir Percy Wyndham, a British soldier of fortune and colonel of the First New Jersey Cavalry. Wyndham was captured and while he was trudging off to the rear under guard, Ashby was killed in a second brush with the enemy.

As Wyndham passed troops along the way, he appeared "much chopfallen, and looking unutterable things in the way of impotent rage, disappointed hopes, and wounded pride," which the laughter of the soldiers did not help to dispel.

One veteran of the Valley campaign later recalled that Sir Percy was "the maddest prisoner I saw during the war" and he was so enraged "that he would have stopped right there in the road and engaged in fisticuff if he could have found a partner."

Sir Percy seemed to have cooled out a bit when he came into General Dick Taylor's view. "A stalwart man, with huge mustaches, cavalry boots adorned with spurs worthy of a caballero, slouched hat, and plume, he strode along with the nonchalant air of one who had wooed Dame Fortune too long to be cast down by her frowns," said Taylor.

Suddenly, Major Wheat who was nearby (Taylor says he was on his horse, Kyd Douglas says he was sitting on a fence) exclaimed: "Percy! Old boy!" As Wheat rushed up to Wyndham, the Britisher recognized him: "Why, Bob!" They exchanged a warm embrace for they were old companions in arms with Garibaldi in Italy.

Kyd Douglas accompanied Wyndham to Jackson's headquarters and he reported Sir Percy in "a most resentful mood" over the way his troops had deserted him in a cowardly way. "He was not an attractive-looking warrior and looked like what he was, a soldier of fortune," said Douglas. Comparing him to Bob Wheat, he added: "Wyndham was still the adventurer, caring little on what side he fought; but Wheat was fighting for a cause in which his whole soul was enlisted." [12]

Two days later, on June 8, Jackson fought Frémont at Cross Keys, with Ewell's division. Taylor's Louisiana Brigade, which was designated the reserve, was not employed during the engagement. Frémont, with characteristic alacrity, withdrew with substantial losses in men and materiel.

The Tigers, after the battle, marched past their old friends, the Twenty-first Georgia Regiment " in quick time . . . in perfect line " and halted. " The captains ordered their men not to wander far, as they would resume the march in a short time," said Captain Jim Nisbet of the Georgians. " Many of these men seized the opportunity to loot. My men had not yet got hardened enough to rob the dead, so they were looking on." [13]

The Louisiana Brigade lingered but briefly, for it had some important business at Port Republic, the little town at the very point of the peninsula where the junction of the North River and South River forms the south fork of the Shenandoah.

There was a bridge across North River into the town, and two fords across South River provided passage when the stream wasn't swollen. Jackson ordered a wagon bridge built, by laying planks on the under structure of wagons, but this proved so rickety that the men could cross South River only in single file.

On the night of June 8 Taylor's Brigade camped near the river. Early the next morning, a bright Sunday, the Louisianians crossed, man after man, with Colonel Henry B. Kelly's Eighth Louisiana leading the way and Wheat's Battalion in third place behind Colonel Leroy Stafford's Ninth Louisiana. The Sixth and Seventh Louisiana followed in that order. The crossing, of necessity, was slow. Accordingly, when firing broke out down the road the delay prevented the troops from reaching the field rapidly, and forced them to be committed to action piecemeal, battalion by battalion.

With the first clatter of small arms, soon to be followed by the booming of the guns, Taylor galloped about a mile forward to see what was happening.

"From the mountain, clothed to its base with under-growth and timber, a level—clear, open and smooth—extended to the river," he said. "This plain was some thousand yards in width. Half a mile north, a gorge, through which flowed a small stream, cut the mountain at a right angle. The north-ern shoulder of this gorge projected farther into the plain than the southern, and on an elevated plateau of the shoulder were placed six guns, sweeping every inch of the plain to the south."

While Taylor watched the powerfully supported Federal line pressing hard on Winder's outnumbered brigade on the plain, Stonewall Jackson came up and said: "Delightful excitement." Taylor said that he told Jackson that "it was pleasant to learn he was enjoying himself, but thought he might have an indigestion of such fun if the six-gun battery was not silenced."

That was all "Old Jack" needed to assign the job of silencing the guns to Taylor. Jackson provided a staff officer, familiar with the terrain, to show Taylor the way.

Meanwhile, Colonel Kelly's Eighth regiment, the most advanced of the Louisiana Brigade, was joined by the Ninth, which formed on Kelly's left. Then Bob Wheat rode up at the head of the Tigers, bringing orders to Kelly from Jackson "to advance and show yourself to the enemy."

With Kelly leading, the two regiments and Wheat's Battalion started up the face of the thickly forested hills. All this while, from the ledge, an abandoned charcoal kiln, the Federal battery was pouring a blistering barrage at the Con-federates. "The fire of that battery was terrible for a while," recalled a Rebel artilleryman. "The thunder of the artillery shook the ground. . . . The shell from the battery on the coaling was ripping the ground open all around us, and the air was full of screaming fragments of exploding shells."

Then, from his point of vantage, this artilleryman saw and heard what Jackson had been waiting for: "After we had been under this dreadful fire about thirty minutes, I

heard a mightly shout on the mountain side in close proximity
to the coaling, and in a few minutes after I saw General
Dick Taylor's Louisianians debouching from the undergrowth,

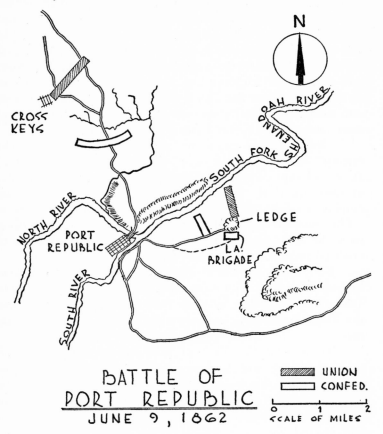

BATTLE OF
PORT REPUBLIC
JUNE 9, 1862

and like a wave crested with shining steel rush toward the
fatal coaling and deadly battery with fixed bayonets, giving
the Rebel yell like mad demons."

Taylor, coming up with the Sixth Louisiana Regiment,
took command of the brigade and ordered the attack on the

battery. Colonel Kelly of the Eighth Louisiana has given a lively picture of the action:

"At the word of command . . . the line moved forward, soon coming into plain view of the batteries and of the infantry of enemy beyond the ravine, which at once opened fire on the advancing brigade. With one volley in reply, and a Confederate yell heard far over the field, the Louisianians rushed down the rough declivity and across the ravine, and carried the batteries like a flash. . . . By the impetus of the charge over the rough ground all formation was lost, and officers and men were all thrown in one unorganized mass around the captured guns."

"Surprise had aided us," said Dick Taylor, "but the enemy's infantry rallied in a moment and drove us out." A second time the guns changed hands in furious fighting at close quarters with fists and stones and knives being employed when other weapons couldn't be brought to bear. "The hand-to-hand conflict raged frightfully, resembling more the onslaught of maddened savages than the fighting of civilized men."

Bob Wheat and his Tigers were in their element. Wheat had his horse shot from under him in the charge and Jackson, "observing this, sent his own horse to take its place," but the Major kept busy afoot among the tangled mass of fighting men.

To prevent the Yankees from taking off the guns if they dislodged the Louisianians a second time, Wheat whipped out a knife and began slashing the throats of the artillery horses. "It was a sickening sight," recalled a veteran of the battle, "men in gray and blue piled up in front of and around the guns and with the horses dying and the blood of men and beasts flowing almost in a stream. Major Wheat was as bloody as a butcher. . . ."

The Federals forced the Confederates off the coaling a second time and succeeded in drawing off one of the guns by hand. But Taylor's men, with even the drummer-boys

getting into the thick of the fight, came surging back with
General Dick Ewell on their heels.

This time, the Federals broke. They had fought bravely,
and in retirement there was no rout, even when Taylor's
men turned the Yankees' own guns on them. They were,
said Dick Taylor, "formidable to the last."

Jackson rode up, "with intense light in his eyes," and
clasped Taylor's hand. The captured guns he turned over
to the Louisiana Brigade, the men cheering madly especially
the Irishmen. One of these, a giant of a fellow with one
eye closed and his whiskers seared with powder burns,
straddled a gun and called to Taylor: "We told you to bet
on your boys."

General Ewell's report gave credit to Taylor's Louisianians for the victory. He said: "Colonel Seymour, of the
Sixth Louisiana, and Major Wheat, of the battalion, on the
left; Colonel Stafford, of the Ninth, in the center, and Colonel
Kelly, of the Eighth, on the right, all acted with the most
determined gallantry and were as gallantly supported by their
officers and men."

The battle of Port Republic ended Jackson's whirlwind
Valley campaign of 1862. General Taylor pridefully recalled
the part his men played in the campaign: "The Louisiana
Brigade marched from its camp near Conrad's store, to join
Jackson at New Market, on the 21st of May. In twenty days
it marched over two hundred miles, fought in five actions,
of which three were severe, and several skirmishes, and,
though it had suffered heavy losses in officers and men, was
yet strong, hard as nails, and full of confidence."

As for Major Wheat, he, too, was proud of commanding
"the toughest battalion in the army," as Freeman called the
Tigers. And at Port Republic the curtain had rung down
for Wheat on the second of "three of the most dramatic scenes
of the drama" in which he was destined to share. The stage
for the third scene was being set by Robert E. Lee on the
Chickahominy.[14]

CHAPTER XVII

"BURY ME ON THE FIELD, BOYS"

Stonewall Jackson had everybody guessing in the middle of
June, 1862.

"Where are we going?" asked Jackson's men, from major
generals down. They got no answer.

"Where is he?." asked the alarmed North. "Is he
marching on Washington?"

"Old Jack," true to his character, kept his plans to
himself. General Lee had sent him reinforcements, Brigadier
Generals William H. C. Whiting's division of eight regiments
and Alexander R. Lawton's of six, and Jackson had made
no attempt to conceal the operation.

When word of it reached Washington, the government
was seized with fear that Jackson, now strongly reinforced,
would come tearing up the Valley again heading for the
Federal capital.

Major Wheat, like every one else in Jackson's army,
speculated on what was up. Shortly after the victory at Port
Republic, Rob and a group of officers dined at Willow Fountain Tavern, about eight miles from Staunton. There was
the usual small talk and then the conversation got around
to Old Jack's intentions.

One officer, a former student of Wheat's father at Chapel
Hill, expressed the general opinion that Jackson with his
strengthened command would move against Washington and,

by threatening the invasion of the North, relieve the pressure
on Richmond.

No, said Wheat, Jackson isn't going to attack Washington. Instead, "like an avalanche he would sweep over the
top of the Blue Ridge upon McClellan's right wing and on
hard fought fields make way for victory." Dr. Wheat's old
student noted "how much sombered and saddened" Major
Wheat appeared as the dinner wore on.[1]

Rob, usually gay and boisterous, was indeed depressed.
His carefree manner was gone. His laughter had lost its
spontaneity. That a stranger should notice this is indicative
of Wheat's low spirits.

Whether he was brooding over the death of John
Thomas or was "sombered and saddened" by his recent
proximity to death on the battlefield, Wheat was seized by
the idea that he would be killed in the next battle.

He could not shake it off and on the march from the
Valley to the Chickahominy—for that indeed was Jackson's
destination and Rob had guessed it—the presentiment that a
soldier's death awaited him on the next battlefield grew
stronger. He talked about his coming death constantly. The
idea haunted him and he begged his intimate friends to see
that he was buried just where he fell. Rob's friends laughed
at him, but the more they laughed, the more insistent he
became.

"But it is so," he insisted. "And you will see that it
will be so."[2]

Before Jackson began his movement to join Lee in the
defense of Richmond, General Dick Taylor had taken up with
with President Davis the matter of a long-delayed and much-
deserved promotion for Major Wheat.

After Manassas, practically every one was certain Rob
would be made a colonel and some even expected him to
become a brigadier general. At one time it was believed
that the Louisiana Zouaves, stationed on the Peninsula, would
be added to Wheat's command, but nothing ever came of it.

Taylor reported to President Davis that the Louisiana Tigers had fallen below a hundred men after the Valley campaign and he suggested that the remnants of several other Louisiana battalions be assigned to Wheat. He reminded Davis of Rob's courage and his services at Manassas. "Nothing could be more just," wrote Taylor, "than to increase his little Battn. to a Regt." And then Taylor added a line which is undoubtedly the key to Rob's failure to receive the long-expected promotion: "I am happy in the belief that his habits have materially changed for the better, and this belief is founded on the experiences of several months past." On June 19, 1862, the President dropped a note to Taylor, acknowledging receipt of his memorandum.

"I have long desired to recognise Major Wheat's service, and once made the attempt by the junction of two battalions to raise his command to a regiment." wrote Davis. "If it can consistently be done in the manner proposed by you, I will gladly avail myself of the opportunity." [3]

Major Wheat was a great favorite in Jackson's army, respected and admired by the foot soldiers and thoroughly loved by his fellow officers. His closest friends, however, were Colonel Leroy Stafford of the Ninth Louisiana and Lieutenant Colonel Billy Peck of the same regiment. "Wheat had formed a strong attachment for Stafford and Peck," said Major David F. Boyd, also of the Ninth Louisiana, "and he usually so managed it that his battalion marched and camped near Stafford's regiment. . . . Indeed, he had begun to mess with them, live with them. . . ." [4]

The Louisiana Brigade moved along in Ewell's Division through Gordonsville, Louisa Court House and Frederickshall and on June 25 went into camp at Ashland, twelve miles from Richmond. That night General Dick Taylor was seized with a severe illness, with pains in the head and loins and the next day he was not able to mount his horse.

Taylor reluctantly turned over command of the brigade to Colonel Isaac Seymour of the Sixth Louisiana and remained in an ambulance, hoping to rejoin the brigade later. Seymour marched the Louisianians to the neighborhood of Pole Green church, where they pitched camp.

As usual, Major Wheat, once he had settled his Tigers for the night, went to the campfire of his friend, Colonel Stafford.

The Confederates had attacked that day at Mechanics-ville, and had met a bloody repulse. During the night, how-ever, the Federals withdrew to the neighborhood of Gaines's Mill, near Cold Harbor, where they entrenched themselves and waited for Lee to resume the fight.

Everyone could feel the imminence of a great battle. It was in the air and in the anxious looks on every face. "The peculiar stillness before a battle, like the lull before a storm, foretold the fury and carnage soon to burst forth," recalled Major Boyd. "Such was the quiet, awful solemnity the night before the battle in the pines of the Chickahominy." [5]

Wheat, Colonel Stafford and Major Boyd slept on the same blanket that night. About daylight, Wheat nudged Boyd into wakefulness.

"Major, wake up, and listen to the ration for the day!" he exclaimed.

Boyd and Stafford rubbed their eyes and sat up. Wheat passed an "eye-opener" to his two friends and then drew from his pocket the Episcopal prayer book his mother had given him at the start of the war.

It was June 27, and the "ration" was a prayer for a "Joyful Resurrection." Wheat read the prayer to his friends, and when he came to the concluding lines, he could not choke back the tears:

"Lord, I commend myself to Thee. Prepare me for living, prepare me for dying. Let me live near Thee in grace now, that I may live with Thee in glory everlasting. Let me be reconciled to endure submissively all that Thy sovereign wisdom and love may see fit to appoint, looking forward through the sorrows and tears of a weeping world to that

better dayspring when I shall behold Thy face in righteous-
ness and be satisfied when I awake in Thy likeness. And all I
ask is for the Redeemer's sake. Amen."

The appropriateness of this prayer for a soldier going
into battle was not lost on Wheat or either of his friends.

"This made Rob's presentiment all the stronger—that
he would surely be killed that day!" wrote Major Boyd.
"Then he began to talk of his mother—he loved her dearly. . . .
He would speak of his mother, and cry like a child, take
another drink and read from his little book again.

"And so he did all through that eventful morning, as
the brigade was marching on against the Federal position on
the Chickahominy. To every intimate friend who came near
him he would read his 'ration for the day' till he knew it by
heart, and would repeat it from memory in that rich, sweet,
musical voice of his. He was to be killed, sure, he said; and
one wish he seemed to have above all others—he wanted to
be buried where he fell! This we had to promise him."

At about 2 P. M. the critical moment came at last.
"Before that poor Bob was full of his presentiment—his little
book, his dear mother and his bottle! But when Jackson gave
orders to form line of battle these were all gone. He was
another man—the Bob Wheat of Manassas and the Valley."[6]

When the chief he idolized passed along the line and
approached the Louisiana Tigers, Wheat, "looking like a
mounted Falstaff," rode up to Jackson with uncovered head
and almost bluntly said:

"General, we are about to get into a hot fight and it
is likely many of us may be killed. I want to ask you for
myself and my Louisianians not to expose yourself so unnecessarily as you often do. What will become of us, down here
in these swamps, if anything happens to you, and what will
become of the country! General, let us do the fighting! Just
let me tell them that you promised me not to expose yourself
and then they'll fight like — er — ah Tigers."

Jackson listened attentively and then grasped Wheat's hand suddenly and shook it.

"Much obliged to you, Major," Stonewall answered softly. "I will try not to go into danger unnecessarily. But Major, you will be in greater danger than I, and I hope you will not get hurt. Each of us had his duty to perform, without regard to consequences; we must perform it and trust in Providence."

As Jackson passed on down the line, he turned to young Kyd Douglas, his aide, and said: "Just like Major Wheat. He thinks of the safety of others, too brave ever to think of himself."

Shortly before the battle of Gaines's Mill opened, Major Boyd rode past Wheat's Battalion and noted that Rob was his old self again. He was "superbly uniformed, as he usually was, his large handsome figure the better set off for the splendid clay-bank horse he was riding."

"Major, just look at my Louisiana 'planters,'" Wheat called to him almost joyously. "I'd like to see any 5000 button makers stand before them this day!"

"His 'planters' were barely 200," said Major Boyd, "and mostly the veriest offscouring of the earth."

Another friend, passing the line of Tigers, waved a greeting. Wheat acknowledged it and said: "Something tells Bob that this is his last." [7]

In a few moments the fury of battle was unleashed in the Chickahominy swamps as Jackson sent his brigades in rapid succession against the entrenched right of McClellan's army. Lee had already launched his attack on the Union left and center and a terrifying din shook the Virginia countryside. "If you can form an idea of a hundred or more cannon and one hundred thousand or more of small arms, and sometimes thousands of men—yelling at the top of their voices," said a Confederate soldier who fought at Gaines's Mill, "then you can begin to understand the raging terror and the roaring, lumbering noise of this big battle. . . ."

Soon the Louisiana Brigade was hurled into the fray,

old Colonel Seymour at their head as they rushed toward the Union breastworks. Under a bitter and galling fire the Louisianians wavered and fell back, leaving Seymour dead on the field.

Wheat's Tigers fell back, too, much to Rob's chagrin. Furious at the setback, Wheat rode forward to get a better view of the enemy's position. His men protested in vain against such exposure, but Wheat gave spur to his horse and rode to within forty paces of the Yankee lines. Suddenly there was a rattle of musketry in Wheat's front and he and his horse fell in a heap. A ball had passed through Wheat's head, and as he died, he murmured: "Bury me on the field, boys." [8]

With Dick Taylor ill and away from the field, with Colonel Seymour and Bob Wheat both dead, the Louisiana Brigade for the first time in its history broke, and General Ewell had to withdraw it from the fight.

Major Boyd rode up to a battle-weary Tiger who was openly crying as he trudged from the front.

"What's the matter?" asked Boyd.

"They have killed the old Major," sobbed the Tiger, "and I am going home."

Throughout the battle and all that night, Rob Wheat lay where he fell. The word passed rapidly through the army, "Poor Wheat is gone!" Many came, of all ranks, to pay respects, under the light of torches, to the remains of "one whose voice and sabre had led in so many dangerous encounters."

Early the following morning Major Boyd returned to the spot to fulfill his promise to Wheat to bury him where he fell.

When he arrived he found Wheat's quartermaster, Captain Sam Dushane and three or four Tigers ahead of him, preparing the burial of their beloved major.

They were working hurriedly, for with Jackson moving forward after McClellan's right, "it was no time for ceremony

or delay . . . and we had no business away from our commands
. . . even to bury the dead."

When the last shovel of earth was scattered over the
grave, and a stone placed to mark it, Captain Dushane turned
to Boyd, saying, " Major, please pray."

" No, Captain," replied Boyd, " you can do that better
than I can."

" Well, if I must, here goes it," exclaimed Dushane,
dropping to his knees. " Kneel down, boys."

They knelt down—Major Boyd, Captain Dushane and
four of Rob Wheat's tough Tigers.

" And never before or since," declared Major Boyd,
" have I heard such a prayer—so short, so telling—coming
straight out from the big, warm heart of a soldier commending
the spirit of his beloved commander and friend to the tender
mercies of God."

Major Boyd dearly loved Chatham Roberdeau Wheat,
as did everyone who knew him. And from his devotion came
this magnificent appraisal of the Gentle Tiger:

" One of the bravest of men, the gentlest and noblest
of gentlemen, modest and refined as a woman, and the truest
of friends." [9]

EPILOGUE

Robert E. Lee had saved the Confederate capital. In the Seven Days Battle around Richmond—Rob Wheat had fallen on the second day—Lee had forced McClellan repeatedly to "change his base," a Federal euphemism for retreating down the Peninsula.

Hardly had the battle ebbed from the gates of the city than Wheat's sister, Josephine May Wheat Shober, hurried from North Carolina to Richmond.

"I went to his grave on the 4th of July just one week after he fell," she wrote her sister, Mrs. Seay, "and oh, then I threw myself on his grave. I wept for us all but most of all for Ma. Oh that she should have to give up two such noble sons does seem so hard."

Mrs. Shober placed a stone with Rob's name on it at his head and scattered flowers on his grave and the graves of Lieutenants W. A. Foley and Charles A. Pittman of the Tigers who slept on either side of their leader, with a private on either side of them.

"Noble pines, like sentinels stand on guard and are continually murmuring, peace, peace, be still," Mrs. Shober told her sister.[1]

197

It was first intended that a fence be built around Wheat's battlefield grave, but the increasing difficulty of tending it during the war prompted Rob's father, in 1863, to transfer the body to Hollywood Cemetery in Richmond. And there Wheat slept in an unmarked grave for seventy years. In 1933 Major Christian of Richmond, "an admirer of valor," erected a handsome stone at his head, eulogizing him as "a Soldier of Freedom . . . Unique for personality, wit, eloquence and genius."

Lee, once the pressure was off Richmond, set about reorganizing his army which had suffered considerable losses in the bloody battle of the Chickahominy. On July 25, less than a month after Wheat's death, Lee wrote President Davis: ". . . The remnants of Wheats battr had better be placed under Captain Atkins." [2]

This was the Irishman with whom Wheat had fought in Garibaldi's army. He had been Wheat's volunteer aide at Manassas and later was elected captain of Company E of the Louisiana Tigers.

Lee's suggestion proved only a temporary measure, for on August 9, 1862, Special Order No. 185 was issued, the ninth article of which read:

"The Battalion of Louisiana volunteers commanded by Major Robert [sic] C. Wheat, deceased, having been reduced to not more than 100 men, will be disbanded, and the men comprising same will be transferred to the Louisiana regiments serving in Virginia." [3]

Thus ended the existence of the Louisiana Tigers, not the least of "that band who fought the first hour of the Battle of Manassas," and who quickly made Stonewall Jackson in the Valley regret he had called them "thoughtless fellows for serious work."

Wheat's Battalion, recalled Major David F. Boyd later, "was a unique body, representing every grade of society and every kind of man, from the princely gentleman who commanded them down to the thief and cutthroat released from

parish prison on condition that he would join Wheat. . . .
Such a motley herd of humanity was probably never got
together before, and may never be again." [4]

General Dick Taylor tried in vain "to decline the honor
of such society" when Joe Johnston assigned the Tigers to
him. But in the end, won by their reckless bravery, he called
them (with as much pride as sarcasm) "the Gentle Tigers."

A civilian who knew the Tigers only by reputation
unknowingly wrote their epitaph:

". . . The wild, looting Tigers of Major Bob Wheat
. . . . made not a pious crew, but they fought." [5]

NOTES

Chapter I

[1] J. E. Reid, *History of the Fourth Regiment of South Carolina Volunteers* (Greenville, S. C., 1892), 53, 57. Hereinafter cited as Reid, *History of the Fourth Regiment*.

[2] General B. T. Johnson, "Memoir of First Maryland Regiment," Paper No. 2, *Southern Historical Society Papers*, IX (1881), 485.

[3] James Cooper Nisbet, *Four Years on the Firing Line* (Chattanooga, 1914), 55–56.

[4] Sergeant Z. Lee Gilmer, Ms. Diary in University of Virginia Library, Charlottesville, Va. W. A. McClendon, *Recollections of War Times by an Old Veteran* (Montgomery, 1909), 37; Samuel Elias Mays, "Sketches from the Journal of a Confederate Soldier" in *Tyler's Quarterly* (Richmond, 1921), V, 50–54.

The Tigers were frequently confused with the Louisiana Zouaves of Major Gaston Coppens. The latter unit's reputation for lawlessness was almost equal to that of Wheat's Battalion. Because of this confusion, the Louisiana Tigers were frequently charged with misbehavior which they were incapable of having committed, such as rioting in Montgomery, en route to Virginia. Wheat's Battalion didn't riot in Montgomery for the very good reason that it didn't pass through Montgomery on its way to Richmond. Coppens' Zouaves did and, moreover, they later ran off with the troop train while their officers were standing in the railroad station. Major Robert Stiles (*Four Years Under Marse Robert*, New York and Washington, 1910, page 80) attributes a particularly brutal atrocity to a couple of Louisiana Tigers at Williamsburg. The Tigers were never near Williamsburg.

[5] *Confederate Veteran*, XIX, 427; Report of Col. J. B. E. Sloan in *War of the Rebellion, Official Records of the Union and Confederate Armies* (Washington, 1889–1901), Series I, Vol. II, 561. Hereinafter cited as *O. R.* An English Combatant, *Battlefields of the South* (2 vols., London, 1863), I, 64.

[6] Joseph A. Joel and Lewis R. Stegman, *Rifle Shots and Bugle Notes* (New York, 1884), 143. Henry Kyd Douglas, *I Rode with Stonewall* (Chapel Hill, N. C., 1940), 102. Lt. Gen. Richard Taylor, *Destruction and Reconstruction* (New York, 1879), 26.

Wheat's first name was pronounced with the accent on the first syllable, *Roberdeau*. Because so many of his friends called him Rob or Bob, his name frequently appeared in contemporary newspapers and memoirs, and even in official correspondence, as Robert C. Wheat or Chatham Robert Wheat. Even so fine a scholar as Douglas S. Freeman miscalls him Roberdeau Chatham Wheat, reversing the proper order of his given names (*Lee's Lieutenants*, I, li). The brilliant young Civil War historian, Frank Vandiver, falls into an aggravated form of the same error, calling him Roberdeau *Cheatham* Wheat, in his admirable biography of Stonewall Jackson, *Mighty Stonewall* (New York, 1957), 303. Another recent offender is Edward S. Wallace, who calls him Chatham Robert Wheat in *Destiny and Glory* (New York, 1956), 72.

⁷ " Diary of a Liberator " (No. VII) in New Orleans *Daily Delta*, June 28, 1850; C. W. Doubleday, *The 'Filibuster War' in Nicaragua* (New York, 1886), 176; Clara Solomon, Diary (Typescript) in Louisiana State University Archives 38; Douglas, *I Rode with Stonewall*, 102; Taylor, *Destruction and Reconstruction*, 26.

⁸ Mrs. Sallie A. B. Putnam (A Richmond Lady), *Richmond During the War* (New York, 1867), 35–36.

⁹ Joel and Stegman, *Rifle Shots and Bugle Notes*, 143.

¹⁰ Information supplied author by J. C. Wheat, Jr., Richmond, Va.; Appleton's *Cyclopedia of American Biography* (New York, 1889), VI, 449; Roberdeau Buchanan, *Roberdeau Genealogy* (Privately printed, 1876). The immediate ancestor of Francis Wheate, founder of Rob Wheat's family in America, is not known, but family tradition traces the descent from Thomas Wheat of Walsall, Staffordshire, who lived in the fifteenth century. From his Roberdeau forbears Wheat inherited his massive frame, and perhaps even his martial tendencies. Rob's maternal great-great-grandfather was Isaac Roberdeau, a Huguenot refugee from LaRochelle, whose wife, Mary Cunyngham, traced her ancestry back to the eleventh-century Earls of Glencairn in Scotland. Their son Daniel Roberdeau was the first Pennsylvania general in the Continental army. A wealthy man, he built and equipped a fort at his own expense. When money was needed to send American envoys to France, General Roberdeau provided it, too. His wife, Mary Bostick, also supplied Wheat with soldier's blood, for one of her ancestors, Edward Hinman, was Sergeant-at-Arms in the bodyguard of Charles I.

¹¹ Rev. Wheat to the Rev. Wilson Waters, quoted in latter's *History of St. Luke's Church, Marietta, Ohio* (Marietta, 1884); Edwin Belknap, *A History of St. Paul's Episcopal Church* (New Orleans, 1926).

¹² Rev. Wheat's Journal (1837), in Wheat-Shober Papers, Southern Historical Collection, University of North Carolina (Chapel Hill); Belknap, *A History of St. Paul's Episcopal Church.*

¹³ *Confederate Veteran*, XIX, 428; Mrs. Wheat to the Rev. Wheat, August 17, 1838, in Craige-Wheat Papers in possession of Mrs. Burton Craige, Winston-Salem, N. C.

¹⁴ Susan P. Lee, *Memoirs of William Nelson Pendleton, D. D.* (Phila-

delphia, 1893), 72–77; Judith W. McGuire, *Diary of a Southern Refugee During the War* (Richmond, 1889), 34; Records of Episcopal High School, Alexandria, Va., 1841–42.

[15] Rev. Wheat to Wheat, November 15, 1841, in Craige-Wheat Papers; Mrs. Wheat to Wheat, December 7, 1841, in Craige-Wheat Papers; Mrs. Wheat to Wheat, March 12, 1842, in Craige-Wheat Papers.

Chapter II

[1] George Peabody College for Teachers: *Historical Bulletin* (Nashville, no date).

[2] Rev. Wheat to Mrs. Wheat, August 7, 1844, in Craige-Wheat Papers.

[3] *Confederate Veteran*, XIX, 428.

[4] Appleton's *Cyclopedia of American Biography*, VI, 449; Unidentified newspaper clipping (Nashville), in possession of Mrs. George A. Washington of New Orleans. Mrs. Washington is the daughter of Marina Cheatham.

[5] Wheat to Mrs. Wheat, October 29, 1845, in Craige-Wheat Papers.

[6] Wheat to Mrs. Wheat, January 2, 1846, in Craige-Wheat Papers.

[7] Wheat to Mrs. Wheat, April 9, 1846, in Craige-Wheat Papers.

[8] Slidell to Polk, quoted in Allan Nevins, *Polk—Diary of a President* (New York, London, Toronto, 1952), xxv; James Schouler, *History of the United States of America under the Constitution* (New York, 1894), IV, 52.

[9] *Confederate Veteran*, XIX, 425; Turner J. Fakes, Jr., "Memphis and the Mexican War," in the *Western Tennessee Historical Society Papers*, II, 124; National Archives: Muster Rolls 1st Tennessee Mounted Regiment—AGO, Records, Mexican War (Record Group 94); Return of Field and Staff Officers of 1st Tennessee Mounted Regiment.

[10] George C. Furber, *The Twelve Months Volunteer* (Cincinnati, 1849), 45. The author, a young Memphis lawyer, was a private in Wheat's company in the First Tennessee Mounted Regiment.

Chapter III

[1] Furber, *The Twelve Months Volunteer*, 44–48, 56, 58–59, 61, 68–78, 80.

[2] Wheat to Dr. and Mrs. Wheat, October 9, 1846, in Craige-Wheat Papers; Wheat to Mrs. George W. Cheatham, October 10, 1846, in possession of Mrs. George A. Washington of New Orleans.

[3] New Orleans *Picayune*, October 21, 1848; Wheat to Dr. and Mrs. Wheat, November 18, 1846, in possession of C. R. Wheat, III, of Devon,

Pa.; Furber, *The Twelve Months Volunteer*, 202; National Archives: Muster Rolls 1st Tennessee National Regiment (Record Group 94); Taylor, *Destruction and Reconstruction*, 25.

⁴ Furber, *The Twelve Months Volunteer*, 492ff; 542–43.

⁵ Dispatch of April 18, from Capt. Milton A. Haynes in Nashville *Republican Banner*, May 14, 1847; Wheat to Mrs. Wheat, November 15, 1852, in Craige-Wheat Papers; Wheat to Dr. and Mrs. Wheat, December 24, 1857, in Craige-Wheat Papers; Gen. Cadmus M. Wilcox, *History of the Mexican War* (Washington, 1892), 305.

⁶ *House Executive Document* 24, 31st Congress 1st Session, 22-c; Wilcox, *History of the Mexican War*, 305; Wheat to Mrs. Wheat, May 3, 1847, in Wheat-Shober Papers; *House Executive Document* 24, 31st Congress 1st Session, 22-h; *House Executive Document* 60, 30th Congress 1st Session, 966; Wheat to Dr. and Mrs. Wheat, April 9, 1860, in Craige-Wheat Papers.

⁷ Wheat to Mrs. Wheat, June 5, 1847, in Craige-Wheat Papers; *Confederate Veteran*, XIX, 425; Buchanan, "Roberdeau Genealogy"; *Southern Historical Society Papers*, Vol. XVII, 47; Wheat to Mrs. Wheat, July 2, 1855, in Craige-Wheat Papers; *Southern Bivouac*, May 1884.

⁸ National Archives: Orders No. 4, Headquarters, Department of Vera Cruz, Record Group No. 94, Book 40; Orders No. 7, Record Group No. 94, Book 41½; General Orders No. 156, Headquarters of Army, March 22, 1847; *Confederate Veteran*, XIX. 425.

⁹ Justin H. Smith, *The War with Mexico* (2 vols., New York, 1919), II, 93; *National Encyclopedia*, IX, 168; John R. Kenly, *Memoirs of a Maryland Volunteer—War with Mexico in the Years 1846–7–8* (Philadelphia, 1873), 366; National Archives: Muster Rolls, Wheat's Company Tennessee Mounted Volunteers, Record Group, No. 94, AGO Records.

¹⁰ Nashville *Republican Banner*, March 3, 1848.

¹¹ National Archives: Returns, Wheat's Company, Tennessee Mounted Volunteers Record Group No. 94, AGO Records; Wheat to Dr. Wheat, May 25, 1848, in Craige-Wheat Papers.

Chapter IV

¹ Wheat to Dr. Wheat, May 25, 1848, in Craige-Wheat Papers.

² David Outlaw to Marina Cheatham, February 7, 1847, in possession of Mrs. George A. Washington.

³ Information supplied author by Mrs. George A. Washington; Dr. Wheat to George Maney, October 11, 1848, in possession of Mrs. George A. Washington.

⁴ Wheat to Mrs. Wheat, December 28, 1852, in Craige-Wheat Papers; Mrs. Wheat to ——(?), May 5, 1849, in Wheat-Shober Papers; Wheat to Mrs. Wheat, September 17, 1849, in Craige-Wheat Papers; Wheat to Mrs. Wheat, January 3, 1853, in Craige-Wheat Papers.

[5] A. Curtis Wilgus, " Official Expression of Manifest Destiny Sentiment Concerning Hispanic America, 1848–1871" in *Louisiana Historical Quarterly*, XV, No. 3 (July 1932); *DeBow's Review*, VI, No. 9 (1848); Chester Stanley Urban, " New Orleans and the Cuban Question During the Lopez Expedition of 1849–51: A Local Study in ' Manifest Destiny ' " in *Louisiana Historical Quarterly*, XXII, No. 4 (October 1929), 1097, 1104.

[6] *Confederate Veteran*, XIX, 425; Robert Granville Caldwell, *The Lopez Expeditions to Cuba, 1848–1851* (Princeton, N. J., 1915), 58. Hereinafter cited as Caldwell, *The Lopez Expedition*. (Lt.) Richardson Hardy, *The History and Adventure of the Cuban Expedition* (Cincinnati, 1850), 3.

[7] Gen. Ambrose José Gonzales, " On to Cuba " in New Orleans *Times-Democrat*, March 30, 1884. *Confederate Veteran*, XIX, 425.

[8] Hardy, *The History and Adventure of the Cuban Expedition*, 10, 12, 16, 31.

[9] " Diary of a Liberator " (No. VII), *loc. cit.*, June 28, 1850.

Chapter V

[1] O. D. D. O., *History of the Late Expedition to Cuba* (New Orleans, 1850), 15–19.

[2] Caldwell, *The Lopez Expedition*, 61ff; Urban, " New Orleans and the Cuban Question," *loc. cit.*, 1125.

[3] Hardy, *The History and Adventure of the Cuban Expedition*, 34–36; O. D. D. O., *History of the Late Expedition to Cuba*, 35–39.

[4] Hardy, *The History and Adventure of the Cuban Expedition*, 36, 38–39; Gonzales, " On to Cuba," *loc. cit.*

[5] Anderson C. Quisenberry, *Lopez's Expedition to Cuba* (Louisville, 1906), 55–56.

[6] O. D. D. O., *History of the Late Expedition to Cuba*, 67; Hardy, *The History and Adventure of the Cuban Expedition*, 40, 42.

[7] Gonzales, " On to Cuba," *loc cit.*; Hardy, *The History and Adventure of the Cuban Expedition*, 46.

[8] Maj. William H. Emory, " Report on the United States and Mexican Boundary Survey," *House Executive Document 135*, 34th Congress 1st Session, 61. Some authors are under the misconception that Wheat was captured by the Spaniards and imprisoned in Spain. William O. Scroggs, in *Filibusters and Financiers* (New York, 1916) makes this error, page 278, and Laurence Greene in *The Filibuster* (Indianapolis, 1937) obviously copied the mistake from Scroggs. Greene has more difficulty with Wheat's name than anyone else, calling him Robert Cheatham Wheat, page 238.

Chapter VI

[1] U. S. Circuit Court Records, Eastern District, Louisiana # 1970.
[2] Quoted in Caldwell, *The Lopez Expedition*, 77–78.
[3] The *Orleanian*, June 8, 1850, quoted in Urban, " New Orleans and the Cuban Question," *loc. cit.*, 1132.
[4] Caldwell, *The Lopez Expedition*, 78–79.
[5] U. S. Circuit Court Records, Eastern District, Louisiana # 1970; Urban, "New Orleans and the Cuban Question," *loc. cit.*, 1135, 1136, 1140, 1141.
[6] Wheat to Dr. and Mrs. Wheat, December 5, 1850, in Craige-Wheat Papers.
[7] Caldwell, *The Lopez Expedition*, 86; J. H. F. Claiborne, *Life and Correspondence of John A. Quitman* (New York, 1860), II, 69; Urban, "New Orleans and the Cuban Question," *loc. cit.*, 1143, 1146, 1149ff; Quisenberry, *Lopez's Expedition*, 101.
[8] New Orleans *Daily Delta*, August 28, 1851; *Daily Delta*, August 27, 1851; *Daily Orleanian*, August 28, 1851; *Louisiana Courier*, August 29, 1851.
[9] Urban, " New Orleans and the Cuban Question," *loc. cit.*, 1163–64.

Chapter VII

[1] Thomas Wolfe to Dr. Wheat, May 9, 1850, in Wheat-Shober Papers.
[2] Ernest C. Shearer, "The Carvajal Disturbances" in *Southwestern Historical Quarterly*, LV, No. 2 (October 1951), 201–03. J. Fred Rippy, *The United States and Mexico* (New York, 1931), 88–89.
[3] Carvajal to J. W. Phelps, October 25, 1851, quoted in Shearer, "The Carvajal Disturbance," *loc. cit.*, 215–16; The New Orleans *Picayune*, November 19, 1851; National Archives: Department of State Consular Reports, Vol. 6, Matamoros, J. F. Waddell to Daniel Webster, October 1, 1851; *ibid.*, November (No date), 1851.
[4] Abbe Emmanuel Demenech, *Missionary Adventures in Texas and Mexico* (London, 1858), 328, quoted in Shearer, "The Carvajal Disturbance," *loc. cit.*, 208; John S. Ford, Memoirs (Transcript), 630, in Archives Collection, University of Texas; National Archives: Waddell to Webster, October 1, 1851.
[5] The New Orleans *Picayune*, December 6, 1851.
[6] *Senate Executive Document, No. 1, Part 1*, 32nd Congress 1st Session; Letcher to Webster, October 29, 1851; *Senate Executive Document No. 97*, 32nd Congress 1st Session, 100–102.
[7] The New Orleans *Picayune*, November 19, 1851.
[8] Wheat to Mrs. Wheat, November 21, 1851, in Craige-Wheat Papers.

[9] See New Orleans *Picayune* for February and March, 1851, for detailed accounts of the "war."

[10] Wheat to Mrs. Wheat, May 25, 1852, in Craige-Wheat Papers.

Chapter VIII

[1] Wheat to Thomas Wheat, July 23, 1852, in Wheat-Shober Papers.

[2] Dr. Wheat to Thomas Wheat, August 17, 1852, in Wheat-Shober Papers.

[3] Wheat to Dr. Wheat, August 30, 1852, in Craige-Wheat Papers; New Orleans *Picayune*, October 30, 1852; Rosette in Craige-Wheat Papers.

[4] Wheat to Dr. Wheat, August 30, 1852, in Craige-Wheat Papers.

[5] New Orleans *Picayune*, November 3, 1852; Wheat to Mrs. Wheat, November 15, 1852, in Craige-Wheat Papers.

[6] New Orleans *Picayune*, December 23, 1852; *ibid.*, December 28, 1852; Wheat to Mrs. Wheat, December 28, 1852, in Craige-Wheat Papers.

[7] Wheat to Mrs. Wheat, January 3, 1853, in Craige-Wheat Papers; Wheat to Mrs. Wheat, January 17, 1853, in Craige-Wheat Papers.

[8] Clarissa E. L. Town, Ms., Diary, in Louisiana State University Archives, entry for February 25, 1853.

[9] *Journal and Official Documents of the House of Representatives of the State of Louisiana, Session of 1853* (New Orleans, 1853).

[10] Wheat to Mrs. Wheat, April 8, 1853, in Craige-Wheat Papers.

[11] *Journal and Official Documents . . . . State of Louisiana, Session of 1853.*

[12] Wheat to Mrs. Wheat, April 29, 1853, in Craige-Wheat Papers.

[13] Selina Wheat Seay to Dr. and Mrs. Wheat, July 3, 1853, in Wheat-Shober Papers; Wheat to Mrs. Wheat, March 14, 1854, in Craige-Wheat Papers.

Chapter IX

[1] Wheat to Mrs. Wheat, March 14, 1854, in Craige-Wheat Papers.

[2] Scroggs, *Filibusters and Financiers*, 9–13, 15–17, 36–37, 42. Scroggs is another reputable scholar who muffed Wheat's name, calling him Robert Chatham Wheat.

[3] San Francisco *Alta California*, January 30, 1854. Quoted in Scroggs, *Filibusters and Financiers*.

[4] Scroggs, *ibid.*, 52, 46–48.

[5] Richard A. Johnson, *The Mexican Revolution of Ayutla, 1854–1855*, Augustana Library Publication No. 17 (Rock Island, Ill., 1939), 81; San Francisco *Herald*, August 2, 1854.

[6] Scroggs, *Filibusters and Financiers*, 62, 65.

[7] San Francisco *Alta California*, August 2, 1854; San Francisco *Herald*, August 2, 1854; San Francisco *Chronicle*, August 2, 1854.

[8] Claiborne, *Life and Correspondence of John A. Quitman*, II, 195.

[9] John Haskell Kemble, *The Panama Route* (Berkeley, Calif., 1943), 166, 47.

[10] New York *Daily Tribune*, September 14, 1854; *ibid.*, September 15, 1854.

[11] Wheat to Quitman, October 13, 1854, in Quitman Papers, Mississippi Archives, Jackson, Miss.; Wheat to Quitman, October 29, 1854, *ibid.*

[12] Shearer, "The Carvajal Disturbance," *loc. cit.*, 209; Claiborne, *Life and Correspondence of John A. Quitman*, 209; San Francisco *Alta California*, June 16, 1855; War Department Archives, Mexico City, marked "Military Operations of 1857."

[13] Wheat to Mrs. Wheat, June 23, 1855, in Craige-Wheat Papers; *Diario Oficial*, March 7, 1854, quoted in Johnson, *The Mexican Revolution of Ayutla*.

[14] Wheat to Mrs. Wheat, June 23, 1855, in Craige-Wheat Papers; Wheat to Mrs. Wheat, July 2, 1855, in Craige-Wheat Papers.

[15] Wheat to Mrs. Wheat, August 14, 1855, in Craige-Wheat Papers.

[16] Wheat to Mrs. Wheat, October 28, 1855, in Craige-Wheat Papers.

[17] Wheat to J. T. Wheat, Jr., March 8, 1856, in Craige-Wheat Papers; Wheat to Mrs. Wheat, June 17, 1856, in Craige-Wheat Papers.

[18] War Department Archives, Mexico City; Dr. Wheat to J. S. Wheat, August 25, 1856, in Wheat-Shober Papers; Dr. Wheat to Miss M. E. Wheat, December 3, 1856, in Wheat-Shober Papers; Dr. Wheat to Miss M. E. Wheat, January 17, 1856, in Wheat-Shober Papers.

Chapter X

[1] Scroggs, *Filibusters and Financiers*, 80, 81, 83, 86, 201, 236.

[2] Buchanan, *Roberdeau Genealogy*, 163.

[3] Doubleday, *The 'Filibuster' War in Nicaragua*, 176–78.

[4] James Carson Jamison, *With Walker in Nicaragua* (Columbia, Mo., 1909), 144; Doubleday, *The 'Filibuster' War in Nicaragua*, 178–80.

[5] Milton Shauman, quoted in New York *Tribune*, April 17, 1857.

[6] Doubleday, *The 'Filibuster' War in Nicaragua*, 180–84, 186–90.

[7] New York *Tribune*, April 30, 1857.

[8] Selina Wheat Seay to Mrs. Wheat, June 12, 1857, in Wheat-Shober Papers.

Chapter XI

[1] Wheat to Dr. and Mrs. Wheat, November 18, 1846, in possession of C. R. Wheat, III; Wheat to J. T. Wheat, Jr., March 8, 1856, in Craige-Wheat Papers.

[2] Wheat to Dr. and Mrs. Wheat, December 24, 1857, in Craige-Wheat Papers.

[3] New York *Tribune*, December 28, 1857.

[4] Wheat to Mrs. Wheat, January 31, 1858, in Wheat-Shober Papers; *National Cyclopedia of American Biography*, XIII, 106.

[5] Wheat to J. B. Floyd, September 28, 1858, National Archives Record Group 94, letters received 322-W, 1858.

[6] Wheat to Mrs. Wheat, January 2, 1858 [1859], in Craige-Wheat Papers; Wheat to Mrs. Wheat, February 9, 1859, in Craige-Wheat Papers.

[7] National Archives: Record Group 156, Entry 320, letters received 323-W; Wheat to Col. Drinkard, May 28, 1859; Wheat to Col. Benjamin Huger, June 9, 1859; Col. Huger's report, June 13, 1859; Capt. Dyer to Col. Craig, September 17, 1859; James R. Haskell to Col. Craig, October 12, 1859; Haskell to Col. Ripley, May 23, 1861.

[8] *The National Cyclopedia of American Biography*, XII, 106.

[9] Wheat to Mrs. Wheat, November 27, 1859, Wheat to Mrs. Wheat, Dec. 27, 1859; Wheat to Dr. and Mrs. Wheat, April 9, 1860; Wheat to Mrs. Wheat, October 28, 1855, all in Craige-Wheat Papers.

[10] *Confederate Veteran*, XIX, 426.

[11] J. T. Wheat to Mrs. Wheat, July 19, 1860, in Wheat-Shober Papers.

Chapter XII

[1] Carl Sandburg, *Abraham Lincoln* (New York, 1954), 174.

[2] Dr. Wheat to Mrs. Wheat, August 20, 1860, in Wheat-Shober Papers; Mrs. Wheat to Leo Wheat, August 28, 1860, in Wheat-Shober Papers.

[3] Dr. Wheat to J. S. Wheat, August 25, 1856, in Wheat-Shober Papers.

[4] George L. Kilmer, American Press Association, in unidentified newspaper clipping in Craige-Wheat Papers; Buchanan, *Roberdeau Genealogy*, 164.

[5] New York *Herald*, September 9, 1860; Buchanan, *Roberdeau Genealogy*, 164; unidentified newspaper clipping in Wheat-Shober Papers.

[6] Dr. Wheat to Leo Wheat, October 2, 1860, in Wheat-Shober Papers.

[7] Wheat to Mrs. Wheat, October 7, 1860, in Craige-Wheat Papers; Mrs. Wheat to Leo Wheat, November 18, 1860, in Wheat-Shober Papers.

[8] *Illustrated London News*, November 3, 1860, p. 410.

[9] Mrs. Wheat to Leo Wheat, November 18, 1860, in Wheat-Shober Papers; Selina Wheat Seay to Leo Wheat, November 25, 1860, in Wheat-

[12] Robert Ritchie to friend in New Orleans *Daily True Delta,* August 15, 1861.

[13] An English Combatant, *Battlefields of South,* I, 40; John Wilcox to W. C. Cook in New Orleans *Daily Delta,* July 28, 1861.

[14] *Confederate Veteran,* XIX, 427; General Evans in his report said Wheat was shot through both lungs.

[15] New Orleans *Picayune,* July 25, 26, 29, 1861.

[16] Francis Shober to wife, July 26, 1861, in Wheat-Shober Papers.

[17] Unidentified clipping in Craige-Wheat Papers.

[18] Francis Shober to wife, July 26, 1861; *Confederate Veteran,* XIX, 427.

[19] John Dimitry, *Confederate Military History* (Atlanta, 1899), X, 210.

[20] New Orleans *Daily True Delta,* August 15, 1861; *Confederate Veteran,* XIX, 427.

[21] Beauregard, "Report on Manassas," *loc. cit.;* Cocke, "Report on Manassas," *loc. cit.,* 30–31; Evans' "Report on Manassas," *loc. cit.*

[22] Alexander, 34n.

Chapter XV

[1] National Archives: Confederate Archives, Pay Voucher, No. 83, July 31, 1861. As a major, Wheat received $150 a month.

[2] Wheat's "Report on Manassas" in Craige-Wheat Papers.

[3] Richmond *Enquirer,* July 26, 1861; New Orleans *Daily True Delta,* August 8, 1861.

[4] Ella Lonn, *Foreigners in the Confederacy* (Chapel Hill, N. C., 1940), 194; Capt. R. G. Atkins to Wheat, August 29, 1861, in Craige-Wheat Papers; Louisiana Military Commission Collection, Book 32, Roster of Officers, 1st Special Battalion.

[5] New Orleans *Picayune,* August 8, 1861; James Barbour to Gov. Letcher(?) August 12, 1861.

[6] Taylor, *Destruction and Reconstruction,* 85.

[7] *Ibid.,* 23–24.

[8] David F. Boyd, in New Orleans *Item,* August 25, 1896. Captain Alex White of the Tigers, according to Boyd, "was a mate on a Vicksburg packet . . . a magnificent specimen in physique . . . of one of the finest old Blue Grass families—his father governor of the State." In a card game he had killed a man, but after trial and conviction, he was pardoned through the influence of his friends and family. "Nor was White his real name," added Boyd. "He had so much respect for his name that he changed it. . . ."

[9] Lynchburg *Virginian,* August 12, 1861.

[10] *Confederate Veteran,* XIX, 427; New Orleans *Daily Delta,* September 3, 1861; Solomon, Diary, 47.

[11] New Orleans *Crescent*, September 26, 1861; Wheat to Mrs. Wheat, October 14, 1861, in Wheat-Shober Papers.

[12] New Orleans *Bee*, August 9, 1861.

[13] Mary Moffett, *Letters of Gen. James Conner, C. S. A.* (no date, no place), 61–62; Taylor, *Destruction and Reconstruction*, 23; National Archives: Box 209, Report of Sick and Wounded, Wheat's Battalion.

[14] Letter to author from Lt. Col. Willard Jones; General P. G. T. Beauregard, *A Commentary on the Campaign and Battle of Manassas of July 1861* (New York and London, 1891), 138.

[15] Nisbet, *Four Years on Firing Line*, 55–56; McClendon, *Recollections of War Times by an Old Veteran*, 37. The Tigers were accused of collecting grisly relics from dead Yankees and carving their bones into finger rings. (See Frank Moore, ed., *Rebellion Record* [New York 1862-1871], Vol. 4, Document 155, 534).

[16] National Archives: Confederate Archives, Provision Returns, Wheat's Battalion, October 18, 1861.

[17] Frederick Skinner, in Harry Worcester Smith, *A Sporting Family of Old South* (Albany, 1936), 320–25.

[18] William M. Owen, *In Camp and Battle with the Washington Artillery of New Orleans* (Boston, 1885), 64–66.

[19] Thomas J. Goree Papers in Louisiana State University Archives, 87; Dunbar Rowland, *Jefferson Davis, Constitutionalist* (Jackson, Miss., 1923), VII, 270; David F. Boyd in New Orleans *Item*, August 25, 1896.

[20] Taylor, *Destruction and Reconstruction*, 25; National Archives: Confederate Records of Courtmartials, Chapter I, Vol. 194, A. & I. G. O. Records, 94 and 246; David F. Boyd, in New Orleans *Item*, August 25, 1896; Z. Lee Gilmer, Diary; McClendon, *Recollections of War Times by an Old Veteran*, 36; B. T. Johnson in *Southern Historical Society Papers*, Vol. IX (1881), 485; New Orleans *Commercial Bulletin*, December 20, 1861.

[21] McClendon, *Recollections of War Times by an old Veteran*, 37.

[22] Wheat to Gen. Cooper, January 20, 1862, in Craige-Wheat Papers.

Chapter XVI

[1] Joseph E. Johnston, *Narrative of Military Operation*, ... , (New York, 1872), 96–97.

[2] Selina Wheat Seay to Dr. Wheat, January 12, 1862, in Wheat-Shober Papers; Dr. Wheat to Mrs. Wheat, February 19, 1862, in Wheat-Shober Papers.

[3] Taylor, *Destruction and Reconstruction*, 35–36, 40.

[4] Savannah *Daily Morning News*, May 14, 1862, quoting Richmond *Dispatch*.

[5] Taylor, *Destruction and Reconstruction*, 49–51; Douglas, *I Rode with Stonewall*, 102.

⁶ Douglas S. Freeman, *Lee's Lieutenants* (New York, 1943–44), I, 374, 376.

⁷ R. L. Dabney, *Life and Campaigns of Lt. Gen. Thomas J. Jackson* (New York, 1866), 364–65. Hereinafter cited as Dabney, *Jackson*; Taylor, *Destruction and Reconstruction*, 51, 54, 80; Douglas, *I Rode with Stonewall*, 52; Lucy Buck, *Diary* (privately printed, 1940), 57–59, 61; Thomas A. Ashby, *The Valley Campaigns* (New York, 1914), 118; Freeman, *Lee's Lieutenants*, I, 381–82.

⁸ Taylor, *Destruction and Reconstruction*, 54–56; Dabney, *Jackson*, 371; Edward A. Moore, *The Story of a Cannoneer Under Stonewall Jackson* (New York and Washington, 1907), 53; O. R., Series I, Vol. XII, Part 1, 703, 576.

⁹ Taylor, *Destruction and Reconstruction*, 56.

¹⁰ Douglas, *I Rode with Stonewall*, 58–59; Taylor, *Destruction and Reconstruction*, 57–59; J. H. Worsham, *One of Jackson's Foot Cavalry* (New York, 1912), 87; O. R., Series I, XII, Part 1, 801.

¹¹ Col. G. F. R. Henderson, *Stonewall Jackson and the American Civil War* (one volume ed., New York, no date), 271, 269; William Allan, *History of the Campaigns of General T. J. (Stonewall) Jackson in the Shenandoah Valley of Virginia* (Philadelphia, 1880), 136.

¹² J. Esten Cooke, *The Life of Stonewall Jackson* (New York, 1863), 168; McClendon, *Recollections of War Times by an Old Veteran*, 64; Taylor, *Destruction and Reconstruction*, 26; Douglas, *I Rode with Stonewall*, 79.

¹³ Nisbet, *Four Years on the Firing Line*, 94.

¹⁴ Col. Henry Kelly, *Port Republic* (Philadelphia, 1886), 15–19; Taylor, *Destruction and Reconstruction*, 74–78; George M. Neese, *Three Years in the Confederate Horse Artillery* (New York, 1911), 74–75; *National Encyclopedia*, Vol. 14, 168; Capt. Samuel D. Buck, *With the Old Confeds., Actual Experiences of a Captain in the Line* (Baltimore, 1925), 38; Freeman, *Lee's Lieutenants*, I, li.

Chapter XVII

¹ Fragment of unidentified letter to Dr. Wheat, March 21, 1863, in Craige-Wheat Papers.

² David F. Boyd, in New Orleans *Item*, August 25, 1896.

³ Unsigned biographical sketch of Wheat in Wheat-Shober Papers; Richard Taylor to Jefferson Davis, no date, in Davis Papers, Louisiana Historical Association Collection, New Orleans; Jefferson Davis to Richard Taylor, June 19, 1862, in Rowland, *Jefferson Davis, Constitutionalist*, V, 280–81.

⁴ David F. Boyd, in Joel and Stegman, *Rifle Shots and Bugle Notes*, 141.

[5] Taylor, *Destruction and Reconstruction*, 83; David F. Boyd in Joel and Stegman, *Rifle Shots and Bugle Notes*, 141–42.

[6] David F. Boyd New Orleans *Item*, August 25, 1896, *Confederate Veteran*, XIX, 428.

[7] Douglas, *I Rode with Stonewall*, 102; David F. Boyd, New Orleans *Item*, August 25, 1896; Alexander, *Military Memoirs of a Confederate*, 34n.

[8] James Huffman, *Ups and Downs of a Confederate Soldier* (New York, 1940), 52; David F. Boyd, in New Orleans *Item*, August 25, 1896; *Confederate Veteran*, XIX, 427.

[9] *O. R.* Series I, Vol. XI, Part 2, 605; David F. Boyd in Joel and Stegman, *Rifle Shots and Bugle Notes*, 143; David F. Boyd, New Orleans *Item*, August 25, 1896; An English Combatant, *Battlefields of the South*, 343–44.

Epilogue

[1] Mrs. May Wheat Shober to Mrs. Selina Wheat Seay, August 1, 1862, in Wheat-Shober Papers.

[2] Douglas S. Freeman, *Lee's Dispatches* (New York, 1915), 36.

[3] Special Orders of the Adjutant and Inspector General Office, Confederate States, 338.

[4] David F. Boyd, in New Orleans *Item*, August 25, 1896.

[5] T. C. DeLeon, *Belles, Beaux and Brains of the Sixties* (New York, 1909), 329.

NOTES ON BIBLIOGRAPHY

*W*heat Manuscripts

There are two main sources for manuscript material on Chatham Roberdeau Wheat. These are, in the order of importance:

1. The Craige-Wheat Papers in the possession of Wheat's grandniece, Mrs. Burton Craige of Winston-Salem, North Carolina.

2. The Wheat-Shober Papers on deposit in the Southern Historical Collection at the University of North Carolina at Chapel Hill.

The Craige-Wheat Papers consist of approximately seventy-five items, about twenty-five of which are letters of Wheat to his family between October, 1845, and July, 1861. About thirty-five items consist of letters of Wheat's mother and father to each other, to him, or to the other children, between 1826 and 1861. A dozen or so items consist of unidentified letters or fragments of letters, newspaper clippings, etc., in which Wheat is mentioned.

The Wheat-Shober Papers, an extensive collection running into the 1890's, has more than three hundred items for the period 1814 to 1862, the bulk of them between the years 1850 and 1862. The collection is most pertinent to this study. It includes the papers of Wheat's father, Dr. John Thomas Wheat, and family correspondence similar to that in the Craige-Wheat Papers. While yielding a number of important letters of Wheat, this collection is valuable essentially for the family letters which are rich in comments on Wheat's activities.

Scattered letters of Wheat are located as follows:

1. National Archives.
2. John A. Quitman Papers in Mississippi Department of Archives and History, Jackson, Mississippi.
3. New-York Historical Society.
4. Mrs. George A. Washington of New Orleans, Louisiana.
5. Chatham Roberdeau Wheat, III, of Devon, Pennsylvania.
6. John A. Quitman Papers in Houghton Library, Harvard University.

Other Manuscripts

The following unpublished diaries and other papers contributed useful and in some cases, valuable, information:

1. Clara Solomon Diary. The original and typescript are in the Department of Archives and Manuscripts, Louisiana State University, Baton Rouge, Louisiana. Clara's father was sutler in Wheat's Battalion.

2. Z. Lee Gilmer Diary. This manuscript diary, owned by Mrs. Louise Horsley Critz of Manteo, Virginia, is on deposit in the Alderman Library at the University of Virginia, Charlottesville, Virginia. Gilmer witnessed, and left a vivid account of the execution of the two Louisiana Tigers at Centreville.

3. The Goree Papers. These consist of letters of Thomas J. Goree from the Virginia theater of war and are located in the Louisiana State University Department of Archives and History, Baton Rouge, Louisiana.

4. Colonel John Ford's Memoirs. Original and typescript are in the Archives Collection of the University of Texas, Austin, Texas. This was useful for material on Wheat's activities on the Rio Grande with Carvajal.

5. Jefferson Davis Papers in Louisiana Historical Association Collection at Tulane University.

Official Records

The following official records were consulted and yielded valuable material in the areas indicated:

1. National Archives, Washington:
    a. Mexican War records.
    b. War Department and Ordnance records, 1858–1860.
    c. Confederate Archives.
    d. Consular reports from Matamoros and Acapulco, 1851–1860.
2. Federal District Court, New Orleans, Louisiana.

Printed Records

1. *War of the Rebellion: A Compilation of the Official Records of the Union and Confederate Armies*, 130 vols. (Washington, 1880-1901).
2. Official House and Senate Documents of the U. S. Congress.
3. Official Journal, Louisiana Legislature, 1853.

Newspapers

The following newspapers were helpful in tracing Wheat's frequent movements:

New Orleans: *The Picayune, Bee, Daily Delta, Daily True Delta, Commercial Bulletin.*
San Francisco: *Chronicle, Alta California, Daily Herald.*
New York: *Herald, Tribune.*
Nashville: *Republican Banner*
London: *Times, Illustrated News.*

Periodicals, Journals, Quarterlies

The following yielded either specific information on Wheat or supplied background material on the events in which he participated:

De Bow's Review.
Confederate Veteran.

Southern Historical Society Papers.
Louisiana Historical Quarterly.
Southwestern Historical Quarterly.
West Tennessee Historical Quarterly.

Biographical Data

Three biographical sketches of Roberdeau Wheat, in the main identical but differing somewhat from each other in a few points, were written in the nineteenth century by Wheat's brother, Leo. They appeared as follows:

1. *Roberdeau Genealogy,* compiled by Roberdeau Buchanan and published privately in 1876.
2. *Southern Historical Society Papers,* Vol. XVII, 47.
3. *Confederate Veteran,* Vol. XIX, 425.

Although these three pieces contain some serious errors in dates and events, and exaggerations stemming from fraternal piety, they are, nonetheless, an important line of departure for a full study of Wheat.

Dr. Douglas S. Freeman paraphrased the last two in writing of Roberdeau Wheat in the first volume of *Lee's Lieutenants.*

Secondary Works

Alexander, E. P. *Military Memoirs of a Confederate.* Scribner, New York, 1907.

Allan, William. *History of the Campaign of General T. J. (Stonewall) Jackson in the Shenendoah Valley of Virginia.* Lippincott, Philadelphia, 1880.

Anderson, J. Q., ed. *Brokenburn: The Journal of Kate Stone, 1861–1868.* Louisiana State University Press, Baton Rouge, 1955.

An English Combatant. *Battlefields of the South.* 2 vols., New York, 1864.

Appleton's *Cylcopedia of American Biography.* Appleton, New York, 1889.

Ashby, Thomas. *The Valley Campaigns.* Neale, New York, 1914.

Bartlett, Napier. *Military Record of Louisiana*. Graham, New Orleans, 1875.

Beauregard, P. G. T. *A Commentary on the Campaign and Battle of Manassas of July 1861*. Putnam, New York and London, 1891.

Belknap, Edwin. *A History of St. Paul's Protestant Episcopal Church*. Privately printed, New Orleans, 1926.

Blackford, Susan Leigh. *Letters from Lee's Army*. Scribner, New York, 1947.

Boggess, F. C. M. *A Veteran of Four Wars*. Privately printed, Arcadia, Florida, 1900.

Bolton, Herbert S. *Guide to Materials for the History of the United States in the Principle Archives of Mexico*. Carnegie Institute, Washington, 1913.

Boyd, David French. In Joel, Joseph A. and Stegman, Lewis R., *Rifle Shots and Bugle Notes*. Grand Army Gazette Publishing Co., New York, 1884.

———. Article on Wheat in *New Orleans Item*, August 25, 1896.

Buchanan, Roberdeau. *Roberdeau Genealogy*. Privately printed, Washington, 1876.

Buck, Captain Samuel D. *With the Old Confeds. Actual Experiences of a Captain in the Line*. Privately printed, Baltimore, 1925.

Buck, Lucy Rebecca. *Diary*. Edited by L. Neville Buck. Privately printed, 1940.

Caldwell, Robert Granville. *The Lopez Expedition to Cuba, 1848–1851*. Princeton University Press, Princeton, N. J., 1915.

Carter, Hodding and Betty. *So Great a Good. A History of the Episcopal Church in Louisiana*. Privately printed, New Orleans, 1955.

Claiborne, J. F. H. *Life and Correspondence of John A. Quitman*. 2 vols., Harper, New York, 1860.

Cooke, J. Esten. *The Life of Stonewall Jackson*. Richardson, New York, 1863.

Coulter, E. Merton. *The Confederate States of America*. (*A History of the South*), Vol. VII. Louisiana State University Press, Baton Rouge, 1950.

Dabney, R. L. *Life and Campaigns of Lieutenant Thomas J. Jackson*. Blelock, New York, 1866.

Davenport, Herbert. "General José Maria Jesus Carvajal." Vol. LV, *Southwestern History Quarterly*, April, 1952.

DeLeon, T. C. *Belles, Beaux and Brains of the Sixties*. Dillingham, New York, 1909.

Diary of a Liberator. Unsigned series of articles in *New Orleans Daily Delta*, June 15–July 20, 1850.

Dimitry, John. *Confederate Military History*. Vol. X, Confederate Publishing Company, Atlanta, 1899.

Domenech, Abbe Emmanuel. *Missionary Adventures in Texas and Mexico*. Longman, London, 1858.

Doubleday, C. W. *Reminiscences of the 'Filibuster' War in Nicaragua*. Putnam, New York, 1886.

Douglas, Henry Kyd. *I Rode with Stonewall*. University of North Carolina Press, Chapel Hill, N. C., 1940.

Dowdey, Clifford. *The Land They Fought For*. Doubleday, Garden City, N. Y., 1955.

———. *Experiment in Rebellion*. Doubleday, Garden City, N. Y., 1946.

Emory, Major William H. "Report of William H. Emory, Major First Cavalry and United States Commissioner, United States and Mexican Boundary Survey." 34th Congress, 1st Session, ex. doc. No. 135, Washington, 1857.

Fakes, Turner J., Jr. "Memphis and the Mexican War." In *West Tennessee Historical Society Papers*, Vol. II, 1948.

Ford, John S. Memoirs. Transcript of Ms. in University of Texas Archives, Austin, Texas.

Freeman, Douglas S. *Lee's Dispatches*. Putnam, New York, 1915.

———. *Lee's Lieutenants*. 3 vols., Scribner, New York, 1943–1944.

———. *Robert E. Lee*. 4 vols., Scribner, New York, 1934–1935.

Furber, George C. *The Twelve Months Volunteer . . . .* J. A. and U. P. Jones, Cincinatti, 1849.

Gill, John. *Reminiscences of Four Years as a Private Soldier in the Confederate Army*. Sun Printing Office, Baltimore, 1904.

Gonzales, General Ambrose José. "On to Cuba." In New Orleans *Times Democrat*, March 30, 1884.

Greene, Laurence. *The Filibuster: The Career of William Walker*. Bobbs Merrill, Indianapolis, 1937.

Hanson, Joseph Mills. *Bull Run Remembers*. National Capitol Publishing Company, Manassas, Virginia, 1953.

Hardy, Lieutenant Richardson. *The History and Adventures of the Cuba Expedition.* . . . Stratton, Cincinatti, 1850.

Henderson, Col. G. F. R. *Stonewall Jackson and the American Civil War.* 1 vol. edition. Grosset and Dunlap, New York, N. Y.

Henry, Robert Selph. *The Story of the Confederacy*. Bobbs-Merrill, Indianapolis, 1931.

History . . . of Funeral Ceremonies in Honor of Calhoun, Clay and Webster. Privately printed, New Orleans, 1853.

Horgan, Paul. *Great River: The Rio Grande*. 2 vols., Rinehart, New York, 1955.

Hotchkiss, Jed. *Confederate Military History*. Vol. III, Confederate Publishing Company, Atlanta, 1899.

Howard, McHenry. *Recollections of a Maryland Confederate Soldier and Staff Officer.* . . . Williams and Wilkins, Baltimore, 1914.

Huffman, James. *Ups and Downs of a Confederate Soldier*. Rudge, New York, 1940.

Jamison, James Carson. *With Walker in Nicaragua*. E. W. Stephens Publishing Company, Columbia, Mo., 1909.

Joel, Joseph A. and Stegman, Lewis R. *Rifle Shots and Bugle Notes*. Grand Army Gazette Publishing Company, New York, 1884.

Johnson, General B. T. "Memoirs of First Maryland Regiment." *Southern Historical Society Papers*, Vol. IX, 1881.

Johnson, Richard A. *The Mexican Revolution of Ayutla. 1854–1855*. Augustana Library Publication No. 17, Rock Island, Illinois, 1939.

Johnston, Joseph E. *Narrative of Military Operation.* . . . Appleton, New York, 1872.

Johnston, R. M. *Bull Run: Its Strategy and Tactics*. Houghton, Mifflin, Boston, 1913.

Kelly, Colonel Henry B. *The Battle of Port Republic*. Lippincott, Philadelphia, 1886.

Kemble, John Haskell. *The Panama Route, 1848–1869.* University of California Press, Berkeley, 1943.

Kenly, John R. *Memoirs of a Maryland Volunteer, War with Mexico in the Years, 1846–1847–1848.* Lippincott, Philadelphia, 1873.

Lee, Susan P. *Memoirs of William Nelson Pendleton, D. D.* Lippincott, Philadelphia, 1893.

Lewis, Lloyd. *Sherman, Fighting Prophet.* Harcourt Brace, New York, 1932.

Logan, John A. *The Great Conspiracy.* Hart, New York, 1886.

Lonn, Ella. *Foreigners in the Confederacy.* University of North Carolina Press, Chapel Hill, N. C., 1940.

McClendon, W. A. *Recollections of War Times by an Old Veteran.* The Paragon Press, Montgomery, 1909.

McGuire, Judith W. *Diary of a Southern Refugee During the War.* Randolph and English, Richmond, 1889.

May, Samuel Elias. "Sketches from the Journal of a Confederate Soldier." In *Tyler's Quarterly.* Vol. V, 50–54, Richmond, 1921.

Mitchell, Lieutenant Colonel Joseph B. *Decisive Battles of the Civil War.* Putnam, New York, 1955.

Moffett, Mary. *Letters of General James Conner, CSA.* No publication facts.

Moore, Edward A. *The Story of a Cannoneer Under Stonewall Jackson.* Neale, New York and Washington, 1907.

Moore, Frank, ed. *The Rebellion Record.* 12 vols., Van Nostrand, New York, 1862-1871.

Neese, George M. *Three Years in the Confederate Horse Artillery.* Neale, New York, 1911.

Nevins, Allan, ed. *Polk—The Diary of a President.* Longmans, Greene, New York, 1952.

Nisbet, James Cooper. *Four Years on the Firing Line.* The Imperial Press, Chattanooga, 1914.

Noll, Rev. Arthur Howard. *History of the Church in the Diocese of Tennessee.* Pott, New York, 1900.

O. D. D. O. (J. C. Davis). *History of the Late Expedition to Cuba.* Daily Delta Publishing Office, New Orleans, 1850.

Owen, William M. *In Camp and Battle with the Washington Artillery of New Orleans.* Ticknor, Boston, 1885.

Peabody College. *Historical Bulletin*, Nashville, No date.

Portell Vila, Hermino. *Narciso Lopez y Su Epoca*. Vol. II, Habana, 1952.

Putnam, Sallie A. (Brock) (A Richmond Lady). *Richmond During the War*. Carleton, New York, 1867.

Quisenberry, Anderson C. *Lopez's Expedition to Cuba*. Morton, Louisville, 1906.

Reid, Jesse Walton. *History of the Fourth Regiment of South Carolina Volunteers*. Shannon, Greenville, 1892.

Rippy, J. Fred. *The United States and Mexico*. Crofts, New York, 1931.

Robarts, William Hugh. *Mexican War Veterans*. Brentano, Washington, 1887.

Rowland, Dunbar. *Jefferson Davis, Constitutionalist*, 10 vols., Mississippi Department of Archives, Jackson, Miss., 1923.

Sandburg, Carl, *Abraham Lincoln*. Harcourt Brace, New York, 1954.

Scroggs, William C. *Filibusters and Financiers*. Macmillan, New York, 1916.

Shearer, Ernest C. "The Carvajal Disturbance." In *Southwestern Historical Quarterly*, Vol. LV, No. 2, October, 1951.

Sherman, W. T. *Memoirs of General W. T. Sherman*. 2 vols., Appleton, New York, 1875.

Skinner, Frederick Gustavus. *Reminiscences of an Old Sportsman*. Reprinted in Harry Worcester Smith's *A Sporting Family of the Old South*. Lyon, Albany, 1936.

Smith, Justin H. *The War with Mexico*. 2 vols., Macmillan, New York, 1919.

Stafford, Dr. G. M. G. *General Leroy Augustus Stafford, His Forbears and Descendants*. Pelican Press, New Orleans, 1943.

Stiles, Major Robert. *Four Years Under Marse Robert*. Neale, New York and Washington, 1910.

Taylor, (Lieutenant General) Richard. *Destruction and Reconstruction*. Appleton, New York, 1879.

Tunnard, W. H. *A Southern Record: The History of the Third Regiment of Louisiana Infantry*. Printed for the author, Baton Rouge, 1866.

Turner, George Edgar. *Victory Rode the Rails*. Bobbs-Merrill, Indianapolis, 1953.

Urban, Chester Stanley. " New Orleans and the Cuban Question
During the Lopez Expeditions of 1849–51: A Local Study
in ' Manifest Destiny.' " In *Louisiana Historical Quarterly*,
Vol. 22, No. 4, October, 1939.

Vielé, Teresa (Griffin). *Following the Drums*. Peterson, Philadelphia, 1864.

Walker, William. *The War in Nicaragua*. Goetzel, Mobile, 1860.

Warder, T. B. and Catlett, Jas. M. *Battle of Young's Branch:
or Manassas Plain*. Enquirer Book and Job Press, Richmond,
1862.

Waters, Wilson. *History of St. Luke's Church, Marietta, Ohio*.
Printed for the author by J. Mueller & Son, Marietta, Ohio,
1884.

Wheat, Silas Carmi. *Wheat Genealogy*. Wheat, Brooklyn, N. Y.,
1903.

Wilcox, (General) Cadmus M. *History of the Mexican War*.
Church News Publishing Company, Washington, D. C.,
1892.

Wiley, Bell I. *The Life of Johnny Reb*. Bobbs-Merrill, Indianapolis, 1943.

Wilgus, A. Curtis. " Official Expression of Manifest Destiny
Sentiment Concerning Hispanic America, 1840–1871." In
Louisiana Historical Quarterly, Vol. XV, No. 3, 1932.

Williams, T. Harry. *Lincoln and the Radicals*. University of
Wisconsin Press, Madison, Wisconsin, 1941.

Wilshin, Francis F. *Manassas (Bull Run) National Battlefield
Park*, National Park Service Historical Handbook Series No.
15, Washington, 1953.

Wise, George. *History of the Seventeenth Virginia Infantry, CSA*.
Kelly, Piet, Baltimore, 1870.

Worsham, John H. *One of Jackson's Foot Cavalry*. Neale, New
York, 1912.

INDEX